AMERICA
AND AMERICANS
IN AUSTRALIA

AMERICA
AND AMERICANS
IN AUSTRALIA

David Mosler and Bob Catley

 PRAEGER

Westport, Connecticut
London

DU
122
.A5
M68
1998

Library of Congress Cataloging-in-Publication Data

Mosler, David, 1941–
   America and Americans in Australia / David Mosler and Bob Catley.
     p. cm.
   Includes bibliographical references (p.) and index.
   ISBN 0–275–96252–0 (alk. paper)
     1. Americans—Australia—History. 2. National characteristics,
  American. 3. Australia—Emigration and immigration. 4. Australia—
  History—20th century. 5. United States—History—20th century.
  I. Catley, Robert. II. Title.
  DU122.A5M68   1998   98–6858
  994′.00413—dc21

British Library Cataloguing in Publication Data is available.

Library of Congress Catalog Card Number: 98–6858

ISBN: 0–275–96252–0

First published in 1998

Praeger Publishers, 88 Post Road West, Westport, CT 06881
An imprint of Greenwood Publishing Group, Inc.

Printed in the United States of America

The paper used in this book complies with the
Permanent Paper Standard issued by the National
Information Standards Organization (Z39.48–1984).

10 9 8 7 6 5 4 3 2 1

To Sharon and Pat

Contents

Tables   ix

Abbreviations and Acronyms   xi

Preface   xiii

1   The Global Context   1

2   Australia in Historical Context   8

3   Modern Australia since World War II   33

4   Why Do People Migrate?   54

5   American Migration to Australia: World War II to the 1990s 66

6   Why Do the Americans Come to Australia?   80

7   Do the Americans Like Australia?   99

8   Cultural Relations   122

9   The Australia Americans Don't Like   140

10   How Do American Migrants Adapt to Australia?   153

11   Conclusion: The Future   179

Appendix   191

Bibliography   195

Index   199

Tables

5.1	American-Born in Australia, 1891–1991	68
5.2	Emigration from the United States, 1940s–1970s	69
5.3	U.S.-Born Migrant Arrivals and Departures in Australia, 1960–92	71
5.4	Age and Sex of 1993 Sample	71
5.5	Marital Status and Place of Birth of Progeny	72
5.6	Place and Region of Birth	73
5.7	Education	73
5.8	Employment: Respondents and Spouses	74
5.9	Decade of Arrival and Assistance	75
5.10	Place of Australian Residence	77
5.11	Summary of Key Characteristics of the 1993 Sample of American Migrants	78
6.1	Reasons for Emigrating from America	82
6.2	Reasons for Choosing Australia	83
6.3	Matrix of Migrant Political Ideology and Miscellaneous Sociocultural Attitudes toward the United States and Australia	85
6.4	Decadal Variations in Reasons for Emigrating to Australia	87
7.1	Level of Satisfaction with Australia	101
7.2	Perceived Levels of Discrimination	102

7.3   Matrix of Political Ideology and Australian Anti-Americanism   109

7.4   The Most Commonly Used Stereotypical Language in the 1993
        Sample of Anecdotal Data by Australians to Describe Americans   111

8.1   Yiddish Words in Common Use in Australia   124

9.1   Common Anti-Australian Stereotypical Language
        Used by American Migrants   141

10.1   Political Preferences of 1993 Sample   155

10.2   Attitudes toward Citizenship   158

10.3   Status of Academics in 1993 Sample   164

10.4   Gender Variations   168

11.1   The Second Generation   180

11.2   Returnees   184

Abbreviations
and Acronyms

ABC	Australian Broadcasting Corporation
ABS	Australian Bureau of Statistics
ACT	Australian Capital Territory
ACTU	Australian Council of Trades Unions
AHR	American Historical Review
ALP	Australian Labour Party
AMP	Australian Mutual Provident Society
ANZUS	Australia–New Zealand–United States
APEC	Asia Pacific Economic Cooperation
BIMPR	Bureau of Immigration, Multicultural and Population Research
BIPR	Bureau of Immigration and Population Research
BIR	Bureau of Immigration Research
CAE	College of Advanced Education
CBD	central business district
CIR	Citizens Initiated Referenda
CPA	Communist Party of Australia
DIEA	Department of Immigration and Ethnic Affairs
DPs	Displaced Persons
EEP	Export Enhancement Program
GATT	General Agreement on Tariffs and Trade
GDP	gross domestic product
MHR	Member of the House of Representatives
NESB	non-English-speaking background

NRA   National Rifle Association
OECD   Organization for Economic Cooperation and Development
PC   political correctness
RSL   Returned Services League
SBS   Special Broadcasting Service
SEATO   South-East Asia Treaty Organization
WTO   World Trade Organization
ZPG   Zero Population Growth

Preface

In September 1971, after one week in Australia, I sat in an interview with the Anglican cleric Headmaster of a most prestigious Adelaide private school. The interview had, I believed, gone well, and with a Master's Degree in History and a nearly completed Ph.D. in European History, I expected to have a reasonable chance of securing a job teaching history in this secondary college. My expectations were to gain a tertiary position, but this would do for the time being. However, the Headmaster, to my consternation, after acknowledging my qualifications as more than respectable, began to make discouraging noises about "there's the sports, you see," by which he meant that I was unfamiliar with the Australian Rules and Rugby codes of football in which I was apparently to be involved in some form or another. My background in American football (up to university level in what I learned was called "gridiron") was not sufficient, and he would be in touch with me about the position. Thus, in what turned out to be an initial failed employment application (one that, fortunately, did not inflict permanent damage on my academic career), I was given a rather abrupt and not particularly pleasant cross-cultural introduction to Australian cultural values and language and to the expectations the society had for "new Australians." I was now clearly an "alien" in a foreign culture.

Thus when, twenty years later, I began to investigate the migration of Americans to Australia since World War II, I could happily combine the compelling motivations of personal experiences with intellectual curiosity. I wished to pursue in a systematic academic manner how my fellow Americans had been assimilated into Australian life. Americans, lacking a visible or coherent community structure, were difficult to locate and investigate in detail, however, and the exercise soon took on a broader scope and interest. I became increasingly fascinated by the general questions surrounding the migration process: Why do people migrate? Under what conditions do people take the very difficult and emotionally wrenching decision to leave their homeland? What variables are most associated with a capacity to adapt and assimilate into the host nation?—In short, the complex questions of migration took on a much broader attraction than the more straightforward desire to place oneself in a framework of migration history.

The object of this study, therefore, is to analyze both the particularities of American migration in the post–World War II period and the general context in which the migration of tens of thousands of people took place. By integrating the individual experiences, social processes, and historical context in which American migration occurred, a holistic picture emerges of the historical pattern.

American migrants to Australia could be perceived as the "invisible migrants." They are thought to be few in number and, being English-speaking, easily assimilated into the mainstream Anglo–Celtic society, with whom they share a common language, history, and culture. The post–World War II "normal" American migrant is thought to be easy to identify: white, of European ancestry, tertiary-educated, English-speaking, and from an urban background. Americans are concentrated spatially in the capital cities and eastern states and occupationally in the white-collar, middle-class professions. Although not often in publicly exposed elite positions—politics, media, education—they are visible in the academic world, business, sports, and in the arts and entertainment. But what is missing from this profile is that they are—in spite of being relatively easily assimilated—still migrants, with all the difficulties, opportunities, and traumas that migration entails. Their relative social "invisibility," therefore, obscures the full story of migration, which I hope to elaborate.

Studies of American migrants to Australia have tended to fall into two categories: general narrative histories that emphasize the particular, and sociological studies that focus on a narrow slice of space and time. This study plots a middle course between general historical narrative and the sociological genre by attempting to combine theoretical and methodological discipline with the experiences of real people facing real problems in an Australian cultural setting: the trials and tribulations caused by crossing from one culture to another: the decision to move or to stay; raising children in a new culture; living with Australians at home and at work and facing "cultural death" as the transplanted family assimilates into Australian society and the first generation raised in Australia matures to be new people: American–Australians. The ugly term "Austericans" will be avoided here.

In a recent sociological analysis of American emigration to Australia, Canada, and Israel, Arnold Dashefsky scolded his fellow American sociologists for not taking American emigration history seriously. Americans, he suggested, seemed to find immigration more exciting and appeared to view emigration as almost an unpatriotic subject.[1] This lack of interest has also applied to Australia, where few ethnographic historians or sociologists, American-born or Australian, have found an interest in the subject. Perhaps, as discussed later in the study, this reflects a desire by American academics in Australia to keep a low profile and a tendency among Australian academics toward anti-Americanism. Whatever the causes for the lack of attention to American migrants in Australia, the subject needs and deserves historical analysis, and it is hoped that the following study—based upon a 1993 questionnaire of 302 American respondents living in Australia—will adequately fill this gap in Australian ethnographic history.

David Mosler, Adelaide

Any person in the English-speaking world must have an attitude toward America. It is the most powerful state in the world and projects an often overwhelming presence—cultural, commercial, technological, and military—into the international system. This has been in so many ways the American Century. For Australia, where I migrated as a young Welsh graduate of the London School of Economics in the mid-1960s, the American impact has been huge, particularly since World War II.

For my generation, the consequences of the American involvement in the War in Vietnam have often been the determining experience, and that was chiefly negative, especially among the intelligentsia. This marks off the people who were then young and protested against the war and who have for the most part retained their anti-American orientation in their now more senior positions, against, on the one hand, the World War II and Korean War generations, who by and large admired the Americans and were to a degree grateful to them, and, on the other hand, younger Australians, whose response to America is principally a cultural one of absorption mixed with resentment. Much has been written about these issues.

When I heard that my colleague David Mosler was researching the experience of Americans in Australia, I thought this was an exciting project on a little-investigated subject. When he asked me to join him in writing this volume, I was more than pleased to provide additional information and fill in some of the contours from my own experience as a member of the Australian federal Parliament in the early 1990s, as a one-time government official, and as a person who has written elsewhere on other dimensions of the American–Australian relationship.

In July 1997 it was found in a survey of American opinion—reported in *The Australian* of 15 July—that Australia was the preferred vacation destination for a majority of respondents. At that time 320,000 Americans were visiting Australia annually, and this figure was expected to double with the Sydney Olympics being held in 2000. Nonetheless few books have been written about Australia for an American audience.

In the mid-1990s context of Australian multiculturalism, concerns about the maintenance of an Australian identity in a globalizing world, and the establishment after the Cold War of a unipolar order dominated by the United States of America, this work seems even more timely.

Bob Catley, Adelaide

Acknowledgments

We would like to thank the University of Adelaide and the Center for Australian and New Zealand Studies at Pennsylvania State University for assistance in the preparation of this volume and our wives for much help and for putting up with the attendant inconveniences. We would also like to thank our colleagues, Hugh Stretton, Lynn Martin, and Henry Albinski, who read the book in draft form and offered many useful suggestions. Appreciation must also go to Judith Saebel, who helped with the statistical data; Sue Brookes and Julie McMahon, who both assisted in typing and other tasks in preparation of the manuscript; and our colleagues Christine Churches and Roger Hainsworth, who provided valuable help with editorial tasks. Finally, we greatly appreciate the professional skills of Greenwood Press and the efficiency of Dr James Sabin and Klara King in completing the project.

NOTE

1. Arnold Dashefsky, *Americans Abroad: A Comparative Study of Emigrants from the United States* (New York, 1992), p. ix.

AMERICA
AND AMERICANS
IN AUSTRALIA

1

The Global Context

This is a book about the impact of the most powerful country in the world, the United States of America, on a medium-sized country, Australia. This influence has been exerted through a number of media—political, strategic, cultural, and economic—and there is a considerable literature devoted to these matters. This volume, however, examines the reception and impact of American citizens in Australia, in particular the over 50,000 who have migrated to Australia since World War II.

Since 1945 there have been great changes in the international system, which have generated waves of migration. These have included the creation of a global economy, improvements in international communications and transportation, the consolidation of English as the dominant language, and the creation of an international labor market in certain skilled occupations, including journalism, trade, electronics, and education. These trends have facilitated the migration of Americans to Australia and the impact of the United States on the development of Australia. A close interchange between America and Australia is in a sense a natural process, since the two countries derive from the same British imperial culture, share a common language, and coexist in the geographic zone of the Pacific Ocean. Yet the interaction between these two modern societies, both formed by migration and then refashioned by multiculturalism, has not usually been placed in the historical and sociological perspective it deserves.

The formation and expansion of the modern international system between the fifteenth and twentieth centuries was accompanied by large-scale migrations. Between 1650 and 1950 the population of Europe increased from 100,000,000 to 500,000,000, and in the same period about 100,000,000 Europeans emigrated permanently from that continent. In the period between 1850 and 1960 alone, 61,000,000 people emigrated from Europe, many to the United States and Australia. After 1945, many of these migrants were skilled, and the wealthy settler-based societies of the Pacific littoral attracted and then generated streams of educated and highly skilled mobile labor. In addition, they attracted people from other regions, including at first involuntary migration from Africa to the United States and later migration to both Australia and the United States from Asia.

Both modern Australia and the modern United States were products of these movements of peoples. In turn, they also generated migration between themselves. The United States, by far the larger of the two countries—being for most of the twentieth century about fifteen times more populous than Australia, with a current population of about 260,000,000 as against 18,000,000—has had both a greater impact on and sent more migrants to Australia than vice-versa. This book is concerned with these two processes: the effect of Americans in Australia, within the larger impact of the United States on Australia. In order to understand these processes, we must begin, however, with a portrayal of the historical evolution of relations between these two societies.

WHAT IS AN AMERICAN?

America began its modern history as a migrant nation in the tidewater region of what is now Virginia with a commercial settlement at Jamestown in 1607. It subsequently became the largest recipient of European migrants, and the character of its laissez faire but powerful state and its variegated culture was formed over the next four centuries by successive waves of migrants from Europe and elsewhere. The resulting characteristics of Americans—individualistic, multicultural, restless—were perceived by important observers of Americans from the earliest days of the independent republic following its defeat of the imperial British and after Crèvecoeur first asked, "What is the American, this new man?"[1]

Americans have long regarded themselves as having a distinct national character, and this is frequently observed by Australians when Americans migrate there. In the 1830s Alexis De Tocqueville viewed Americans as chauvinist, garrulous, ethnocentric, always on the move, and "impatient of the smallest censure and insatiable of praise. . . . Their vanity is not only greedy but restless and jealous."[2] The American historian George Bancroft later believed that "Providence had conducted the United States to its present happiness and glory."[3] By the twentieth century many observers depicted Americans as restless, aggressive, expansionist, ethnocentric, and imbued with a sense of a national mission and ethnic superiority. Yet because, perhaps, of America's multicultural character, citizenship itself assumed a unique importance in the fusion of American nationality from its various cultural subgroups, and its symbols—the flag, the constitution, the armed forces, and the rejection of "un-

Americanisms"—became important components of delivering the national identity from the melting pot. America itself had attained a national ideology that was more egalitarian, classless, mobile, capitalist, and individualistic than any of the older national component parts from which its citizens were derived.

At the onset of the twentieth century, following a period of mass immigration (only curtailed in the 1920s) and the resulting rapid population growth, industrialization accompanied by the development of giant corporations, and territorial expansion to encompass the natural frontiers of the North American continent and colonial acquisition in the Pacific and Caribbean regions, America was ready to become a great power. For most of the twentieth century, indeed, it has been the most powerful state in the world. It intervened decisively in World War I; it was drawn into World War II, determined its outcome, and emerged from it as one of the two global superpowers; and then it comprehensively defeated the Soviet Union in the Cold War. By the 1990s only the United States was a global superpower.

The accompanying growth of the American population, which made it by the end of the Cold War the third most populous nation on earth after the ancient and poor Asian peasant-based civilization/states of China and India, was achieved by a prolonged pattern of mass migration both from overseas and within the United States, which was slowed but not stopped by the 1920s discriminatory legislation. This had made the country's cities truly multicultural by the latter part of the twentieth century. The new population diversity generated ideas and habits of democratic pluralism and institutional and legal structures that accommodated the different origins of American citizens and made their generally peaceful cohabitation possible. It was also accompanied by the growth of the American corporate economy, the creation of many of the world's largest and first truly global companies, and the establishment of a resulting level of individual wealth and national technological development that is almost unmatched in the rest of the world. To be American was to work hard and be rewarded with material success.

Also unlike much of the rest of the world, the United States generated no significant socialist movement in the twentieth century, a phenomenon that has attracted intellectual curiosity since Werner Sombart wrote, *Why Is There No Socialism in the United States?*[4] America's nationalist ideology had emerged from its eighteenth-century and mostly affluent origins as egalitarian but also antistatist and without the strong socialist and social democratic movements characteristic of Europe and Australia in the twentieth century. For many left-wing American and foreign observers, this has also meant that America ignored the seamier underside of its materialist success in the form of disadvantaged sectors of the population—blacks, American Indians, poor whites, non-English-speaking communities, the laboring classes, and some lower-class women—who began to be encompassed by the American political system, and for that matter its historiography, only in the latter part of the twentieth century. In the meantime most foreigners—including Australians—and many Americans found the

American political culture to the right of that of most other comparable countries, its economy less regulated, and its culture more materialistic and individualistic.

Nonetheless, America developed the first mass education system in the world and by the start of the twentieth century had the largest postsecondary system of education of any country. In 1910 there were 3,000 postsecondary American tertiary institutions with 300,000 students, compared, for example, to France, which had 7,000 postsecondary students with a population nearly half as large. This educational system with its combination of mass delivery and elite excellence was one of the key contributing factors to the twentieth-century success story of the U.S. economy and society, providing as it did a uniquely large and homogeneous cohort of educated people. As Lord Bryce anticipated late in the nineteenth century,[5] this mass of educated Americans was to have an unprecedented impact on the history of the world—particularly after World War II, when the university system was expanded to encompass a larger proportion of the American population than ever before and serve its world-leading economy and system of technological innovation.

This process also served to make Americans, already among the most mobile people in human history, even more on the move. In 1870, 23 percent of Americans were not born in the state where they lived; by 1970 the figure was 32 percent and by the late 1980s about 40 percent. They were searching for better employment, a richer lifestyle, or merely adventure. The great American cities, particularly on the West Coast, were being inhabited by people from somewhere else. It was a modern culture of mobility based on the highest world level of car ownership, which helped fuel internal migration, as blacks moved from the South to the North, Hispanics into the United States, Europeans to the East Coast and Asians to the West Coast, whites from the countryside and to the suburbs, and blacks to the inner cities. The society of America had become individualistic, culturally variegated, ethnically semisegregated, mass-educated, and incomparably mobile.

THE "CRISIS" OF MODERN AMERICA

Many sociological observers came to see these phenomena as representing a crisis for modern America. Unlike the developed countries of Europe and Australia, the United States did not develop an extended state sector with public welfare services and fiscal responsibility for pursuing full employment. The American way was the private economy, except when this clearly failed and generated the New Deal in the 1930s. During normal peacetime the American state remained largely noninterventionist, and the quasi–New Deal administrations of John F. Kennedy and Lyndon B. Johnson left little impact in a country where the fiscal conservatism of Dwight Eisenhower and Ronald Reagan were more the norm. Of course, the military expansion of the Reagan years, while strategically enormously successful, left a national debt of considerable proportions, leaping as it did from $500 billion in 1970, to $1 trillion in 1980 and to $4.3 trillion by 1992. Much of this, of course, sprang from the willingness of Americans to spend money in order to wage and win the Cold War against the Soviets while being decidedly unprepared to pay the cost in current taxes as against future debt.

By the early 1990s there were therefore signs that Americans were beginning to lose their traditional optimism and their faith in their political institutions as these social and fiscal problems were compounded by a long pause in the growth of personal incomes and a series of scandals that shook the legitimacy of their political leaders, including some presidents. The Vietnam defeat, the Watergate crisis, and the Iran–Contra affair took their toll on public confidence.

At the end of the Cold War and following the disintegration of the Soviet Union in December 1991, many Americans came to believe that in the absence of an identifiable enemy, the United States was militarily overextended throughout the world, running large and unsustainable budget and trade deficits and allowing its society to become increasingly unequal and therefore unmanageable. While triumphalists like Francis Fukuyama[6] had their day in the sun, Cold War victor George Bush lost the 1992 presidential election to a more domestically attuned Bill Clinton. Intellectual critics increasingly portrayed a divided and unequal society from which an underclass, based on ethnicity, skills, culture, and often gender, was being excluded. From the 1970s on, left-wing historians began describing a nation for which this had always been the case but whose cultural elite had instead depicted a successful melting pot in which the rags-to-riches dream could become a widespread reality. For social critics in the early 1990s the social consensus of America appeared to weaken in the face of these pressures, and the coherent national objectives and historical self-confidence seemed to disintegrate. Did these problems contribute to the willingness of some Americans to migrate from a country that had been historically the largest recipient of migrants in human history? And if so, did they increase the likelihood of their migrating to Australia?

AMERICAN MIGRATION

Of course, even were one to take the most optimistic view of the American condition, one would expect some emigration to take place from the United States because of the mobility of the American population and the relentless search for personal improvement displayed by its citizens. Nonetheless, by and large Americans are not an emigrating people. In most surveys they remain the proudest and most chauvinistic about their nation in the developed world and the most reluctant to leave what they continue to see as the "best nation in the world." Americans, whether by self-delusion, ignorance, or perceptiveness, remain intensely reluctant to leave their nation as migrants, and while movement to the suburbs or interstate is very common, overseas migration appears to risk detribalization, the severing of contact with the symbols of American nationality, and the loss of cultural identity. In the post–World War II era, Australia, however, did present a special kind of destination to some tens of thousands of Americans who did leave. Australia was perceived as a part of the American cultural universe—a kind of fifty-first state and further extension of the long-trodden path to, and then beyond, the West Coast.

Marshall Green, the former U.S. troubleshooter and U.S. ambassador to Australia at the time of the most serious political crisis in the country since World War II, the 1975 sacking of the Whitlam Labour government, had decades of experience that prompted him to comment that "one can emigrate from Australia to America or from America to Australia without ever leaving home."[7] Australia was similarly well known to millions of Americans from World War II service and by resulting repute, as a sprawling nation in an underpopulated continent in the South Pacific, alluring to Americans looking for employment, adventure, and, in the 1990s perhaps, seeking an escape or respite from the problems of urban America. Australia often appeared to Americans as an atavistic example of the American past: untamed, egalitarian, unspoiled, peaceful, a land of free and democratic peoples, even if the reality of both was considerably more complicated.

In 1994 Robert Zoellick, former under secretary of state in the Bush administration, viewed "Australia as 'America West' . . . a wide-open country, with energetic people who love the outdoors, with a good sense of humor."[8] In the popular press, in movies, on television, and in some clever Australian-funded advertising campaigns designed to attract tourists, Australia was portrayed as nearly paradise. For many Americans, notoriously ill-informed about the outside world in a way often unique to a nearly self-contained continental civilization, Australia would become among the most popular actual and aspired-to destinations for travel and settlement. But the destination they attained was not uniformly Nirvana.

THE IDEA OF THE AMERICAN STATE

The Americans who migrated to Australia, like migrants everywhere, had to coexist with the views that the receiving society held of their national characteristics, culture, and state. For Americans the dimensions of this problem assumed larger proportions than were common for other nationalities. During the twentieth century America has been a great power, since World War II the most powerful country, and in the 1990s the dominant, even hegemonic, power of the international system. Its citizens are often judged by the behavior of their state.

The modern impact of the American state on Australia has been particularly profound. Until World War II a component of the British Empire, after 1945 Australia emerged with its own independent interests. In the strategic sphere this coincided with the development of the U.S. policy of containment of communism in East Asia. Australia aligned with America in pursuit of this objective and joined the United States in the Korean and Vietnam Wars and other lesser conflicts. Australia also supported the United States in its intensified confrontation with the Soviet Union in the 1980s and in the 1991–92 Gulf War. As in the United States, these activities produced some domestic opposition and critics, particularly on the political Left. As in most other countries, the political Left has been historically stronger in Australia than in America, particularly in intellectual circles.

Since the end of the Cold War the international dominance of the United States has become even more pronounced and the hostility of the intellectual Left, if anything, more intense, although often masked in the guise of postcolonial or postmodernist theory. This American hegemony has extended from its military preponderance, through its unrivaled political ascendancy, including in the United Nations, to its economic status as easily the largest national economy and host for many of the largest global companies, to the cultural preponderance of American production in television, movies, fashions, and tastes in fields as widely cast as music, clothing, and fast food. In the wider Australian population this has generated an ambivalence toward individual Americans who are often well liked for their characteristics while being simultaneously resented for the power they are perceived, however vicariously, to represent.

The effect of this background mosaic on Australia, the impact of America, and the reception of American migrants to Australia has been multifaceted. Americans have left a homeland that has, according to critics and to some of the migrants themselves, exhibited a continuing social and economic crisis. They have come to an Australia, however, where America understandably appears as a dominant power the strength of whose culture threatens almost the existence of the Australian identity. Yet the obvious similarities between Australians and Americans would dictate the ready assimilation of American migrants into Australian society on equitable terms. It is within the parameters dictated by these paradoxes that the American migrants to Australia must survive.

NOTES

1. Quoted in Peter Marshall, "The Emergence of American Nationalism," in Michael McGiffert and Robert Skotheim, eds., *American Social Thought* (London, 1972), p. 22.

2. Alexis De Tocqueville, *Democracy in America* (London, 1956 edition), p. 252.

3. Quoted by Marshall, "American Nationalism," p. 227.

4. Werner Sombart, *Why Is There No Socialism in the United States?* (White Plains, NY, [1906] 1976).

5. Lord Bryce, *The American Commonwealth* (second ed., revised) (London, 1891).

6. F. Fukuyama, *The End of History and the Last Man* (London, 1992).

7. Quoted in Philip and Roger Bell, *Implicated, the United States in Australia* (Melbourne, 1993), p. 111.

8. *The Australian*, 3 September 1994, p. 12.

2

Australia in Historical Context

AUSTRALIA: ANOTHER AMERICA?

Although the first European settlement in Australia was a convict colony established at Sydney in 1788, in a striking number of ways America and Australia have traveled parallel historical paths—a fact that has not gone unnoticed from the middle of the nineteenth century down to the present. Both were peripheral colonial Anglo-Saxon cultures with a huge frontier to settle in the nineteenth century; they shared a common linguistic and cultural heritage; neither could avoid the historical record of rather ruthless and brutal treatment of their indigenous peoples, whose state of health and social welfare is still acutely poor; both now have robust and pluralistic dominant political cultures; both now have multicultural societies resulting from mass European and, to a lesser extent, Asian immigration; they have developed a similar post–World War II culture shaped by the social forces of hyperconsumption, suburbanization, and ideological liberal capitalism while sharing a shrinking Asian–Pacific Basin; and the two "cousins" have similar national characters.

In the mid–nineteenth century one observer commented: "the people of this colony [Australia] resemble the Americans in their presumption, arrogance, ignorance and conceit." Many other travelers in the Empire found British colonials, like Americans, to be brash, crude, egalitarian, materialistic, provincial, and braggarts—a list not unfamiliar to students of the American character. Matthew Arnold once suggested, as commented upon by Richard White, that Australia, rather than America, represented the nadir of cultural debasement. The two nations, therefore, are often lumped together in space and time, and the

evolution of the two national cultures is a "natural" for juxtaposition by historians, sociologists, and countless observers and scribblers of all types.[1]

Americans and Australians have been looking at one another with a critical
eye for over two centuries. In trade, diplomacy, the arts, and academic life the
nationals from both cultures have analyzed the respective economies, laws,
mores, values, ethics, and cultural strengths of each nation. These observations
always reveal the values of the observer and the observed; to examine them
over time serves a dual purpose for comprehending the judgments of Americans
and Australians about each other and the cultural position from which these
judgments are derived. They serve, therefore, as a means by which to gain
an understanding not only of the mutual relationship between Australia and
America but a window through which may be viewed the evolving cultural
landscape of each.

From the early nineteenth century to the 1990s some transcendent themes
emerge in the interplay between the two former British colonial societies. Settled
much earlier, America was always the stronger economic and geopolitical
power, and consequently Australia invariably is more concerned about how it is
perceived by the United States than the reverse. Australians and Americans
perceive each other as part of a common democratic and pluralistic experiment
and achievement. Australians have been ambivalent about copying American
models and have, throughout their history, had the contradictory habit of simultaneously embracing some American standards and rejecting others, including in
the same area. Both societies have viewed the other through selective ideological
prisms, so that individual observers utilize evidence to reinforce or denigrate
political positions from internal political debates in their respective nations.
And, finally, any examination of the attitudes of Americans and Australians
to one another will reveal the marvelous kaleidoscope of changing cultures as
from 1800 to the 1990s both societies go through the extraordinary challenges of
colonial societies, nation-building, war, depression, modernization, and finally
the looming twenty-first century, with the difficult problems of urban overpopu-
lation, pollution, and economic dislocation and reorganization compelling both
nations to rethink their own identities.

AMERICA AND AUSTRALIA: THE EARLY YEARS

Early contacts between Americans and Australians provide examples of most
of these themes and raise issues that would continue down to the present. White
Americans throughout their history have been ethnocentric and limited in their
knowledge about the world outside their borders. In a speech to a Joint Session
of Congress in 1955, an honor given to few foreign leaders, Sir Robert Menzies,
the Australian prime minister, remarked that he had met "a gentleman in San
Francisco [who] understood quite plainly [that Australia] was on the East Coast
of the United States; a sort of off-shore island."[2] The Australian continent,
therefore, was a subject about which Americans in the nineteenth century knew

little; as Menzies discovered in the 1950s, this would persist well into the modern period and, as discussed below, even to the 1990s. Australia, as a distant land, would never impinge greatly on American consciousness, and, as already indicated, American migrants in the post–World War II period would generally come to Australia with a low knowledge base and a hazy notion of Australia, which was generally perceived as resembling another American state or a replication of an earlier, more pristine, form of America.

Australians, on the other hand, although better informed about the imperial metropolitan culture of the Pacific Basin than Americans are about Australia, have often viewed America through stereotypical images projected in popular culture. In the nineteenth century minstrel shows, circuses, dime novels, and the popular press circulated simplistic views of America; the twentieth-century equivalents of television, film, and popular magazines continue to project often distorted views of American culture. Ideologically tainted analyses of America frequently exaggerate the violent, predatory, and corrupt aspects of American society from the Left, and the Right counters with equally hyperbolic interpretations of the successes of antistatist, liberal capitalist America. Periodic monarchist warnings about the dangers of the American presidential system have done little to cultivate pro-American attitudes. A historical analysis of the perceptions Australia and America have of each other must attempt, therefore, to cut through the ethnocentric and epistemological limitations of both cultures in order to grasp what they do and do not know about each other.

Early contacts between the two countries date from the very beginnings of colonization in New South Wales. With the establishment of the penal colony in 1788, American ships were quick to develop trade between Australia and America as part of the Western Pacific trade pattern. Even though there were restrictions placed on trade by the East India Company, trade contacts were regular and profitable between Sydney and the United States to the 1820s. A triangular trade developed between Australia, the United States, and China, and with the termination of the East India Company's monopoly in 1813, a brisk trade grew around sealing, whaling, fishing, guano, and later gold. Even in this early period, an inverse balance of trade developed on the Australian side, a phenomenon that is a transcendent theme and source of friction between the two nations down to the 1990s.[3]

In this earliest phase of American–Australian interactions the conceptions the two countries had of one another were rather primitive and simplistic but instructive. Of course the two societies had quite different origins in that most of the early American settlers were fleeing the power of overly oppressive states and seeking to establish colonies free from religious restrictions, whereas the settlement of New South Wales was controlled by the British imperial state and was in the first instance dominated by convicts and their jailers. No one came voluntarily. During the following half-century 160,00 convicts arrived in the Australian penal settlements and provided much of the labor particularly for the construction of infrastructure.

In 1839, when the American Charles Wilkes visited Sydney, he observed that "New South Wales is known in the United States almost by its name alone."[4] By that time the settlement was more diverse and prosperous after the discovery of the Murray–Darling Basin had made it one of the world's major wool exporters. People from both nations recognized the commonality of the two cultures, but Australians, while acknowledging that Americans were optimistic and energetic go-getters, were suspicious and somewhat hostile about their alleged radicalism on the monarchy and found them to be especially pushy and materialistic. Americans were trading with Australia to gain the maximum advantage and profitability, and the Australians were quick to gain as much advantage as possible from their Anglo-Saxon cousins, about whom they had ambivalent opinions.[5]

Friction was common between American traders and merchants based in Sydney and the local people and authority. When whaling and sealing crews were ashore, brawls took place in the taverns and the narrow streets of Sydney. Even though the rights of citizenship were restrictive for Americans, a few American merchants became citizens and took up permanent residence in Australia. In South Australia, settled after 1836, one whalers' sanctuary on Kangaroo Island is named "American River" after the early-nineteenth-century use of the sheltered anchorage. The influence of American culture, however, even though small, was to be inexorable. In the 1820s American missionaries began to arrive, and American constitutional and political ideas served as models for Australia in the 1830s as representative government evolved in the colonies. Americans were moving westward in their own nation, and their influence was rapidly spilling over into the Pacific Basin. The first United States consul, James Hartwell Williams, arrived on the *Draco* in 1837 to take up his post in Sydney; he was followed by colleagues in Hobart in 1843 and Melbourne in 1852. The pattern for the future, then, was already set between the two nations, with an expanding and powerful America and a young Australia low in population density and economic strength willing, or even anxious, to accept Americans but always suspicious of the motives, power, and national characteristics of their Yankee cousins.[6]

THE GOLD RUSHES

The next phase of the relationship between Australia and America revolved almost entirely around the discovery of gold in America in 1849 and in Australia in 1851. The gold rushes in California, New South Wales, and Victoria would greatly accelerate the flow of people, trade, and ideas across the Pacific. This trans-Pacific activity would heighten and extend the tensions between the two as well as develop reciprocal exchanges of common political and social concerns. The cultural dynamic (especially significant in later analysis of post–World War II Australia) of American influence producing fears about Americanization, and the concomitant reaction of anti-Americanism associated with Australian nationalistic search for identity, can be observed as early as the 1850s. The foundations of the modern relationship can, therefore, be traced back to the economic and migration changes produced by the search for gold and the increased trade as part of the process, for intrinsic to this pattern was anxiety in Australia about being swamped by American economic dominance and cultural forms.

English-born Edward Hargraves was drawn from Australia to America by the discovery of gold near Sacramento in 1849. He returned to Australia in the early 1850s, bringing with him the techniques of panning and cradling he had utilized in California. When he discovered gold in New South Wales in 1851, Australians flocked to the gold fields from around the nation. This stemmed the flow of gold-seekers to America, and miners who had been to America returned to Australia. Also from America came American migrants of all types—black and white, skilled tradesmen and laborers, merchants with capital to invest and entrepreneurs to promote trade and commerce.

Some 5,000–6,000 Americans would migrate to Australia in the 1850s, although the exact number is impossible to establish, for the terms "American," "Californian," and "Yankee" were used loosely to denote American nationals as well as Australians or Europeans who had temporary residence in America. It was the first large-scale migration of Americans to Australia and would also engender a debate about the desirability of the American influence on Australian society.[7] This coincided with the evolution of representative government structures in Australia, which the British authorities—in some measure because they were mindful of the experience of the American Revolution, which they did not wish to repeat—made no effort to resist. By the 1850s all five eastern colonies had parliamentary systems, and Western Australia was to follow shortly thereafter.

Trade increased dramatically, with manufactured goods flowing to the gold fields from America and primary products going to the West Coast of America. Axes, shovels, agricultural and mining equipment throughout the colonies increasingly bore the imprint "Made in America." Indigenous manufacturers of joinery complained of the flooding of Australia by American products—symptomatic of the generalized fears about American competition. Protectionists pushed for greater controls over cheaper American goods, and throughout the 1850s the balance of trade was clearly in America's favor.[8] The Australian population continued to grow, but fewer could find employment on the gold fields, which were increasingly worked with higher technology that required capital; so the work force demanded of their politicians a protected industry policy. By the 1890s protectionism had produced some industrialization in the southern colonies of Victoria and South Australia in particular.

Individual Americans also began to appear in the saga of Australian history as the population expanded during the gold rushes and opportunities beckoned for the already mobile, opportunistic, and materialistic Americans. Adams and Company was a successful transport company in America specializing in the shipment of gold and merchandise. The opportunities in Australia were obvious, and in 1853 a Melbourne office was opened; the first direct gold shipment to America went on the *Bavaria* in that year. In 1854 two of the directors of the company, Samuel Cutler and Freeman Cobb, took over management of the firm, and for the next two years a new company, Cobb and Co., would offer coach transportation throughout the colonies. Freeman Cobb popularized American-style coaches and offered an efficient and popular service. The Melbourne *Age* praised him as "the pioneer of coach traveling" in Australia, and Freeman Cobb became the first of many Americans who would have an impact on the economic development of the Australian colonies from the 1850s to Federation in 1901.[9] He was later to be immortalized as the star of a popular television series in the 1960s.

Social and political values and institutional forms were also imported from America. Entertainment from the United States included circuses, minstrel shows, live theater, and individual traveling entertainers. American cultural imperialism was quick to draw animosity in the colonies, where the importing of American actors, productions, and techniques was resisted and resented by Australian theatrical companies and actors. From the mid–nineteenth century on to the 1990s, an essential ingredient in anti-Americanism was the fear of Americanization of the arts and entertainment; as one 1850s editorial in the *Hobart Courier* put it, the persistent question by the defenders of Australian culture would always be, "What do we want with Americans?"[10]

Americans also brought with them the egalitarian—for white people—political values of a republican society. Questions were raised in the colonies about the dangers to Australian colonial stability from Yankee-inspired radicalism. Although a great deal of controversy exists on the impact of Americans on the Eureka rebellion in 1854, one can conclude that a few Americans participated in and gave encouragement to radical political activity in and around the gold fields. Overall, however, the American connections with Australian political change in the 1850s were superficial and relatively insignificant.[11]

The issue of race in the gold rushes in both countries reveals patterns of behavior of greater substance and more transcendent importance to both societies. Black Americans also went to Australia and were keenly aware of the position of free and slave blacks in America in the 1850s. These free blacks numbered in the hundreds in Australia and were to be found among miners and tradesmen in the colonies, though very few would remain in Australia. (The reactions of Australians to black Americans and the relationship between black and white Americans in Australia is considered in detail in later sections on World War II and post–World War II migration.) Black Americans expressed some sympathy with indigenous Aborigines in Australia, but little substantive evidence exists on their relationship with the general white Australian community.[12]

A clearer pattern, however, emerges on the Chinese in Australia, paralleled by American attitudes and legislation on Asians in the nineteenth century in both nations. Throughout the 1850s, friction existed between Australians, Europeans,

Americans, and Chinese in the search for gold. Americans brought with them the prevailing nineteenth-century Anglo-Saxon conceptions of the superiority of Europeans—ideas that were, of course, virtually identical to those of white Australians. American egalitarianism did not transcend racial lines in the 1850s —nor, for that matter, always in the 1990s. In the violence against the Chinese, especially in the riots at Bendigo (1854) and Buckland (1857) in Victoria, and in Lambing Flat, New South Wales (1860–61), Americans were implicated but probably not the prime movers in the anti-Chinese actions.

What these incidents clearly reveal, however, is the common racism of Americans and Australians, a fact that is reflected in the anti-Chinese–Japanese–Asian legislation and immigration restrictions implemented in both countries from the mid-nineteenth century, through the White Australia policy established in the 1901 Australian Immigration Act, to the American Immigration Acts of 1921 and 1924 and the internment of the Japanese in World War II. Americans and Australians may have differed on many things, but on race in the 1850s these Anglo-Saxon cultures were on common ground.[13]

By the end of the 1850s the American connection faded again. As the gold rushes came to a close, Americans returned to the United States without having made a permanent impression on Australian culture. Americans took back with them impressions of Australians as a proud, independent, and somewhat prickly people with whom they shared a common culture and interest in gambling, drinking, and general style of life. Australians accepted Americans as kindred people but to be watched carefully for their propensities to work excessively and exercise their power and influence in a manner that threatened the autonomy of Australian society. In the 1860s American attention would be totally focused on the great domestic crisis of the Civil War, and they would withdraw into their own national sphere, but with the resurgence of a unified America in the period from the 1870s to World War I, America was soon to draw Australia within its geographic orbit.[14]

AUSTRALIA MOVES TOWARD NATIONHOOD

In the second half of the nineteenth century America emerged as a world power and multiethnic society, while Australia evolved toward an independent nation within the British Empire based upon an Anglo-Celtic cultural and ethnic base. Contacts throughout this period between America and Australia continued to grow in frequency and substantive importance as the confluent forces of the two cultures became stronger. As the British Empire reached its apogee (and unbeknownst to most contemporaries its imminent rapid decline), the historical changes that would see the replacement of European power in the Asian–Pacific region by the Pax Americana were already in place.

Industrialization in the United States would alter the underlying structures of the economy and consequently and correspondingly transform the social order and ideological structures. Those sections of the society uprooted by enormous change would attempt to retard, mold, or seek accommodation to the alterations of their social position and financial prospects in an industrial society. The rural revolt of farmers, facing high interest rates, low incomes, and growing transportation costs, was led by William Jennings Bryan and the Populist movement and Party. In the cities the popular protests built up in the period between 1870 and 1910 and produced the progressive movement, with great consequences for both major political parties. The Republicans would be led by the progressive President Theodore Roosevelt (1901–09) and the Democrats would nominate and successfully see elected the progressive Woodrow Wilson, president from 1913 to 1921.

The industrial culture would also produce a growing union movement, and the full spectrum of ideological positions—embracing the traditional unionism of Samuel Gompers, the socialism of Daniel De Leon and Eugene V. Debs, the anarcho-syndicalism of Bill Haywood and the Industrial Workers of the World (IWW or Wobblies), and a kaleidoscope of left-wing ideas from figures such as Henry George, Emma Goldman, and Edward Bellamy—would make up the union–left industrial culture of the urban working classes. The conviction of Wobblie activists on arson charges and the possible persecution of the IWW has been subjected to close scrutiny by the former Australian Communist Ian Turner in his book, *Sydney's Burning*.[15] In a society dominated by a conservative capitalist hegemony, these reformist elements presented at least a moderate challenge to the prevailing ideology; reform politics in the United States would also result in the distribution of these ideas across American borders to nations like Australia.

Australians responded with interest, but also ambivalence, to constitutional and political models emanating from the United States. As the world was moving inexorably to the "American century," Australians could not ignore ubiquitous paradigms of culture and society coming from America. In many ways the global model of modernization in the twentieth century would be American, so that Americanization was not so much a simple aping of U.S. culture as conformity to prevailing global technological and cultural forms. By the end of the process, Australia—indeed America itself—would be enveloped by the twentieth-century "American" global pattern of mass consumption, multinational capital, information-based technology, and transnational social values.[16]

The intellectual ferment produced by industrialization of the European–American world included, of course, Australia, and men and ideas migrated across national boundaries. The most notable late-nineteenth-century visit by an American, a central figure in radical thought, was in 1890 by the writer and economist Henry George. His book *Progress and Poverty* (1879) was read widely in Australia, and his theories, revolving around a tax on land, were popular in the labor movement. George lectured in Australia to enthusiastic audiences, and Henry George and Single Tax Leagues were established in this period and survived to the 1990s. The socialist thought of Daniel De Leon of the Socialist Labor Party of America (1895) and the radical unionism of the Industrial Workers of the World (the IWW), established in 1905, also found fertile ground, and an IWW—or "Wobblies"—chapter was set up in Australia. Interest also existed in Australia in populist, progressive and radical thought on issues concerning banking, education, women, and the environment. Australia, therefore, was an amalgam of European and British intellectual traditions, but in the final decades of the nineteenth century it increasingly embraced the products of social change and protest from America.[17]

FEDERATION

In the late nineteenth century, with the approaching challenge of national unity and Federation in 1901, the issues of constitutional and political forms became of prime importance in Australia. The traditions of Britain, Canada, and America would, of course, all be examined for possible structures and principles relevant to Australian constitutional requirements for a federation of states. In the convention of 1897–98 there were vigorous and protracted debates about the competing and multiple traditions upon which Australia could draw in formulating the new constitution. Then, as now, the British and U.S. cultural models offered both complementary and conflicting solutions, and radicals, liberals, and conservatives alike would claim to be representing Australian national interests. Some delegates were antagonistic to the inordinate influence of the U.S. Constitution on the convention, but in the end that document was to be a primary source for the Australian Constitution. As is probable with the republic debate in the 1990s, the pressures of Americanization came from the "right side of history," and the British imperial tradition was doomed to be "on the wrong side."

In crucial areas the constitutional structure was based on the U.S. model: a federal union; three branches of government—executive, legislative, and judicial; the lower house elected on a popular basis, the House of Representatives, and an upper house composed of representatives elected from each state but with equal numbers, the Senate; a supreme court replicated by a High Court in Australia with powers to establish subordinate district courts; a division between federal powers at the center of government and the remaining powers reserved for the states; and a federal capital territory based upon the model of Washington DC.

There were also some notable differences, however, which continue to be debated through to the 1990s. The Australian Constitution did not contain a Bill of Rights, nor did it break with the British constitutional monarchy. American republicanism was rejected, and the Westminster traditions of authority from the Crown, the status of the governor-general, the choice and origins of cabinet, and the appeal to the Privy Council were all retained. The Commonwealth of Australia in 1901 was based, then, upon a hybrid constitution with a dominant American influence but retaining some central elements of the Westminster system.[18]

Much has been written, and continues to be written, about the relative deficiencies and strengths of the two constitutions. Both contain the chronic and sometimes crippling tensions between central and state government powers. Both nations can experience "gridlock" in the legislative arena, and the capacities of both political structures for producing rapid change are limited. The Australian Constitution is actually an Act of the British Parliament. The U.S. Constitution directly contains provisions and protection conducive to libertarian democracy and in that respect is superior to the Australian Constitution. However, historically, the American hostility to an interventionist state has inhibited moves toward social justice. The Australian Constitution, on the other hand, lacks a Bill of Rights, but Australia generally has a more equitable society— with the exception of indigenous Aborigines—because of a strong collectivist, social democratic British–European tradition. The Australian Constitution is partly a derivative of the U.S. model; both nations experience problems instituting social change, and the respective political systems experience, in particular policy areas, difficulties that are a complex combination of historical factors and constitutional structures unique to both societies. But throughout the twentieth century both have been assertive and raucous democracies.

The American influence in the deliberations and structure of the Australian Constitution was matched by its growing physical presence in the Western Pacific. The victory over Spain in 1898 gave it a base in the region in the Philippines and Guam and, together with its control of Hawaii and Samoa, firmly established the United States as a Western Pacific power. This led indubitably to greater recognition by Australia of U.S. power, and when President Theodore Roosevelt sent a fleet in 1908 to tour the region, this "Great White Fleet," as it was called by the Australian press, was welcomed warmly in Australia by Prime Minister Alfred Deakin, a progressive liberal. It also gave the opportunity to stage the world heavyweight boxing title bout in Sydney, which the giant Jack Johnson, who was black, won by pulverizing the smaller Tommy Burns, who was white.

Even though this pro-American enthusiasm was a shift away from British imperial ties, it was also a clear recognition of American power and an expression of solidarity with America against resurgent Asian (especially Japanese) power. Australia was to align itself subsequently with the United States in two World Wars, the Cold War era (Korea, Vietnam), and its post–Cold War aspirations. With the American naval visit in 1908 one can already see adumbrated the ties of geopolitical, ideological, and cultural commonality between Australia and the United States.[19]

SOCIALISM IN AUSTRALIA

Unlike the United States, which, it has often been noted, did not produce a socialist movement, Australia developed an indigenous and unique socialist tradition, particularly around the Australian Labour Party, which was to have a significant and distinctive impact on Australian development. Also unlike America, Australia developed a regulated, protected, and statist political economy, which meant that however alike the two peoples were in other respects, their societies projected distinct values and structures. Whereas observers of America —from the Baron de Montesquieu to Thomas Paine to De Tocqueville—were impressed by the commercial vigor of American liberal civilization and often wanted to reimport its egalitarian and democratic temper to Europe, it was the socialist nature of the new Australian society that most impressed visitors. The English Fabian Socialist Webbs were to visit Australia at the turn of the century and be impressed with the social and franchise gains, although they were often made at the expense of what the middle-class radicals believed to be excessive class collaboration. Albert Metin, a noted French observer, was sufficiently impressed to entitle his book *Socialisme sans doctrines*,[20] in recognition of the practical nature of the Australian laboring classes and their political doctrines. Lenin, ever the fanatic, was critical for exactly the same reason.

The roots of this strong development of social democratic practices in Australia were to be found in Europe, particularly Britain. During the second British Empire, London had no intention of repeating its American mistake and quickly granted self-government to the Australian colonists, mostly by the 1850s and 1860s. The workers who flooded Australia during the gold-rush boom of the late eighteenth century came from an England where it was the conflict between emerging industrial capital and labor that was predominant, not the nineteenth-century battle against the absolutist monarchic state. Trade unions were quickly formed and legalized, and the franchise was extended such that it was effectively universal by the end of the century, including women, but not the Aboriginals— though sometimes in the colonies including even them. The Australian unions became embroiled in some quite bitter industrial struggles in the 1890s economic depression and, as in much of contemporary Europe, set up their own political party in 1891—the Australian Labour Party (ALP).

In 1901, after extensive discussions and debates throughout the continent and a series of referenda, the six colonies united into the Commonwealth of Australia by Act of the compliant British Parliament. But unlike in America over a hundred years previously, no one seriously believed this to be a revolutionary and earth-shattering event. During the first decade of its existence the Australian Parliament was dominated by the ALP and a loosely aligned group of social liberals who together constructed the basic contours of the Australian state. Unlike the American Founding Fathers, the early Australian politicians wanted to use the state's powers to improve the condition of civil society. The five pillars that formed the basis of what Kelly has called the Australian Settlement[21] were to survive until the 1980s.

While the creation of the nation rested on free trade between the former colonies (and now states), it had been achieved only by the pro–free-trade states led by New South Wales agreeing to the imposition of a national tariff to continue the protection of the southern state manufacturing industry. The tariff was then, of course, a common means for accelerating industrialization among late developers, including the United States. This mechanism for protecting wage rates was buttressed by the White Australia policy, demanded by the unions and supported by manufacturers as a trade-off for tariff protection. Wage rates, in turn—since they were not in any case related to productivity—were determined after 1907 by a uniquely Australian institution, the Arbitration Commission, which set the just and legal wage rate in each trade. The use of such regulatory bodies quickly spread throughout the economy, together with the use of state-owned corporations like the Commonwealth Bank and later the Qantas airline, to provide for a market failure or to encourage competition. Finally, the whole structure was closely linked to the British imperial system with whom Australia did most of its trade and for whom it went to both World Wars.

This economic system has been called *dirigiste* and could survive quite well as an effectively dual economy. The exporting sectors in agriculture and mining were world-competitive and usually earned sufficient foreign exchange to keep the nation solvent. During the 1930s depression this failed with the collapse of commodity prices, and Australia began to regulate even more heavily. After World War II it took this process a step further and undertook to broaden the industrial base.

Although Americans had been active in the primary and trading sectors of the Australian economy since the nineteenth century, the first U.S. industrial presence in Australia came after World War I, when the protected and high-income domestic market proved attractive for American companies that emerged from the conflict with capital to export. As Australian cities suburbanized, so the early products of the automobile age spread from America, although English capital remained dominant. After World War II American capital entered in earnest, and the United States soon surpassed the United Kingdom as the principal source of foreign investment—a status it maintained through the 1950s and 1960s.[22]

AMERICANS IN AUSTRALIA

The ties between the two nations were also extended in the early twentieth century by a trickle of Americans settling in Australia and a growing reciprocal affection between the Anglo-Saxon cousins. This may have been detracted from by anger in Australia over America's late entry into World War I and subsequent disputes at Versailles, including Australian resistance to the principle of racial equality, but in the end the shared victory over German militarism was remembered more than the trifling arguments.[23]

In this period a few individuals from America made an impact on Australian history; those who did deserve to be considered insofar as they contributed to the image of Americans in Australia and to Australian public life. It is possibly an irony, and one that is explored in detail in subsequent sections, that two of them—John Greely Jenkins and King O'Malley—achieved positions that have never been equaled subsequently by any other American migrants.

The most famous American visitor in this period was the global star of literature, Mark Twain, who entertained packed houses throughout Australia and New Zealand during a tour in the last months of 1895. He was welcomed by the governing elite of Australia and dined at private clubs in Sydney, Melbourne, and Adelaide with men like the two future prime ministers, Edward Barton and Alfred Deakin. Aspiring writers, journalists, editors, and assorted intelligentsia besieged the author throughout the tour with anxious questions about Australian writing, national character, and the bonds of Australian–American culture. Twain, always with a perceptive sense of his audience and his income, charmed the Australians by praising their journals, which were at that time particularly numerous, including the very nationalistic *Bulletin.* Twain—anxious, as ever, to please—remarked that "Australians did not seem to me to differ noticeably from Americans either in dress, carriage, ways, pronunciations, inflection, or general appearances." While it may be doubted that Australians at that or any other time actually sounded like Americans, Twain's tour did reveal other familiar themes: the friendly reception of Americans in Australia, but always tinged with insecurity about Australian national identity.[24]

Herbert Clark Hoover, elected president of the United States in 1928, was symptomatic of the emerging symbiosis between America and Australia. Hoover, like James Rutherford in the steel industry in the 1880s before him and Julius Kruttschmitt, who was general manager of Mount Isa Mines Ltd, after him in the 1930s, was a mining engineer drawn to Australia in the late 1890s. Between 1896 and 1898, and again between 1905 and 1907, he worked in Western Australia near Kalgoorlie and later in New South Wales. This was his first overseas experience in mining, and he went on to work in China, Africa, Russia, and Latin America. He would become U.S. secretary of commerce in 1921 under President Harding, but some of his fellow Americans would stay permanently in Australia and achieve a comparable political status in the Australian political system.[25]

John Greely Jenkins (1851–1923) was the only person of American birth ever to be elected premier of an Australian state. He was born in Pennsylvania of Welsh migrant parents, who had come to America in the 1830s. He was educated in a Wyoming seminary and came to South Australia as a publisher's traveler in 1878. He entered politics in 1886 in Unley and became mayor in 1888. Elected to the South Australian Parliament in 1887 as a protectionist, he was considered to be a "shrewd long-headed Yankee." He became a minister in Thomas Playford's government in 1891 and premier in 1901, and he was elected in his own right in 1902. He resigned from Parliament in 1908 to become agent-general in London, where he died in 1923 after a late career as a steel importer. In politics and in business he was agile—he was described by noted psephologist Dean Jaensch as a "political acrobat."[26]

Of far greater significance and controversy was the career and life of King O'Malley, whose origins and impact—from his obscure beginnings down to the play *The Legend of King O'Malley,* by Michael Buddy and Robert Ellis, in

1971—remain a subject of dispute. O'Malley was probably born in America in 1858, although he later claimed to be Canadian so that he could run for parliament in South Australia. He came to Australia in 1888, at the age of 30, and he was elected to the South Australian House of Assembly from the seat of Encounter Bay, having been a real estate salesman up to that time. He served from 1896, but, as a strong federationist, in 1901 he stood for the federal parliament in Tasmania from the mining seat of Lyell. When Andrew Fisher was elected Labour prime minister in 1910, O'Malley became minister for home affairs, although Fisher had no great love for him.[27]

O'Malley's career in federal politics was almost a caricature of Yankee stereotypical behavior. He was larger than life, garrulous, and a curious mixture of huckster, visionary, and, in the American vernacular, just plain "screwball." John Molony claims that he "fluctuated from the sane and wise to the flamboyant and unbalanced."[28] He was at the center of many crucial issues in the building of an Australian nation and achieved the highest political office of any American-born Australian politician. Only twice since (and possibly because of opprobrium from O'Malley's career) have Americans been elected to federal parliament—and this low participation rate is discussed in a subsequent chapter. From O'Malley to some high-profile American elite business figures in the 1990s—like "chainsaw" Al Dunlap working for Kerry Packer's Australian Consolidated Holdings—Americans have been both admired and despised for aggressive "zaniness."

In 1910, as minister for home affairs, O'Malley was put in charge of organizing the planning for the Australian Capital Territory. He supported the plan submitted by his fellow American Walter Burley Griffin, and in May 1912 Griffin won the international competition to design the new national capital to be built in New South Wales, but more than a hundred miles from Sydney—the compromise solution in the Constitution that had satisfied both old Sydney town and the newer, powerful Melbourne built on gold and other mining successes. Both O'Malley and Griffin were then involved in years of battling, caught up in internecine warfare in the Labour Party, and eventually both were removed from the process of building the national capital at Canberra. O'Malley had favored the now seemingly rather bizarre names for the territory of "Shakespeare" or "Myola," but both were rejected. O'Malley lost his ministry under the pro-imperial Prime Minister Billy Hughes in November, 1916, partly over the conscription issue and his general antiwar position. In 1917 he lost his seat in a proconscription electorate, and subsequently he lost twice in succession, in Denison in 1919 and in Bass in 1922. O'Malley, the last surviving member of the first Commonwealth Parliament of Australia, died in 1953 and left a reasonable estate made from a career in property.

O'Malley's period in federal politics, however, is associated with one other permanent feature of Australian life in addition to beginning the process of building Canberra. Throughout his career he had an interest in banking and a powerful social democratic vision of a "people's" bank. This partly came to fruition in the National Bank set up in 1911, which did not totally embrace O'Malley's ideas but encompassed his conception of making capital available to the masses. O'Malley's ideas on banking would eventually be implemented in the Commonwealth and Reserve banks, and—as claimed by his biographer A. R. Hoyle—he can justifiably claim to be the "father" of the Commonwealth Bank.[29] This was established in true Australian rather than American tradition to curb the power of the private banks.

Much of this "American" presence in federal politics of King O'Malley included the career of Walter Burley Griffin. Griffin's career, then and now, was almost as controversial as that of his fellow eccentric, O'Malley. Born in 1876 in Chicago, he graduated from the University of Illinois in 1899. In his early years he worked with Frank Lloyd Wright, and his style put him in the Prairie School of Architecture. He came to Australia with an international reputation, having been involved in large-scale construction in Shanghai. Griffin's plan sought to create a human capital city without intruding on and destroying the natural physical environment, a tendency that was already becoming typical of American cities. When he arrived to begin work in 1913, the controversy began almost immediately, and it was to be a leitmotif of his stay in Australia.

In 1913–14 the atmosphere toward Americans in Australia was not particularly favorable. W. O. Archibald, minister for home affairs in September 1914, who temporarily replaced O'Malley, considered Griffin an unpleasant outsider, "a Yankee bounder," not only reflecting xenophobia but also the general antagonism for America's unwillingness to enter World War I. As controversy followed controversy, a Royal Commission was established over Griffin's plan, and the results were not favorable to O'Malley and Griffin. With the Welsh-born Billy Hughes now prime minister, both Griffin and O'Malley were pushed aside, but Griffin struggled on through the war in an attempt to influence the construction of the new capital. By 1920, however, he was thoroughly alienated, and he resigned, only to be sacked by the prime minister from his contract with the Federal Capital Commission.

Griffin's career in Australia was not just limited to the planning of Canberra. He had commissions in Sydney and Melbourne, which included many houses in Sydney, the interior of Cafe Australia in Melbourne, and two commercial projects: the seven-story Leonard House (1924) and the Capitol Theater (1924), both in the Victorian capital. By the late 1920s Griffin had become disillusioned, and he considered the Federal Capital Commission to have "violated the aesthetic, social, and economic principles in almost every act" that it implemented for the new capital. When an opportunity presented itself to leave Australia in 1935, Griffin went to work in India, but he subsequently became ill and died there in 1937.[30]

Another American who sparked public debate in this period was the railroad engineer William A. Webb, who was recruited as the commissioner of railways (1922–30) by the South Australian government. Webb was born in Ohio in 1878; he became an engineer of some note, with elite political connections, including Charles Evans Hughes, the Republican presidential candidate in 1916, secretary of state in the Harding administration in 1921, and later chief justice of the U.S. Supreme Court (1930–41). When Webb was selected as commissioner, it produced a political storm in South Australia, during which he was attacked violently by both conservative and labor politicians. Lionel Hill, Labour premier in 1926, despised Webb and rejected the need for any non-British subject to be in the position. Webb, appointed with what was perceived to be very favorable conditions, was disliked by the labor movement, which was, according to Webb's biographer, "scared of him and intimidated by his bluntness." Webb, in turn, was not fond of the Australian working man and "was highly suspicious [of] the average Australian's idea of what constituted a fair day's work." When Webb returned to America, there was a witch-hunt into the railways, and the Labour government was very happy to see him leave.[31]

The careers of these Americans illustrate the cultural ambivalence expressed by both Americans and Australians in their interactions with one another. In this period of transition in Australia, from the British imperial political and cultural orbit to that of an independent nation greatly influenced by America, Americans in Australia would be both welcomed for their expertise and vigor and resented for their aggression, arrogance, and threatening presence. Americans, on the other hand, would find Australia a desirable place in which to work and to further their careers but would often clash with Australians over the latter's work habits, monarchical political system, and general nationalistic pride and independence. In the 1930s the international situation, with the growing threat of Fascism in Europe and Japan and the results of the Great Depression in 1929, would eventually combine to push the two nations closer together—after some quite protracted trade disputes[32]—but, as with O'Malley and Griffin, conflict and tension would arise over the style and power of Americans and the American imperial order.[33]

THE INTERWAR YEARS

In the 1920s the United States had an ambivalent role in international affairs. The U.S. Senate and the nation had rejected the League of Nations, even though Woodrow Wilson had so strenuously attempted to convince the American people that it would create "a new world order" (a phrase recycled by George Bush in the 1990s). This began a relative retreat, or isolation, from some European affairs, but this aspect of U.S. foreign policy did not preclude the highly interventionist international role of the United States in Latin America and the Asian–Pacific region. America perceived Australia in this period as being within the British imperial Pacific sphere, and it was not until 1918 that Australia sent a trade commission to America—albeit this was the first such act by Australia outside the Empire.

In the Washington Naval Conference of 1922, which attempted to stabilize rivalries on the seas between the great powers of the Pacific, particularly Britain, the United States, and Japan, Australia was not allowed to participate as a separate nation but only as a Dominion within the British Empire. Given that Australian defense planning was undertaken almost wholly within an imperial framework, this was understandable and probably reasonable. Throughout the 1920s, therefore, Australia would be in an uncertain position in the Pacific region, with Britain less than fully committed to its naval base in Singapore, a threatening Japan, and Australia's relations with America not clearly defined.[34]

Trade conflicts with America heightened with the crisis of the Great Depression and the interventionist policies of the Roosevelt administration, which began in early 1933. The Ottawa Agreement of 1932 had set in place mutual preferences in trade between Britain and the Dominions, and this created conflicts with the United States under its protectionist policies emerging from the Hawley–Smoot tariff regime in 1930. (Again, similar problems were to be discussed later with respect to GATT in 1993.) In the 1930s the tensions in the trade relationship were the subject of numerous bilateral negotiations, none of which was concluded to the satisfaction of both parties. When the world picture was transformed by war in 1939, the bilateral trade relationship between America and Australia was still a source of friction,[35] although Raymond Esthus probably goes too far when he describes the relationship as being initially one of "enmity."[36]

The spread of American culture between the wars was a global phenomenon, and Australia was one of the most willing absorbers of Yankee cultural forms. With the film industry in America propagating a worldwide image of the American Dream—ironically created mostly by eastern European migrant Jews like Sam Goldwyn, Louis B. Mayer, and the Warner brothers, who all but invented Hollywood, with its new union-free industrial structure—the first talkies arrived in 1929, with Al Jolson's *Jazz Singer*. These displaced the nascent Australian film industry of the pre-1914 period and almost completely destroyed it in the 1930s. The Australian public, often to the alarm of the Anglo–Australian ruling elites, was saturated with American values and material aspirations on screens throughout the nation's cinemas. The increasing affluence of the 1920s allowed Australians to indulge themselves and use their surplus capital in purchasing sundaes, Life Savers, and Kellogg's Cornflakes as the benefits of U.S. marketing and manufacturing flowed to the Southern Hemisphere. The American Dream as portrayed by the advertising industry was becoming the world model for affluence and success, and after the interruption of the Depression and World War II, it would become almost indistinguishable from the Australian Dream.[37]

Increased contacts between the two nations resulted in greater sophistication and rising frequency of analyses of each other's strengths and weaknesses. C. Hartley Grattan, one of the architects of scholarship about Australia in America, came to Australia as a Carnegie Research Fellow in 1936. He encouraged Australians and Americans to take a greater interest in their respective nations' talents, attitudes, and geopolitical profiles. Throughout his career as a historian of the Pacific region he would promote the study of Australia, and in his *The United States and the Southwest Pacific* (1961) he summarizes his views of the Australian national character: "They are, ordinarily, an easy people with whom to get along, but they insist upon a decent respect for their own conception of their worth and opinions, occasionally with fierceness."[38]

P. G. Edwards, in his *Australia Through American Eyes*, also provides an insight into American perceptions about Australia in the 1930s. In these documents of American diplomats, which he has edited, one is struck by an extraordinary mixture of ethnocentrism, negativism, but fondness for Australia —themes that will be repeated again and again by postwar migrants in the 1950s. Edwards concludes by summarizing the observations of these diplomats about Australia, portraying it "frequently in terms more applicable to a backward colony or at best a newly emergent nation." J. Pierrepont Moffat, from an elite Groton School and Harvard College background, who was sent to Australia in 1935, praises the Australians' egalitarianism in his correspondence but condemns their enthusiastic monarchist views. Nelson Johnson, a Mid-Westerner, complains about many features of Australian society: their handout mentality, their socialistic ideas, such as those of H. C. Coombs, and their strong tendencies to place holidays above work, no matter the consequences. The correspondence frequently reveals astonishment about the "she'll be right" attitude in Australia, and the American diplomats strongly recommended doses of the work ethic to be distributed liberally. As the greatest Australian–American crisis loomed at the end of the 1930s, Americans, therefore, viewed their potential allies in the Asian–Pacific region as people for whom they had fondness and feelings of solidarity, but they were critical of what was perceived as the Australians' reluctance to embrace American conceptions of work, leisure, and efficiency.[39]

WORLD WAR II

The sweep of world history tends not to be altered by a few dramatic events, but surely the events of 1940–42 must be an exception to the rule when applied to the Australian–American world in those years. The rise of imperial Japanese power in Asia in the 1930s culminated in the bombing of Pearl Harbor on 7 December 1941, and the fall of Singapore on 15 February 1942 ended the Asian geopolitical power of Britain and brought the United States into World War II as the dominant Asian–Pacific nation.

On 17 March, General Douglas MacArthur landed in Darwin; he had left the Philippines, which would fall in April, promising to return and liberate the islands. As the Labour prime minister, John Curtin, sought to bring Australian troops back from overseas theaters to defend Australia, the Japanese—from 19 February to July—bombed Darwin, Katherine, Newcastle, and Townsville. The United States, too, was fighting for its survival: for the first time since the War of 1812, its immediate physical security was threatened as the Japanese occupied the Aleutian Islands in Alaska and German submarines roamed the North Atlantic.

Roosevelt was to use Australia as the southern base from which to roll back the Japanese Empire, and soon millions of American troops would pass through on their way to the front. The world for Australia would never be the same again, for in the crisis of World War II would be forged the new American alliance, and with the victories at sea at the Battles of Coral Sea and Midway (5–8 May and 4–6 June) the alliance of war would take on a sentimental and mythic quality. Australia, an Anglo–Celtic nation, would be transformed into an Anglo–Celtic–American syncretistic culture.

All the aspects of historical interactions between the two nations would be accentuated by World War II: clashes over economic interests, conflicts over cultural values, Australian anti-Americanism, American anti-Australianism, and political and strategic conflicts over war tactics and aims. The pressures of war tensions would heighten all the social contradictions of both societies, and this would be reflected in war relationships between the politicians, generals, and the troops, black and white, on both sides.

The story of U.S. migration to Australia in the post–World War II period begins, therefore, with the stationing of American forces in Australia between 1942 and 1945. This brought Americans to Australia in large numbers for the first time, and knowledge about Australia flowed back to America; thousands of Americans would stay in Australia after the war as husbands and, in some cases, wives. In the 1980s many descendants of these troops would locate their original ideas of migration as coming to them in the 1950s from war reminiscences of their parents about the delights of north Queensland, Sydney, and Melbourne. Australia was now part of American consciousness, dim and hazy as these conceptions of it might be for the majority of Americans. All of this would result from—as Studs Terkel, the Chicago radio broadcaster and writer, called it—the last of the "Good Wars."[40]

Australia was now recognized as a fully independent nation by the Americans. On 5 March 1940, R. G. Casey presented his credentials to President Roosevelt, thus establishing full bilateral diplomatic relations between Australia and America. It is possibly a historical irony that at the very moment when Australia was forced back upon its own resources for survival, without the traditional support within the British Empire, and recognized as a mature society, it was embraced and enveloped by the American giant. But when the Yankees came "down under," that would be precisely the dilemma faced by Australians, particularly the intellectuals, not just during World War II, but through to the 1990s.

The search for an Australian identity, therefore, emerged in a concentrated way out of the wartime alliance with America. This area of social criticism and historiography—including the plethora of questions surrounding Americanization—has become a separate intellectual growth industry in Australia, as it has in America, on the issues of national identity in the second half of the nineteenth century. From the 1950s to the 1990s, Russel Ward, Robin Boyd, Donald Horne, Geoffrey Blainey, Craig McGregor, Humphrey McQueen, Ronald Conway, Geoffrey Serle, David Walker, Richard White, John Carroll, Bruce Grant, Philip and Roger Bell, and Tony Griffiths, among others, employed their considerable intellectual talents at dissecting and exploring the etiology and future of the Australian national character and "peoplehood." The challenges of the war, the emergence of a multiethnic Australia, the pressures from Asian populations and economies, and the republic debate have kept the subject of Australian national character alive and ideologically intense. These extraordinarily complex and rapid social changes, although a boon for booksellers, have produced strains within Australian society and, albeit not as threatening as in America, with its huge population and racial divisions, caused strong centrifugal forces to develop in the social order.[41]

The debate over Australian national identity has been long—having originated in earnest in the 1890s—and intellectually complex, and it strikes at the very heart of the national culture. Some, like Russel Ward, have argued for a persistent rural ideal, based upon Bush culture for Australian identity as a working-class idealization of Australian rural life, which, like the American Western myth, became the norm for a culture without a clear ethnic identity. Richard White, in *Inventing Australia* (1981), recognized the search for an Australian identity as a transcendent, cyclical obsession in Australian culture and historiography. But Donald Horne, in 1994, jumped into the debate with characteristic pugnacity and declared: "It is certainly time for the idea of 'national identity' to be abandoned. There never has been, and there never will be, something called the Australian national identity. Australia is a diverse and distinct society, like any others." Horne calls for a new "civic identity," a kind of civil contract of mutual respect and dignity in a multicultural society. The debate will, however, not be terminated, and as Australia moves closer to an Asian–Pacific identity, the contradictions and tensions on identity, race, multicultural-ism, and the republic will, undoubtedly, be exacerbated and engender further intellectual combat on the question of an Australian national identity.[42]

When the American troops arrived in 1941–42, however, they were unable to anticipate the national debates of the postwar era; all thoughts were on the war to be fought together. Australians welcomed their American allies, and the premier of New South Wales, W. J. McKell, expressed the general sentiment when he said that the Americans were "our cousins by blood and should be treated as such."[43] Hospitality was to be extended, and all the warmth of the Australian nation was to make the Yanks feel as much at home as possible. By the tens of thousands the boys from Maine and Mississippi, Kansas and California, Washington and Florida poured in to help defend Australia. Raw and mostly overseas for the first time, these mainly provincial Americans would put the warm inner glow of Australians in 1942–43 to the test. The Yanks, when disembarking, would sing "Australia, Australia, we've come / To help you fight, fight, fight!" but the positive vibrations in this refrain would not last for long.[44]

Americans in Australia immediately produced, as they did in the rest of the world in the war years, a dynamic of conflict and antagonism with the nationals of the countries in which they served.[45] By mid-1942 there were over 100,000 American troops in Australia, and the peak number would be close to 500,000. Complaints about them, as expressed in the judgment that they were "overpaid, oversexed, and over here," centered on the high levels of surplus capital they could spend in Australia, thus seizing the advantage in relationships with Australian women over local males. The G.I.s could also make liberal use of their PX goodies—cigarettes, liquor, silk stockings, and chocolates—to curry favor in the Australian community. Australians, therefore, responded with ambivalence to these Yanks with riches, with many Australians more than willing to share in American largesse. But a pattern of jealousy and resentment would also be sparked off with some vehemence from most Australians, many of whom were not reluctant to fleece American troops when possible.[46]

During World War II, violence between Americans and Australians in Australia took many forms. There were the usual brawls in the pubs on Saturday night, but often these fights turned into serious confrontations such as the "Battle of Brisbane" in November 1942, in which there was one fatality. Wherever there were heavy concentrations of Americans, especially in Brisbane, Townsville, and Cairns, there were physical conflicts between Yanks and Aussies. The war meant that these confrontations were not given any press coverage, and the Australians and Americans both kept the less than amiable relationship between the troops very quiet during the war.[47]

There is a persistent anecdotal account of a violent conflict between troops from Australian and American troop trains that had stopped simultaneously on parallel tracks, in which troops poured out, grenades were thrown, and a mass brawl took place. We have not been able to authenticate this in any historical record, even though it has become part of folklore, and it must therefore be considered apocryphal.

Another source of violence and social tensions was the presence of tens of thousands of black American soldiers in Australia. The racial questions inherent in the stationing of black troops encompass the whole range of Australian and American attitudes toward race: the segregation of troops in the American forces; conflicts between black and white Americans; conflicts between black Americans and white Australians; conflicts between white Americans and white Australians, who failed at times to accept white Jim Crowism brought from America; and black American contacts with and attitudes toward Australian Aborigines.

The Australian government did not want black troops sent to Australia, and Curtin had unsuccessfully attempted to persuade Roosevelt not to do so. The proportion of black troops, in segregated sections of the American forces, was about one in ten; these were large numbers, in the tens of thousands, and they presented all the problems of oppression and racism caused by the white American majority. Violence between black and white Americans was common, especially when color lines were crossed with respect to women and in desegregated Australian facilities. Although Australians, in general, were not as overtly racist as the Americans, some incidents that appear to be racial in nature did occur between white Australians and black troops. Black Americans expressed some sympathy with Aborigines, and, like so much of the relationship between Americans and Australia, the impact of black Americans on Aboriginal activism in Australia dates from those World War II contacts. All the stresses and strains of American–Australian culture, then, are revealed by these racial tensions in Australia, and the domestic conflicts in the 1960s in America and Australia over race were clearly adumbrated in the war years of 1942–45 in these tripartite race relationships in Australia.[48]

As the war dragged on through 1943–44, the American troops grew increasingly homesick and critical of Australia. Like the 1930s diplomatic observers, Moffat and Johnson, wartime observers considered Australia to be a backward nation in which the indigenous (white) peoples were not as friendly as they had first believed. There were complaints about the food, especially mutton, the weather, and the flies. One wrote home that Australia was "like what I've heard of U.S. history 30 years ago"—a persistent theme in American observations about Australia. One commentator writing in *Collier's* remarked that Australians were "more carefree," but this trait did not make for great national achievements. By 1945 the Americans were quite happy to return to their bastion of affluence and civilization in North America, but when V-J Day came on the 15th of August thousands would remain, having established, in spite of the "harsh" conditions of Australia, more permanent ties.[49]

By the time America dropped the atom bomb on Hiroshima, some 7,000 Australian women had married American nationals; this number would rise to about 12,000, emerging out of wartime relationships. The overwhelming majority of these (80 percent) would go to America, although even by 1945 some Australian war brides had already returned, disappointed, to Australia. The 20 percent of Americans who stayed in Australia with their war brides numbered about 2,400, and most would remain in Australia permanently. The core of the small post–World War II American migrant community, along with business and diplomatic personnel, would be formed by these Americans remaining in Australia and by American women who had formed attachments with or married Australian nationals. World War II would produce for the first time a steadier and more continuous exchange of peoples between Australia and America and mark the beginning of new relationship in all areas between the two nations.[50]

The strategic and geopolitical results of World War II in the Asian–Pacific region had, of course, profound implications for the defense positions of America and Australia. There were, and are, great differences between the views of American and Australian partisans on the conduct of the war, on who did or who did not fight most valiantly, and on the political and tactical battles involving Curtin, Roosevelt, and their respective military commanders. These arguments, as vigorous and contentious as they are, are beyond the scope of this introductory summary on Australia, but the crucial consequences of the war for the Australian–American alliance are of greater significance and of long-term import for modern Australian history. In the patterns of Australian society in the post–World War II decade the impact of Americanization would transform the consumption styles of Australia; the migrant population would increase rapidly, and its ethnic composition would alter the Anglo–Celtic base of the society; and the Cold War would produce treaty alliances and ties with America that would involve Australia, along with America, in a costly war in Korea and in the most divisive unpopular foreign war in their history in Vietnam. All these factors would shift Australia along a spectrum toward an American model of society and culture and, in the perceptions of prospective migrants from America, a more attractive place in which Americans could live and work.

NOTES

1. Richard White, *Inventing Australia, Images and Identity, 1788–1980* (Sydney, 1981), pp. 47, 48, 49, 50, 57.

2. Quoted in Dennis Cuddy, *The Yanks are Coming* (San Francisco, CA, 1977), p. 17 and fn. 60.

3. C. Hartley Grattan, *The United States and the Southwest Pacific* (Cambridge, MA, 1961), pp. 71, 82, 95; Norman Harper, "A Historical Perspective," in Norman Harper, ed., *Pacific Orbit* (Melbourne, 1968), pp. 176–177.

4. Quoted in Harper, *Pacific Orbit*, p. 178.

5. Bell and Bell, *Implicated*, pp. 19–20, 24; E. & A. Potts, *Young America and Australian Gold* (St. Lucia, 1974), pp. 4, 32; Richard White, *Inventing Australia* (Sydney, 1981), pp. 48–50.

6. Ray Aitchison, *The Americans in Australia* (Blackburn, Victoria, 1986), pp. 26–30; Potts and Potts, *Gold*, p. 1; Harper, *Pacific Orbit*, p. 177.

7. John Molony, *The Penguin History of Australia* (Melbourne, 1987), p. 103; Potts and Potts, *Gold*, pp. 51, 52, 66, 201–202.

8. Potts and Potts, *Gold*, pp. 113 and 118.

9. Potts and Potts, *Gold*, pp. 89–92.

10. Potts and Potts, *Gold*, pp. 25, 123–153; it is interesting to note that the final issue at dispute in the Uruguay Round of the GATT Treaty of December, 1993, was over American cultural imperialism in Europe, especially French objections to U.S. film companies.

11. Aitchison, *Americans*, pp. 34, 61–65; Potts and Potts, *Gold*, pp. 89, 189, 199.

12. Potts and Potts, *Gold*, pp. 29–30, 46, 56–57, 157, 217–218.

13. Potts and Potts, *Gold*, p. 129; Bell and Bell, *Implicated*, pp. 51–59, 64, fn. 69; Arthur Huck, *The Chinese in Australia* (Melbourne, 1968), pp. 1–5; Molony, *Australia*, pp. 116, 133, 146; C. A. Price, *The Great White Walls Are Built: Restrictive Immigration to North America and Australia, 1836–1888* (Canberra, 1974), *passim*; Sherington, *Immigrants*, p. 67.

14. Molony, *Australia*, pp. 59, 103, 109; Potts and Potts, *Gold*, pp. 199, 216.

15. Ian Turner, *Sydney's Burning* (London, 1967).

16. See Bill Bryson, *Made in America* (Melbourne, 1994); Bell and Bell, *Implicated*, p. 2 and *passim.*

17. Bell and Bell, *Implicated*, pp. 31–39; Molony, *Australia*, p. 168; for a general discussion of American left-wing influences in Australia, see L. G. Churchyard, *Australia and America, 1788–1972: An Alternative History* (Sydney, 1979); for World War I, see Joseph

Conlin, *Big Bill Haywood* (Syracuse, 1969); Melvyn Dubofsky, *We Shall Be All: A History of the Industrial Workers of the World* (Urbana, IL, 1988).

18. Bell and Bell, *Implicated*, pp. 47–51; Zelman Cowen, "Two Federations," in Harper, *Pacific Orbit*, pp. 189–206; E. M. Hunt, *American Precedents in Australian Federation* (New York, 1968).

19. Bell and Bell, *Implicated*, pp. 56–57; see also Neville Meaney, *The Search for Security in the Pacific, 1901–1914* (Sydney, 1976).

20. Albert Metin, *Socialism Without Doctrines*, trans. Russell Ward, APCOL (Sydney, 1977).

21. Paul Kelly, *The End of Certainty* (Sydney, 1992).

22. Donald Brash, *American Investment in Australian Industry* (Australian National University, 1966).

23. Richard Cotter, "War, Boom and Depression," in *Essays in Economic History of Australia*, James Griffin, ed. (Ryde, NSW, 1967), pp. 270–271.

24. Quotation from Norman Bartlett, *1776–1976: Australia and America through Two Hundred Years* (Sydney, 1976), p. 182; see Miriam Shillingsburg, *At Home Abroad, Mark Twain in Australasia* (Jackson, MS, 1988).

25. Aitchison, *Americans*, pp. 70–71.

26. Dean Jaensch, "John Greeley Jenkins," *Australian Dictionary of Biography* (Melbourne, 1966–1991), pp. 478–479.

27. The section on O'Malley is based upon *ADB*, pp. 84–86; Aitchison, *Americans*, pp. 81–83; Dorothy Catts, *King O'Malley: Man and Statesman* (Sydney, 1957); A. R. Hoyle, *King O'Malley: "The American Bounder"* (Melbourne, 1981); Molony, *Australia*, pp. 207, 209–211.

28. Molony, *Australia*, p. 207.

29. A. R. Hoyle, "King O'Malley," *ADB*, pp. 84–86.

30. Quotation from *ADB*, p. 108; and the section based upon Aitchison, *Americans*, pp. 83–90; *ADB*, pp. 107–110; James P. Birrell, *Walter Burley Griffin* (Brisbane, 1965).

31. Reece I. Jennings, *William A. Webb* (Adelaide, 1973), pp. 86, 87, 91, 161, 162.

32. See Raymond A. Esthus, *From Enmity to Alliance; US–Australian Relations, 1931–1941* (Melbourne, 1964).

33. For another American migrant whose career illustrates these themes, see E. D. and A. Potts, "Thomas Welton Stanford (1832–1918) and American–Australian Business and Cultural Relations," *Historical Studies*, 17 (1976), pp. 193–209.

34. Bell and Bell, *Implicated*, pp. 58–59; Robert Thornton "The Semblance of Security: Australia and the Washington Conference, 1921–22," *Australian Outlook*, 32 (1978), 65–83.

35. J. G. Crawford, "Partnership in Trade," in *Pacific Orbit*, pp. 45–48.

36. Esthus, *Enmity to Alliance*, 1964.

37. Molony, *Australia*, pp. 239–241; see also Neal Gabler, *An Empire of Their Own* (New York, 1989), for the story of how Jews "invented" Hollywood and the American Dream; Stuart Macintyre, *Oxford History of Australia*, Vol. 4 (Melbourne, 1986), p. 206.

38. C. Hartley Grattan, *The United States and the Southwest Pacific* (Cambridge, MA, 1961), p. 36; Richard White, *Inventing Australia* (Sydney, 1981), pp. 150–151.

39. P. G. Edwards, *Australia through American Eyes* (St. Lucia, 1979), p. 18, and diplomats' comments on pp. 4, 12–13, 14–15, 16 and 17.

40. Studs Terkel, *The Good War* (New York, 1984).

41. Russel Ward, *The Australian Legend* (Melbourne, 1958); Robin Boyd, *The Australian Ugliness* (Melbourne, 1960); Donald Horne, *The Lucky Country* (Melbourne, 1964); Geoffrey Blainey, *The Tyranny of Distance* (Melbourne, 1966); Craig McGregor, *Profile of Australia* (London, 1966); Humphrey McQueen, *A New Britannia* (Melbourne, 1970);

Ronald Conway, *The Great Australian Stupor* (Melbourne, 1971); Geoffrey Serle, *From Deserts the Prophets Come: The Creative Spirit in Australia, 1788–1972* (Melbourne, 1974); David Walker, *Dream and Disillusion: A Search for the Australian Cultural Identity* (Canberra, 1976); Richard White, *Inventing Australia: Images and Identity, 1688–1980* (Sydney, 1981); John Carroll, ed., *Intruders in the Bush: The Australian Quest for Identity* (Melbourne, 1982); Bruce Grant, *The Australian Dilemma: A New Kind of Western Society* (Sydney, 1983); Bruce Grant, *What Kind of Country* (Ringwood, Victoria, 1988); Philip and Roger Bell, *Implicated, the United States in Australia* (Melbourne, 1993); Tony Griffiths, *Beautiful Lies: Australia from Kokoda to Keating* (London, 1993), an updated version of *Contemporary Australia* published in 1972. For the same issues in Canada, see Ian Lumsden, ed., *The Americanization of Canada* (Toronto, 1990). This search for an Australian identity continued in 1993 with the "I Am an Australian" campaign launched to define "Australianness" for the nation. See also the kind of continuing *angst* about national identity, as in Kate Legge's Australia Day special, "Rediscovering Australia," *The Australian Magazine*, 22 January 1994, pp. 8–12, and Morris West writing in the *Bulletin*, 25 January 1994, pp. 26–29, sounding a despairing note in "The Sunburnt Country: Broke, Bewildered, Besieged."

42. Russel Ward, *The Australian Legend* (Melbourne, 1958); Richard White, *Inventing Australia* (Sydney, 1981); *The Australian*, 8 February 1994, p. 9. The Academy of Social Sciences is currently undertaking a massive study of Australian identity in the *Australian National Identity* project, with contributors such as Ken Inglis, Charles Price, and Gillian Bottomley; this, and other work, will certainly keep the debate going: see *The Australian Magazine*, 28 May 1994, pp. 11–16. Hugh Mackay, like some American pessimists, sees a deep crisis in Australian culture with a breakdown of community: *The Australian Magazine*, 1 October 1994, 14–20; Robert Manne makes the same point in his book, *The Shadow of 1917*, as revealed in his piece in *The Adelaide Review* (October 1994), pp. 22–23; Peter Coleman echoes all of these themes in his "Talking about Australian Civilization Again," *The Adelaide Review* (November 1994), pp. 24–25. See also Patrick O'Farrell, "Australian Races Towards an Identity Crisis," *The Adelaide Review* (February 1995), pp. 10–11.

43. Quoted in Potts and Potts, *WWII*, p. 175.

44. Potts and Potts, *WWII*, p. 11.

45. For a similar story in New Zealand, see Harry Bioletti, *The Yanks Are Coming: The American Invasion of New Zealand, 1942–1944* (Auckland, 1989), *passim*.

46. John Moore, *Over-Sexed, Over-Paid and Over Here, Americans in Australia 1941–45* (St. Lucia, 1981); Molony, *Australia*, p. 287; Potts and Potts, *WWII*, p. 29; Paul Hasluck, *The Government and the People, 1942–1945* (Canberra, 1970), p. 225, fn. 6.

47. Potts and Potts, *WWII*, pp. 303, 309; Aitchison, *Americans*, 105–107.

48. Bell and Bell, *Implicated*, p. 100; for conflicts between black and white Americans, see Potts and Potts, *WWII*, pp. 31, 40, 48–50, 109, 110–113, 188, 191, 299, 300; for black Americans and white Australians, see pp. 14, 146, 190; for attitudes towards Aborigines, see p. 190. See also Joanna Penglase and David Horner, *When the War Came to Australia* (St. Leonards, 1992), pp. 167–182.

49. Potts and Potts, *WWII*, pp. 88–89, 196–197.

50. Potts and Potts, *WWII*, pp. 362, 384, 398.

3

Modern Australia since World War II

POST–WORLD WAR II: RELATIONS BETWEEN AMERICA AND AUSTRALIA AND THE 1951 ANZUS TREATY

The geopolitical struggles in Central Europe and East Asia between 1945 and 1949 created a dynamic of conflict between the United States and the Soviet Union that would ripple around the world for the next forty years. Regardless of the causality of the Cold War and the relative culpability of Harry S. Truman and Joseph Stalin in inaugurating and perpetuating it—and the historiography in this area is now one of the most dense in modern history,[1] with the most recent squarely blaming Stalin—its consequence in the Asian–Pacific region was the creation of alliances reflecting a bipolar world. In the struggle between the American and Soviet alliance systems and interests, Australia, extending the World War II alliance with the United States, would fall firmly into the U.S. orbit. The extraordinary vehemence of domestic anti-Communism in America would also be replicated in Australia, though possibly in a less virulent form.

American foreign policy, after Truman enunciated his containment doctrine to the U.S. Congress in March 1947, would pursue a military policy to resist the expansion of Communist power throughout the world. This required a massive expansion of the American military budget and the active engagement of Soviet influence at all levels of society and in every strategic corner of the world. Truman accepted a recommended expansion of these principles in a National Security Council report (NSC–68) in April 1950, in which alliances were to be formed with like-minded countries—a policy that the next president, Dwight D.

Eisenhower (1953–61), pursued with particular vigor. Eisenhower's secretary of state, John Foster Dulles, and his brother as Director of the CIA, Allen Dulles, implemented these activist policies of American bipartisan anti-Communism, the results of which were to include alliance with Australia in an Asian–Pacific anti-Communist front. Norman Harper, a historian also noted for his support of the spread of American studies in Australia in the post–World War II decades, has written that this enthusiasm of Australia for the American alliance came only after the requirements of Australia's strategic needs in the region necessitated the abandonment of sentimental attachments to the British Empire.

The positioning of Australia under the American nuclear defense umbrella was not an easy decision, but once it was made, Australia would match any nation in the world for its fervent pro-American, anti-Soviet foreign policy.[2] At first the ANZUS Treaty was conceived as a trade-off for Australia's accepting a lenient peace treaty with a Japan that Washington now wished to revive as a major anti-Communist bulwark in East Asia. In exchange for Canberra's compliance in this shift away from a punitive peace being imposed on Japan, America gave Australia what then amounted to a security guarantee. But the alliance relationship progressively evolved into a much wider security partnership involving intelligence dimensions, the building of important electronic information-gathering facilities on Australian soil, and combined military operations in two major Asian wars, in Korea and Vietnam.

THE KOREAN WAR

When Robert Menzies led the Liberals to victory against the Labour Party in 1949, Australia began a period of 23 years of conservative political hegemony, matching the ideological complexion of governments in North America and Europe. Australia would cement itself into the global American alliance system with the signing of the ANZUS (1951) and then SEATO (1954) treaties, thus overtly committing Australia to an American defense strategy to contain Communism in Asia and the Pacific. The logic and the letter of these obligations would involve Australia in the Korean and Vietnam Wars. The latter was the most divisive foreign war in the history of both America and Australia. With Australia extending the "spiritual" bonds of World War II, established through the bloodletting of New Guinea and the Battle of Coral Sea, to an emotional bonding with America in the world anti-Communist crusade, the opposition to these policies would not develop to a high level until the strains of the Vietnam War in the late 1960s.

Australia was the first country after the United States to commit forces from all three military arms to Korea in defense of the Southern regime under United Nations auspices. While Australia suffered casualties in the progress of the war, it united the nation, and few outside the extreme Left and Communist Party opposed Australian participation. The generation of Australians who lived through the successful prosecution of the war remained pro-American and saw no need to alter their strategic or ideological disposition. This generation was generally retired by the 1990s.

During the Korean War, Menzies also tried unsuccessfully to make the Communist Party of Australia (CPA) illegal. The referendum required by the Constitution for such an act failed narrowly to pass.[3] The CPA was among the most powerful in the English-speaking world, reflecting the leftish culture of the early–twentieth-century Australian labor movement. It had been formed in the early 1920s and thoroughly Stalinized by a Russian with an American passport, Harry Wicks—also known in Australia as Herbert Moore—sent by the Comintern to do the job in 1929–31.[4] After being made illegal for supporting the Nazis between 1939 and 1941, the CPA grew rapidly during the alliance with the Soviet state. In the late 1940s it closed the vital New South Wales coalfield with strikes, and some of its leaders were jailed during the ALP government. It remained loyal to the Soviets until a splinter group formed a pro-China party in the early 1960s. Both parties were, needless to say, despised by the general Australian public. Only one Communist was ever elected to an Australian Parliament: a war hero doctor, to the Queensland House in the mid-1940s.[5]

The CPA's real influence was among the intelligentsia—which was always more amenable to the theoretical doctrines of Marxism than the proletariat. There it concentrated particularly on cultivating social scientists in universities, and it achieved considerable success. Much of the national historical school in Australia has consisted of scholars who were either close to or members of the CPA—Russell Ward, Manning Clark, Robin Gollan, Eric Fry, Ian Turner, Humphrey McQueen, Stuart McIntyre, Jean Curthoys—which in part explains the dominant anti-Americanism of its temper and the virulence with which right-wing historians like Geoffrey Blainey have been attacked. They formed the rump of what was to become a mass movement against the Vietnam War.

THE VIETNAM WAR

America moved unwisely into the political vacuum left by the disintegration of French imperial power in the Indo–Chinese peninsula. Throughout the late 1950s it was increasingly committed to the maintenance of an anti-Communist regime in South Vietnam created by the peace settlement of the French Indo–China War in 1954. The successor to Menzies, Harold Holt, prime minister from 1966 to 1967, continued the pro-American foreign policy of the Cold War and expressed his determination to go "all the way with LBJ." Johnson's visit to Australia in October 1966 was, indeed, the first by a U.S. president. In 1965 Australia had decided that its troops would join U.S. forces in Vietnam. This entanglement would have profound political and social consequences for Australia, which, again, matched the events in America, for out of this Asian war would emerge a general and more popular critique of America.[6]

Australia's involvement in the Vietnam War did not, it should be stressed, result from American pressure on its ally. Australia had its own strategy of defense in depth, which involved fighting Communism as far to the north as possible, and during the American debates about whether to escalate the war in 1964 Australia continually pressed for a greater engagement.[7] Australia suffered 500 casualties in the war and, despite successfully pacifying Phuoc Tuy Province, eventually suffered the defeat with America. At home also a vast antiwar movement, led from the university campuses, had developed by the late 1960s and became virulently anti-American. This generation of intellectuals were to retain that orientation into the 1990s, by which time the protesters had made the long march through the institutions and propagated anti-Americanism from more senior and influential positions. Anti-Americanism in Australia assumed its modern left-wing form during the protests against the Vietnam War.

AUSTRALIA IN GLOBAL STRATEGY

The Cold War alliance would involve Australia directly in American global nuclear strategy by hosting U.S. communication bases at North-West Cape, Pine Gap, and Nurrungar. These all aroused great controversy and leftist opposition, which has continued through the 1990s. These communications facilities were established in Australia in the 1960s and were progressively upgraded during the following decades. The function of Harold E. Holt base at North-West Cape was to communicate with American nuclear-armed and -powered submarines operating in the Indian Ocean and targeting Soviet missile silos in central Asia. That of the Pine Gap base, to which the one at Nurrungar is connected, was to download data collected by satellite reconnaissance over East and Central Asia. Pine Gap was valuable for eavesdropping and war fighting; it was located in central Australia to avoid cloud cover, Soviet jamming from naval vessels, and hostility from the domestic population.[8]

When President Reagan reactivated the Cold War in the early 1980s, with the eventual effect of defeating the Soviet Union without having to fight a generalized war, these facilities became very important to American strategy. The Left organized in Australia against Reagan's strategy and, as in Europe and New Zealand, tried to withdraw from the Western alliance system. In New Zealand this succeeded in taking the country out of ANZUS, but in Australia the Labour government stood firm despite very large demonstrations and the election of a few candidates from the Peace Party—which was later openly taken over by Trotskyites—to Parliament. These developments only served to deepen the anti-Americanism of the Left and of the intelligentsia and extend it into another generation.

ANTI-AMERICANISM IN AUSTRALIA

Anti-Americanism is a term that can embrace an enormous variety of meanings within the context of the post–World War II decades. It includes leftist, nationalistic views that are opposed to American political and military imperialism; rightist, nationalistic views, such as those of the Gaullists in France, opposed to all aspects of U.S. power and culture; the leftist critique of American culture as decadent, crude, and destructive to civilized society; the institutionalized Communist–Marxist conception of the United States as the leading bourgeois capitalist world power; the declinist views of the debate already discussed above; and the minority but persistent Anglo-Saxon Tory view that America is a vulgar society in which excessive democracy and republicanism render it ultimately unstable. This latter view was still expressed in Australia in the 1990s republic debate when W. C. Wentworth, the former Liberal minister, claimed that "the United States' immunity from presidential-dictatorship may well be in jeopardy."[9] The domestic and foreign pressures in both Australia and the United States would weave all these strains of anti-Americanism together, resulting in opposition to the Vietnam War in the 1960s and to pressures in the 1990s for structural changes to the social and political order.[10]

Indeed anti-Americanism exists; it was arguably invented in America and was not a new nor an "un-American" viewpoint. From the mid-nineteenth-century Marxist and left-wing tradition through the socialist writers of the 1920s such as Theodore Dreiser and Upton Sinclair, a persistent leftist, intellectual tradition had attacked the excesses of American "bourgeois imperialist society." When the radical movement in America (and Australia) in the mid-1960s mobilized students, academics, writers, and a growing proportion of the electorate against the Vietnam War, they drew on a long and important tradition of American anti-Americanism. Leftist writers such as Noam Chomsky, Howard P. Zinn, Paul Goodman, and others were critical of all aspects of capitalist America as well as its imperialist policies in the Vietnam War. These ideas were as widely circulated in Australia as in America and formed a common left-wing–intellectual bridge between the two nations.[11]

Australians drew upon these leftist traditions when, especially in the radical wing of the Labour Party grouped around its deputy leader, Jim Cairns, the political forces mobilized against the Vietnam War.[12] This was part of a general pattern of change in Australian society that would culminate in the election in 1972 of Gough Whitlam as the first Labour prime minister since 1949. This began a process of nationalistic cultural change the results of which are considered below, and a lessening of the warmth with which the American alliance was regarded.

Whitlam's government represented a challenge to close ties with America, and the United States government was concerned about the future of American bases in Australia (North-West Cape, Pine Gap, and Nurrungar) and the general orientation of the Labour government.[13]

Whether America did or did not influence the removal of Whitlam by the governor-general in November 1975 is a subject of much debate. Many on the left continue to believe so, although no evidence has been produced for this claim. It has been added to the catalogue of alleged American crimes against the Australian people, to rank alongside conflicts such as those involving the horse Phar Lap, the boxer Les Darcy, the Vietnam War, and others that are considered below. But the result of this constitutional coup d'état was a return to a more traditional pro-American stance by the new Liberal Prime Minister Malcolm Fraser (1975–83) and by the Hawke–Keating Labour governments (1983–96) through the late stages of the Cold War as well as the Gulf War in 1991.

THE ECONOMY AND SOCIETY

The nature of American influence in Australia, against which the anti-Americanism of the 1960s was also directed, included many aspects of Australian culture beyond foreign policy entanglements in Asia. The two key areas were the economy and the general structure of Australian culture—both popular and elite culture—which were increasingly perceived as swamped by American imperial power. It was the resistance to these forces that, when combined with a critique of Cold War strategies, formed the basis of a generalized cultural anti-Americanism in Australia in the postwar decades.

The victory of the Allies in 1945 in Europe and Japan gave the United States an unequaled position in history to dominate world trade: untouched by war devastation, it had nuclear weapons, the largest military machine, and 40–45 percent of the total world production and trade. American technological prowess, which had been building up for two generations, gave it additional advantages, and American manufacturing industries reigned supreme in automobiles, white goods, steel, electronics, and many others. The products of American farms and mines were exported at unprecedented levels, and America ran huge balance of trade and payments surpluses. Americans had the highest per capita incomes, the most cars, and the widest distribution of telephones; the national economy boomed. Why would Australia not look to the American model as a social form to emulate?

Even in the 1930s, many aspects of the Australian economy were beginning to feel the impact of American capital investment, management techniques, and multinational corporations. Australia increasingly shifted toward the importation of American goods and capital and away from its traditional trade with Britain. The World War II years would see an acceleration of these trends, and, as noted by Philip and Roger Bell, the consequences were enormous, with "more than two-thirds of local imports . . . from America, [and] . . . Australian exports to that nation doubling to approximately one-quarter of its total export effort." As trade increased in volume, so did the impact of American corporations investing in manufacturing and selling products in Australia. As the style and message of marketing were Americanized, Australians became avid consumers of Coke,

Heinz ketchup, General Electric equipment, and the products of the Detroit automobile giants. The mode and sources of consumption in the post–World War II decades, therefore, were already becoming established when the struggles in the Pacific ended in 1945.[14]

During that postwar boom the same companies that were fueling American consumerism began operating in Australia. This was encouraged by the policy regime that encouraged direct foreign investment and ownership but made private foreign borrowings difficult and subject to official licensing. The automobile industry was to take off in 1948, when, with a government subsidy, General Motors Holden began production in Australia of a reject Chevrolet design that was to dominate for a decade the previously British-controlled market. Ford and Chrysler soon followed with their own plants and the Falcon and Valiant. America's oil giants also grew, as did the American tobacco, electronics, aviation, movie, and household consumer goods companies. With a similar per capita income, Australian workers were soon enjoying a consumption pattern similar to that of their American counterparts. While some industries—including banking, insurance and much of the media—were wholly protected from foreign ownership, the American corporate presence grew hugely during the postwar decades of American economic primacy and the first phase of the creation of multinational corporations.

For most Australians this process was of great benefit, and Australian living standards and habits changed considerably and for the better during these Menzies years. At the time of federation, the Australian people had enjoyed, on the resource-rich and very large continent which they had conquered, exploited, and sparsely settled, an income level that was probably the highest in the world. By the 1950s this had been exceeded somewhat by the Americans, who had built a vast industrial base—but the differences were marginal, and consumption patterns were more remarkable for their similarities than their discrepancies. This was the nearest Australia came to being a New America.

The postwar decade witnessed the global exportation of the American Dream. The two-car family, education for all, endless hyperconsumption, and the promise of unlimited growth—these could be had, it seemed, by all who adopted the American free enterprise system. The alluring glitter and wealth of America was propagated on film and then after 1956 on television, to be beamed into homes throughout Australia. To have the "latest" from America became the standard against which were judged all aspects of style, consumption, technology, as well as—spreading into broader cultural areas—the arts, education, sport, and what became known later in the exported American catchphrase as "lifestyle."

The Australian economy of the 1950s and 1960s would feel the American presence in virtually every dimension of economic activity. Australia became a major target of U.S. investment, and the value in investment of American dollars soon exceeded that of British pounds. By the mid-1960s, as noted by W. J. Hudson, American interests wholly owned more than 70 of the top 300 manufacturing companies in Australia and held a majority interest in a further 20. Key industries, such as auto manufacturing, would fall under American control, and by the 1960s automobile production was 75 percent controlled by U.S. companies.[15]

In trade, the shifts were equally portentous: in 1948–49 the United States accounted for only 10 percent of imports to Australia; by 1966–67 this had jumped to 25.1 percent. Australia was exporting goods to the value of $37 million to America but importing $783 million in goods from the United States. This adverse balance of trade for Australia was to continue and be exacerbated by American competition in third markets in key areas of Australian exports in tobacco, sugar, wool, and beef—thus creating a cycle of conflicts over trade that would persist for the duration of the century in international trade competition, negotiations, and treaties like GATT. It would not just be the Left in Australia from the 1950s to the 1990s who would view these developments with alarm. By the early 1990s a growing consensus was emerging that the economic imperialism of America was not just a threat propagated by the traditional left-wing antagonists toward America or the anti-Americanism of political economists like Ted Wheelwright.[16]

Without adopting a simplistic application of the Marxist model of culture—the conception of the superstructure of culture as always a direct reflection of the underlying substructure of the economy and its ownership and control—one cannot but conclude that the shift to greater American control of the Australian economy also brought a broad-based impact of cultural domination by America. These two phenomena do not seem to be separable; they seemed to come as a "package deal." In film, television, radio, advertising, architecture, town planning, education, tertiary curriculum—including left-wing curriculum—monetarist economic thought, sport—the list is almost endless—the ubiquitous influence of U.S. culture spread in Australia.[17] Critics of American English, including the influential Adelaide writer, columnist, and bookshop owner, Max Harris, protested not only at the enveloping cultural models, but the very words, phrases, and intrinsic patterns of thought by which American society was "coopting"—another American word—Australian culture.[18]

Americans were appearing as personalities on television. The popular Bob Dyer, who was also famous for catching, with his wife Dolly, a huge shark in Moreton Bay in the mid-1950s, was the leading quiz program compère. It was on his show that the later president of the Labour Party [1993] and minister of science, Barry Jones, was to become famous. The programming content of television was to make American cowboys, variety performers, and soap stars as recognizable in Australia as they were in the United States.

Australians raised in the post–World War II era were being socialized to be Australian–American hybrids by the relentless globalization of North American culture. The reaction to this process was to become especially pronounced in the 1970s in the nationalist wave, which, in part, brought Gough Whitlam to the prime ministership in 1972. Although it would be overly simplistic in the extreme to explain the victory of the Labour Party solely in terms of anti-Americanism, it did represent a break from traditional Cold War values and policies, of which a constituent element had been exuberant pro-American policies and attitudes.

Geoffrey Serle, writing in 1974, sensed a new confidence in Australia under the Labour government and a growing consensus among intellectuals—people like Donald Horne, Craig McGregor, and Robin Boyd—that a renaissance of Australian culture was in progress. The cultural model of the 1970s and 1980s would be more Australian—not British or American, but the expression of a mature and independent (and now possibly republican?) nation.[19] The renaissance in the film industry, initially government-supported, the Ocker movement in advertising, comedy, and television programming, and the increasingly Australian fare in literature and the arts, all reflected rising nationalist feelings in Australia. Anti-Americanism was no longer merely the province of the Left but had become a leitmotif of Australian culture and part of the context of Australian national identity. The changing nature of this cultural and intellectual environment would, of course, impact on thousands of American migrants moving to and living in Australia in the post–World War II decades. The consequence of this cultural interaction is taken up subsequently in some detail. But the very fluid nature of the debate about Australian society would create a general sense of unease for all Australians. Like America, part of this national navel-gazing involved a sense of decline, of a culture reaching its limits, and, especially after the "banana republic" currency crisis of 1986 and the stock market crash in 1987, of the ending of postwar prosperity.

Perhaps Bruce Grant—someone with broad experience of America and Australia and no radical—writing in 1988, should have the last word on these changes. He summarizes:

American dependence . . . induced laziness and a lack of integrity in Australian policy making, a mistaken sense of racial superiority and a readiness to model Australian social and economic development thoughtlessly on the United States.

. . . It is impossible for the relationship to be one of equals, to be other than asymmetrical. It is important for Australia in the longer term to free itself of emotional and intellectual dependence on the United States and to explore more deeply its relations with other countries in the region. This is not in order to reject the United States. . . . [but] to improve the efficiency of . . . Australia's ability to contribute as a different kind of western society in the Pacific.[20]

The convergence of the two societies with similar income levels was not just cultural and economic—they were also becoming virtually indistinguishable physically. With the advent of the automobile, Australian cities, with their suburban sprawl and multistoried buildings, came to look like comparably sized American cities.[21]

Australians have been among the first to take up new consumer technologies, and as a result the Australian Way of Life—with refrigerators, washing machines, televisions (later VCRs and then personal computers and the World Wide Web), and multiple car ownership—became more and more a Southern-Hemispheric clone of the American Way of Life. In the 1980s Australia was an Anglo–Celtic/British culture with a superimposed American style of life, attempting to integrate its economy with ancient Asian civilizations; no wonder that the "Generation X" of the 1990s is characterized as confused and having difficulties defining their ethical and social values.

SCHOLARSHIP

This cross-fertilization of cultures was, of course, recognized and analyzed by historians and social critics, as already discussed, but in addition this would stimulate interest in formal academic studies in Australia about America and conversely the expansion of Australian studies in America. Historical studies in Australia expanded in the decade after World War II as the universities moved to levels of postgraduate education to match the American model of large multi-purpose universities with growing Ph.D. programs.

The first full university course in Australian history was introduced at Melbourne in 1946, and this was symptomatic of an emerging nationalism and sophistication in the tertiary system.[22] The comparative study of America and Australia, therefore, emerged as part of a general expansion of historical studies and a growing consciousness on both sides of the Pacific of the commonality and convergent features of the two nations. It was another indication of the shift of Australia out of the British intellectual framework and toward a greater knowledge of the American, and of the exchange, at all levels, of ideas and personnel between the United States and Australia.

The exploration of the Turner thesis—which argues for the great effect of vast quantities of free and available land on the growth and character of America—was explored in Fred Alexander's *Moving Frontier: An American Theme and Its Application to Australian History,* published in 1947. The first major comparative study of the development of Australian and American development was, however, by an Englishman: H. C. Allen, in his *Bush and Backwoods,* published over a decade later in 1959, analyzed and juxtaposed the frontier experiences of the two nations. The areas for useful comparative analysis and research were obvious—urbanization, immigration, Anglo-Saxon cultural heritage, popular culture, political institutions—and many of these were subjects of scholarship in the 1970s and 1980s.

One of the most fruitful topics for comparative historical work has been that of immigration, beginning with Charles Price's *Southern Europeans in Australia* (1963), to the writings of James Jupp and the many others who have all drawn upon the dense ethnic historiography of the two nations. The usefulness of comparative history has also been recognized in America, where in the past decade Australian studies have been given institutional status at the University of Texas (Austin) and at Harvard University, and earlier at Pennsylvania State University through the active sponsorship of the doyen of U.S. Australianists, Henry Albinski. Plans are now underway for a major center of Australian and New Zealand studies at Georgetown University in Washington DC, with the encouragement of the Australian Jesuit scholar, Father John Eddy. On both sides of the Pacific the commonality and exchange of ideas and people between Australia and America has been commensurate with the related trends of Americanization of Australia and the continuing search for an Australian identity.[23]

IMMIGRATION

A crucial component stimulating the reevaluation of Australian national identity lay in the social and historical causes and consequences of the mass migration of non-English-speaking peoples to Australia since World War II. This transformation of Australia to a multiethnic society has touched off an enormous range of debates and public policy dilemmas: the questions of migration levels; multiculturalism and Australian identity; the so-called "Blainey debate" on Asian immigration; the economic effects of migration on levels of productivity, unemployment, and social welfare spending; the potential strains of a multiethnic society on levels of tolerance and intolerance; and the debate over the republic, now that almost one-quarter of Australians were born overseas (one-fifth of non-Anglo-Celtic heritage). To place the migration of Americans in this general context, one must examine in detail the pattern of evolution of Australian migration and the ramifications of these changes on contemporary Australian society.

Australia, of course, began its early colonial history, as did America, as an Anglo-Saxon culture, with migrants almost exclusively from the British Isles. In colonial America (1607–1783) this also included large numbers of Germans, Scandinavians, and other northern Europeans; although Australia did have migrants from these groups (and numerous Italians), in the nineteenth century the numbers were generally small and did not greatly alter the essentially Anglo–Celtic character of colonial Australian society. Australia by Federation was a white British and Irish culture, and the overseas-born were overwhelmingly from the British Isles. In 1891, 90 percent of overseas-born were from Britain in most states.[24] When the new constitution and nation were proclaimed in 1901, Australia was to be a white Christian nation firmly within the Anglo-Saxon British Empire.

As Americans were in the midst of the peak decades of the Great Migration between the 1870s and the 1920s, Australians debated and finalized the new constitution and the need for immigration legislation for the Commonwealth of Australia. American ethnic and racial thought in the nineteenth century had a long tradition of xenophobia and white Anglo-Saxonism, going back to the anti-Catholic and anti-immigration movements of the 1840s, which had produced the

Know-Nothing or American Party. The American Party reached its peak of national popularity when its presidential candidate, Millard Fillmore (U.S. president, 1850–53), achieved 25 percent of the vote in 1856; at the state level they reached a high with 63 percent of the popular vote in their strongest state of Massachusetts in the elections of 1854.[25] The Social Darwinist, William Graham Summer, a Yale political science professor, combined Americanism with Darwinist evolutionary ideals to propagate a view of both the biological and the historical superiority of the white Christian American, thus echoing his English counterpart, Herbert Spencer, who had published his seminal *Social Statics* in 1850.[26]

Racial views found even more extreme expression in the Ku Klux Klan—in the first Klan of the post–Civil War era (1860s) but more consequentially in the second rising of the Klan in the World War I period. The Klan was the most violent and terroristic element in the Red Scare of the early 1920s, which blended anti-Catholic, anti-Semitic, anti-Left, anti-black and generally xenophobic elements.[27] All the strains of racism also drew upon the "evidence" of science—pseudo-science—like phrenology, which allegedly "proved" the inferiority of non-white "mongrel" races (in the case of phrenology through cranial sizes and skull physiognomy). This terminology survived to the late twentieth century, when in 1997 the reelected mayor of Port Lincoln in South Australia referred to part Aboriginal and other mixed-race people as "mongrels." Shortly afterwards a new Liberal senator, Ross Lightfoot of Western Australia, insisted that Aboriginals were the lowest color on the spectrum of human civilization, until he was forced to apologize by Prime Minister John Howard.

In America the position of blacks under Jim Crowism, and the reduction of the Native American population over four centuries from around 2.5 million to 237,000 in 1900, provided ample evidence that America was, and intended to remain, a white man's country.[28] The Immigration Bills of 1921 and 1924 intended it to be, furthermore, not just white, but Protestant.

With the exception of the treatment of the indigenous Aboriginal population, Australia did not, of course, have a history quite as replete with institutional racism as did America, nor did it have the tradition and legacy of mass slavery. But it did have fainter echoes. In the nineteenth century the Queensland sugarcane industry had practiced "blackbirding"—that is, importing Kanak or Melanesian indentured labor from the South Pacific. It also decimated the Aboriginal population with at least the same thoroughness as the Americans had used on indigenous peoples, reducing them from at least 251,000 in 1788 to 60,000 by 1921.[29] The benign disposition within the settler community itself may be chiefly attributed to the White Australia policy. Australians clearly intended to remain a white nation, for, as Ron Norris has written in his book on Federation, "the belief in a racially homogenous White society was an article of faith held by all strata of Australian society."

The Immigration Restriction Act of 1901 was structured, through the subterfuge of a language test—based on the Natal model but also echoing southern

American techniques to disenfranchise blacks—to exclude non-Europeans from entering Australia. Any migrant could be tested for proficiency in any European language and refused entry on failure. Throughout the debates, again from Norris, "politicians openly stated the purpose of the legislation in the plainest racist language inside and outside parliament." In Queensland the labor movement especially feared competition from cheap white and Pacific Islander labor; the Northern Territory was sensitive about the propinquity of the Chinese and Asians in general; and the Victorians and New South Welshmen had particular objections to Afghan and Indian hawkers and the recent experience of Chinese in the gold fields. All the colonies, therefore, wished urgently to restrict immigration, and most already had anti-Asian labor and immigration legislation. The language and intellectual environment revealed the same Anglo-Saxonism and racial views that were pervasive in America, and with the White Australia policy established by the Immigration Act of 1901, Australia overtly presented itself to the world, like its American cousin, as a white Christian (preferably Protestant) nation.[30]

Under the White Australia policy the character of immigration until World War II was predominantly Anglo–Celtic. Australia encouraged British migration, and when the British parliament passed the Empire Settlement Act, which came into effect in 1922, the chief destination of British migrants shifted from the United States to Australia, New Zealand, and Canada. The U.S. immigration legislation of 1921 and 1924 was intended to restrict Catholic southern European migration, but the quota system it established also resulted in reducing British migration, with the result that the surplus intending migrants went increasingly to Australasia. In the 1920s, another 282,000 British migrants entered Australia, with 212,000 receiving assistance under the Empire Settlement Act. Australia seemed secure in its desire to remain part of the white British imperial orbit.[31]

But the pressures for change were already apparent on the eve of World War II. Australia, in the Asian–Pacific region, would not be able to ignore its Asian propinquity forever; the population and economic pressures were slowly building from the north. The European non-Anglo–Celtic element was also beginning to increase, with some 8,000 Italians arriving by the 1920s and small communities of Greeks, Yugoslavs, Maltese, and Jews appearing in Australian cities and regional centers. When the world was turned upside down by the events of 7 December 1941, Australians turned their attention to survival, but the inexorable process of broadening the Australian ethnic base and its position in the world was under way. After V-J Day Australia would have to face its geographic position in the economy of the Asian–Pacific region and inevitably to abandon the isolation and racist image of its White Australia policy.[32]

The policy changes brought into effect by the Labour Party after World War II would inaugurate an entire chain of social changes in Australian society. When Arthur Calwell, the newly created minister for immigration who formed a new department, announced a policy of large-scale immigration, including assisted passage in 1946, he not only set in train a move toward a multiethnic society but departed from traditional Labour Party and Australian immigration policy. The scheme was to bring in 70,000 migrants per year by 1948; those from Britain were expected to pay 10 pounds, with the British and Australian governments to pay the rest of the costs. Thus was achieved what John Molony has described, with exaggeration, as the "most remarkable and far-reaching effect of the Second World War", the implications of which are still being revealed in the mid-1990s.[33]

Calwell had no intention of abandoning the White Australia policy, and his antipathy toward Asian or black American migration was widely known—he excused the exclusion of one Chinese with the expression, "two wongs don't make a White," and on another occasion he referred to Asians as "living off the smell of an oily rag."[34] But his desire to increase rapidly the population base of Australia from 8,000,000, for economic and strategic reasons, would almost immediately result in an increase in non-Anglo–Celtic and non-Christian migration. The increasingly numerous Jews came in for some general hostility, as displaced persons or DPs,[35] and Calwell's agreements with the International Refugee Organization in 1947 would bring 120,000 Baltic peoples to Australia. Postwar economic expansion required large numbers of unskilled laborers to work in the factories, farms, and mines, and large-scale projects, such as the Snowy Mountain Scheme, would be a source of work for European migrants eager to live in Australia. Thus began the evolution of Australia toward a multicultural society in which the traditional British-derived culture would inexorably lose its social and cultural hegemony.

The conservative governments (1949–72) of the Menzies era (1949–66) continued the immigration changes begun by the Labour government, and by the early 1970s a few significant shifts—both legal and political—had been made in the White Australia policy. Indeed, one may conclude, as did Herb London,[36] that by the late 1960s the Coalition government had effectively ended the White Australia policy, although it continued to favor British and European migrants. Between the late 1940s and the early 1970s, hundreds of thousands of people of Baltic origin, Greeks, Italians, Serbs, Croats, Russians, Poles, and scores of other ethnic groups would make Australia their new and permanent home (80 percent of those arriving during these years would stay). There was still a large British component in the migrant intake (42 percent between 1947 and 1969), but the pattern was changing.

The cities of Australia—like U.S. cities in the 1890s—were taking on a multicultural character, and by the late 1960s the population of Sydney was 42 percent overseas-born, that of Melbourne 51 percent, Adelaide 48 percent, Perth 35 percent, and, the lowest, Brisbane 18 percent. Consecutive Australian governments from World War II to 1972 expanded the assisted passage scheme, and during this period agreements were negotiated with the Netherlands (1951), Italy (1951), Austria, Greece, and West Germany (1952), Spain (1958), Belgium (1961), Turkey (1967), and Yugoslavia (1970). Small numbers of Americans were also beginning to arrive (6 percent of the total in the 1960s), but they were represented at a much higher level as a percentage of the professionals entering Australia (16 percent). Pressures for further change to Australia's immigration policies were mounting as the volume and variety of migration increased.[37]

As discussed above, the 1960s represented a period in which there was a world-wide atmosphere of radical change, especially in the Anglo-Saxon and European world. In America, Lyndon Johnson (president, 1963–69) pressed the reforms of the Great Society, including immigration changes, which increased numbers and loosened restrictions on Asian immigration as a consequence of the 1965 changes to the Immigration Act. Political pressures from the black Civil Rights movement and other radical reform movements were intense and combined with the anti-Vietnam War upheavals. In Australia the pressures for reform were also building: the prime ministers following the 1966 retirement of Menzies—Harold Holt, John Gorton, and William McMahon—were also subjected to prolonged and intense pressures over the need for reforms of immigration, education, and policies on women, all within the transcendent and growing pressure against Australia's role in Vietnam.

By the early 1970s, administrative and political actions had weakened the White Australia policy. Already in 1958 the Migration Act had rescinded the dictation test from the 1901 Act, and Australia's participation in the Colombo Plan, the migration of Turks to Australia, the admission of some Asians with educational qualifications (1966), had all built up pressures in Australia to abandon its White Australia policy. This image and immigration stance were an embarrassment to the nation, and by the early 1970s they were increasingly perceived as harmful to the growing trade with Asia. Consequently, with the election of Gough Whitlam in 1972 and the appointment of Al Grassby as the highly visible activist minister for immigration, the nation was prepared to bury, as the major political parties had already done, the moribund White Australia policy.

From the 1970s to the 1990s Australian immigration policy continued along a number of lines set by the Whitlam government: a continuation of large-scale levels of migration; a commitment to multiculturalism; a growing percentage of Asian migrants as prosperity reduced migration from Europe; a growing debate within the Australian community on all aspects of migration; and a strong commitment to racial justice, as exemplified by the Racial Discrimination Act (1975). The level of intake of migrants in this period has been related to perceptions by Liberal and Labour governments of the economic capacity of Australia to assimilate large-scale migration and the political sensibilities of the Australian community. In the recession period of the mid-1970s, the immigration level was lowered by Labour to 56,000 per annum, from 1971 to 1976; in the more expansionist late 1970s and early 1980s under the Liberals this was increased to 100,000 each year. Similar fluctuations took place in the economic expansion of late 1980s, when under the regime of Immigration Minister Chris Hurford and in search of a growing economy the intake went up to reach a figure of over

140,000 in one year. This was then wound back in the recession of the early 1990s, when it fell to 60,000 annually under the Hawke–Keating Labour governments. This lower figure was to be maintained under the Coalition government when it was reelected in 1996.

By the 1980s Australia was almost as multiethnic as America, with 140 ethnic groups, 40 languages other than English spoken in Australian homes, and almost one-quarter of the population born overseas. Nonetheless the overwhelming majority of the population, unlike in America, remained ethnic Europeans and Anglophones.

With these dramatic changes has also come divisive debate, especially since the 1984 speech by Professor Geoffrey Blainey, which began the so-called Blainey debate on Asian immigration. In the 1990s, migration has seldom been out of the public eye, and the large proportion of Asian migrants, largely from South-East Asia and the Indian subcontinent in the intakes of the late 1980s (close to 40 percent) compared to British (19 percent) and European (12 percent), continues to be, implicitly, at least, a subject of divisive political debate.[38] The issue of multiculturalism in the 1990s engenders an ideological split in Australian society in which the Left defends multiculturalism and republicanism against the Right increasingly committed to implicit monoculturalism and British monarchist traditions. In the 1990s, the republic debate has deepened and exacerbated these divisions within Australian culture.

Looking back from the 1990s to World War II at these changes in immigration policies, one must conclude that, overall, Australia has very effectively assimilated a large number of diverse people and changed itself in the process. Multicultural/multireligious nations—Ireland, Lebanon, Sri Lanka, to name a few—do not inspire much hope for racial and ethnic harmony; however, the Australian record of harmony must include the rather less than edifying story of Aborigines, non-Anglo–Celtic migrants, Muslims, and Jews and the way they have been treated by the white Australian population. The success story is much less impressive considering the discrimination against groups who came to Australia but were not always greeted warmly, nor, as their numbers grew and social visibility increased in Australian society, have they always been treated equitably. Migration, therefore, is always a difficult and complex process, and even in a relatively benign environment like Australia it requires subtle and complicated modes of analysis.

GLOBALIZING AUSTRALIA

As these great changes in the ethnic composition of the Australian nation were taking place, the country also embarked on a profound restructuring of the economy. In the 1980s Australia, too, began a transformation in response to the forces of globalization and the end of the Cold War. But the first indications of the need for these changes emerged in the 1970s, when the dual economy created by the Australian settlement at the time of federation began to encounter strains with which it could not deal.

These strains first became evident during the Whitlam government, when the 400 percent increase in the price of oil engineered by the OPEC countries led to a surge in the value of Australian commodity exports and drove the Australian dollar to a peak of $U.S.1.53. The following international recession pushed the Australian economy into its first serious economic slump since the 1930s. The Whitlam government lost the 1975 election largely because it had been unable to revive the economy, despite Treasurer Hayden's belated embrace of what he called "economic rationalism," thereby settling the term for future Australian usage. Inflation increased, and unemployment rose to around 5 percent.

The succeeding Fraser government tried to revive the Australian economy by increasing protection against foreign imports, driving down wages, and increasing the profits of Australian industry. It also tried to engineer a minerals and energy boom in the late 1970s. It succeeded in fact only in producing a condition of stagflation similar to that then prevailing in the United States. In the next global recession of 1981–83 the Fraser government was swept from office in a wave of strikes designed to restore real wages to earlier levels, which helped to produce double-digit inflation and unemployment. The incoming Labour government, led by the right wing under Prime Minister Bob Hawke and Treasurer Paul Keating, arrived at quite a different diagnosis of the problem and applied a new remedy.

Australia, having locked its foreign exports into commodities that constituted a declining share of world trade, faced uncertain, unstable, but usually falling prices. These commodities—including wool, wheat, beef, and minerals—could no longer be depended on to provide the foreign exchange earnings on which the entire Australian economy had depended. During 1984 the Australian dollar was heavily traded, and the government was forced to float it alongside most other developed country currencies; it accordingly slipped downwards in recognition of its commodity dependence. In 1985–86 Australia then faced an acute balance of payments problem as its external earnings dived and with them the Australian dollar, to 60 American cents. Keating warned that the country risked becoming a banana republic, and a new economic direction was charted.[39]

The dual economy had to be dismantled, the dependence on the primary sector for foreign trade reduced, and the protected regulated domestic economy made more internationally competitive in recognition that it could no longer be subsidized by agriculture and mining. Three quarters of a century of regulatory economic mechanisms were progressively dismantled. The tariff walls were brought down annually, to reach, it was planned, zero in 2010. The Australian dollar was floated and the financial sector effectively deregulated. Government-owned industries and institutions like the Commonwealth Bank and Qantas Airlines were sold off, and regulated sectors like the wool industry and domestic airlines were exposed to the market. Efforts were made to make the traded goods sector more efficient by changing work practices in the ports and factories, and the entire wage-fixing structure was assaulted to make wage rates more closely match production. And the state share of the GDP, which had reached a high under Whitlam, was wound back by cutting some welfare programs but more often by trimming them through the application of tough assets and incomes tests, in order to control "middle-class welfare."

Australia was, of course, not the only country undertaking these liberalizing measures. The adoption of such free-trade and market-oriented policies was to be the mark of many countries after the end of the Cold War and in few areas as clearly as in the Asia–Pacific region. The enthusiasm of Australians, having become new converts, knew few bounds, and it was instrumental in creating the Asia Pacific Economic Cooperation (APEC) in 1989 and urging the extension of the free-trade principles of GATT to agriculture and services in 1994. The result was an Australia abandoning the dual economy for a competitive globalized structure during the 1990s, which integrated it more closely into the Asia-Pacific region.

The driving force behind this process of globalization was, of course, the United States. As described earlier, the liberal world order was revived after the defeat of the Soviet Union and the doctrines of free trade brushed off from the 1940s. This time the absence of a serious Communist challenge and the massive improvements in technology combined to make a global economy truly possible. The innovations—in transport, including jumbo jets, supertankers, and mammoth container vessels, in communications, with faxes, mobile phones, linked stock exchanges, computers, and the Net, in information dissemination, with satellites and fiber-optic cables, and in production, with the enhanced mobility of capital—all combined to bring the American global liberal order within sight.

In these circumstances it is hardly surprising that American personnel should play a leading role in the transformation of the Australian economy from a protected and regulated one to one that is being globalized. Since America was the first globalizing economy, its citizens were first exposed to the process and were recruited in increasing numbers to assist the process in Australia as chief executive officers of corporatized former publicly owned enterprises and as new management and owners in private Australian companies going offshore for commercial advantage. Finally, American ideas began to emerge more widely as the bedrock of the globalizing mentality driving the quest for greater efficiency in the new Australia. It was Americans who produced the new doctrines of monetarist or rational economics and the "Washington consensus" on liberal economic reform that swept through Australia in the 1980s and 1990s. And it was often Americans who were blamed, particularly by the Left, for the adverse repercussions that followed the dismantling of a dual economy whose time had, in fact, come and gone.

AUSTRALIA IN THE 1990S

In the final decade of the twentieth century Australia can, in many respects, look back over the past 40 years with some satisfaction. It has matured to a culturally sophisticated, independent middle-level power; it has an enviable record as a humane society; the private welfare system and state sector have created an equitable distribution of social services and provide a safety net for most people even after the trimming of the 1980s; and Australia has a relatively successful record as an egalitarian, multicultural society. It has also undergone quite massive structural changes to its ethnic composition and economic character within a generation without widespread social dysfunction, the glaring exception to this otherwise quite positive record being the continuing poor situation of the indigenous Aboriginal Australians.

But, as with all Western nations, there are still serious problems: marginal groups are growing with the globalized economy, and a nascent underclass has already been established; income gaps induced by policies of economic rationalism between rich and poor have widened; environmental degradation is at serious levels in water quality, beach erosion, soil degradation, and air quality control; and the structural problems of unemployment in a post–Cold War economy show no signs of abating. From World War II to the 1980s Australia was a land of hope and opportunity to millions of migrants; in the 1990s this reputation has been somewhat tarnished, but in global terms it remains, if not the "lucky country," certainly an extraordinarily pleasant one. Against that background, it perhaps seems superfluous to ask our next question: why do people migrate?[40]

NOTES

1. One could, however, start with Melvyn P. Leffler, "The American Conception of National Security and the Beginnings of the Cold War, 1945–48," *A.H.R.*, 89 (1984), pp. 346–381.

2. Norman Harper, *Pacific Orbit*, pp. 8–9; Norman Harper, *A Great and Powerful Friend: A Study of Australian–American Relations Between 1900 and 1975* (St. Lucia, 1987). A recent conference in London, "Australia and the End of Overseas Empires, 1945–75," has confirmed the *angst* at the end of the British alliance: *The Australian*, 18 May 1994, p. 27.

3. Leicester Webb, *Communism and Democracy in Australia, A Survey of the Referendum of 1951* (Melbourne, 1954).

4. Alistair Davidson, *The Communist Party of Australia, A Short History* (Stanford, CA, 1969), especially pp. 51 ff.

5. See Ross Fitzgerald, *The People's Champion; Fred Paterson, Australia's Only Communist Member of Parliament* (St. Lucia, 1997), for a naive hagiographic biography.

6. Recent books on Australia's involvement in Vietnam are highly critical and reject the need for Australia to follow America's strategic policies: Terry Burstall, *Vietnam: The Australian Dilemma* (St. Lucia, 1993), and John Murphy, *Harvest of Fear: A History of Australia's Vietnam War* (St. Leonards, 1993).

7. Michael Sexton, *War for the Asking, Australia's Vietnam Secrets* (Ringwood, 1981).

8. Des Ball, *A Base For Debate* (St. Leonards, 1987).

9. W. C. Wentworth, "Australia and the Monarchy—A Liberal View," in Geoffrey Dutton, ed., *Republican Australia*? (Melbourne, 1977), p. 122.

10. See Stephen Haseler, *The Varieties of Anti-Americanism* (Washington, DC, 1985).

11. For an overview, see William L. O'Neil, *Coming Apart* (Chicago, IL, 1971); Allen Matusow, *The Unraveling of America* (New York, 1984); for how these perceptions impinged on Australia, see Roger Bell, *Unequal Allies: Australian–American Relations and the Pacific War* (Melbourne, 1977); Catley's E-mail system has the address "Chomsky," reflecting the transcendent influence of the American Left on even university senior management today.

12. See Jim Cairns, *The Eagle and the Lotus, Western Intervention in Vietnam, 1847–1968* (Melbourne, 1969).

13. See Aitchison, *Americans*, pp. 134–135; see also Bell and Bell, *Implicated*, pp. 146–147; the works of Australia's foremost authority Desmond Ball, including *A Suitable Piece of Real Estate: American Installations in Australia* (Sydney, 1980); *A Base for Debate: The US Satellite Station at Nurrungar* (Sydney, 1987); *Pine Gap* (Sydney, 1988); *The Intelligence War in the Gulf* (Canberra, 1991). President Nixon ordered the CIA to investigate the Whitlam government after its re-election in 1974 because of concern over the bases: *Australian,* 26 December 1995, p. 1.

14. Bell and Bell, *Implicated*, p. 105.

15. W. J. Hudson, section covering 1951–72, in Frank Crowley, ed., *A New History of Australia* (Adelaide, 1980), p. 526.

16. J. G. Crawford, "Partnership in Trade," in Harper, *Pacific Orbit*, pp. 45, 50, 54, 56–57.

17. For film, see Bell and Bell, *Implicated*, pp. 188, 194–195, and Molony, *Australia*, p. 382; for the other mass media, see Bell and Bell, *Implicated*, pp. 71, 81, 82, 167–168, 183, 189; for education, see A. G. Austin, "The American Impact on Education," in Harper, *Pacific Orbit*, pp. 91–107, especially p. 104, on Australian ambivalence to U.S. models; on monetarism, known in Australia as economic rationalism, see Michael Pusey, *Economic Rationalism in Canberra* (Canberra, 1991).

18. Max Harris felt the language would "finish up as poor man's American": quoted in Bell and Bell, *Implicated*, p. 204; for discussion of this area, see also pp. 203–206.

19. Geoffrey Serle, *From Deserts the Prophets Come, the Creative Spirit in Australia, 1788–1972* (Melbourne, 1974), pp. 216–218.

20. Bruce Grant, *What Kind of Country? Australia and the Twenty-First Century* (Ringwood, Victoria, 1988), p. 142.

21. See M. Neutze, *Urbanization in Australia* (Sydney, 1977).

22. Molony, *Australia*, p. 309.

23. For these works cited and others, see Ian Bickerton, "The United States and Australia: Some Points of Comparison," in Norman Harper and Elaine Barry, eds., *American Studies Down Under* (Kensington, NSW, 1976), pp. 42–57; Bell and Bell, *Implicated*, pp. 10–14; for James Jupp's latest Australian–American immigration study, see James Jupp and Gary Freeman, eds., *Nations of Immigrants: Australia, the United States, and International Migration* (Melbourne, 1992); for Georgetown's plans, see *The Australian*, 27 April 1994, p. 25; Joe Siracusa views U.S. studies in Australia as now having an "Aussie flavor": *The Australian,* 16 November 1994, p. 36. For reports of a conference on Australian studies in the United States, see *The Australian*, 18 September 1996, p. 38.

24. Geoffrey Sherington, *Australia's Immigrants* (Sydney, 1990), p. 85.

25. Michael F. Holt, "The Politics of Impatience: The Origins of Know-Nothingism," *Journal of American History* 60 (1973), pp. 309–331.

26. See Robert Bannister, *Social Darwinism* (Philadelphia, PA, 1979).

27. Allen Trelease, *White Terror: KKK* (New York, 1971).

28. As with Aboriginal history in Australia, the pre-European numbers of Native Americans, and how long they have inhabited their land, has been hotly debated. Especially Native American historians have rightly seen these points as indicative of the scale of European decimation of native culture and the proprietary rights of indigenous peoples: see Francis Prucha, *American Indian Policy in the Formative Years* (Cambridge, MA, 1962); Edward Spicer, *A Short History of the Indians of the United States* (New York, 1969).

29. See C. D. Rowley, *The Destruction of Aboriginal Society* (Canberra, 1970), p. 384. The figure of 60,000 is probably too low, and Aboriginals may now number over a quarter of a million; but it is also now often postulated that there were probably nearly a million in Australia in 1788.

30. Ron Norris, *The Emergent Commonwealth, Australian Federation: Expectations and Fulfilment, 1889–1910* (Melbourne, 1975), quotations on pp. 80, 91, and see also pp. 45, 49, 60, 62.

31. Sherington, *Immigrants,* pp. 107, 117, 118.

32. Sherington, *Immigrants,* pp. 120–125; W. D. Borrie, *Italians and Germans in Australia* (Melbourne, 1954), p. 51.

33. Molony, *Australia*, p. 294.

34. The White Australia policy was clearly understood in the black press in America such as *Ebony Magazine*, see Cuddy, *Yanks,* pp. 12–13, and fn. 30.

35. Paul Bartrop's recent book *Australia and the Holocaust, 1933–45* (Kew, 1994), paints a sorry picture of the Australian government's anti-Semitism in the 1930s when, in spite of Nazi atrocities being fully known, they rejected Jewish emigration to Australia on the grounds that Jews were not racially acceptable.

36. H. T. London, *Non-White Immigration and the "White Australia" Policy* (Sydney, 1970).

37. Sherington, *Immigrants*, pp. 142, 149.

38. Sherington, *Immigrants*, p. 168. By 2020, some projections place the percentage of the population of Asian origin to be 27 percent of the Australian total: *The Australian Magazine*, 22 January 1994, p. 10; Stephen Castles and Mark Miller, *The Age of Migration* (Sydney, 1993), pp. 83–84.

39. For a more detailed description of the issues raised in this section, see Bob Catley, *Globalising Australian Capitalism* (Cambridge, 1996).

40. For recent studies on Australia's relative success as a multicultural society, see Liz Thompson, *From Somewhere Else* (Oatley, 1993); Anne Henderson, *From All Corners—Six Migrant Stories* (St. Leonards, 1993).

4

Why Do People Migrate?

This question appears to be one that would lend itself to an easy answer, or at least one with no more than two or three historical dimensions required to exhaust the possibilities. Most people would quickly respond that migration is a way for people "to get employment and a better life for their children," or "to see a new part of the world and seek better opportunities," or something similar. However, over the past few decades the best historical minds, including scholars like the mega-historian William McNeill, have attempted to create a theoretical framework for this intriguing question, only to find that the intensity of the scholarship has heightened rather than reduced the uncertainties.[1] Historians, sociologists, geographers, demographers, economists, ethnographers, population biologists, and others have all contributed to the attempts to explain why people move from point A to point B, and the consequent methodological problems have continued to multiply. Before moving from the historical context of Americans migrating to Australia to the actual empirical data on American migration, we should pause to examine where, in the 1990s, these historiographical and theoretical attempts have brought the migration historian.

THEORIES OF MIGRATION

The areas of inquiry on which the theoreticians of migration have concentrated are, first, problems of global causality—why do people migrate, and what factors push people out of one culture and pull them to another?—and, second, problems that make up the constituent elements of the migration process: what are the costs, material and human, of migration; how, and over what time period, do migrants assimilate; and what factors affect remigration and/or permanent settlement in a new culture? All of these issues have produced a proliferation of explanatory models, but one should begin by first examining some typologies that have been advanced for explaining global migration.

Models for global migration have attempted to explain why large numbers of people move across the globe. The underlying presuppositions in these models dealing with large units of space and time are complex and present enormous methodological difficulties. They attempt to address key philosophical issues that motivate human behavior and to resolve questions regarding intrinsic biological traits as opposed to environmental conditioning ("nature versus nurture"), volitional human historical patterns juxtaposed with deterministic models of world history, and whether people migrate of their own free will or are pushed along by social forces that they only vaguely comprehend, let alone control. Increasingly, theorists of migration have moved to more holistic or multivariate models to explain migration patterns, and in the 1980s a consensus emerged that migration is caused by both volitional and macrohistorical factors.[2]

Some of the global causal models of migration emphasize psychological, sociological, and economic variables. Psychological models emphasize the state of mind of the intending migrant. These elements include alienation from the home culture, desire for adventure, psychosocial maladaptive traits, and overt pathological states. Sociological models have concentrated on social and environmental changes such as religious persecution, family breakdown, social class deprivation, war dislocation, and extreme environmental disruptions such as famine and natural disasters. Economic models have concentrated on labor markets, on relative differences in standard of living in host and migrant-producing regions/nations, and on other empirically measurable differentials in income, land distribution, and perceived economic advantages between nations. All of these models hope to explain the patterns of migration and partially elucidate the timing, volume, settlement patterns, and assimilation rates of migrants in their host nations.

The second area of migration theory—the more finite questions of the costs of migration and adaptation—also present the ethnographic historian with a multiplicity of difficulties. To analyze the costs of migration, one must elaborate complex cost of living models and judgments on the relative value of goods and labor in different countries over long periods of time. Subjective elements—loneliness, alienation, and fear—are of crucial importance but cannot be easily, if at all, quantified. Assimilation patterns raise thorny methodological questions on the definitions of a migrant, ethnicity, and value judgments on the desirability or otherwise of assimilation. Remigration is also difficult, for data in this area are always hard to obtain and motivational patterns hard to document adequately.

Migration theorists, therefore, have struggled valiantly in the past two decades to overcome these interpretive difficulties. Often progress has been hampered by the reluctance of researchers to make full use of the variety of specialists in the field and their findings. Cross-fertilization between historical studies and social sciences has, however, begun to increase in the past decade. Recent migration scholarship has revealed historians more open to theory and to the quantitative work of sociologists, and sociologists have become more receptive to a broader historical framework in their theoretical models and empirical data. This blending of disciplines has resulted in a far greater understanding of migration, and there have been considerable shifts in major interpretations since ethnographic history was established in the 1940s as a mainstream historical discipline.

ETHNIC HISTORY IN AMERICA AND AUSTRALIA

The density of ethnographic historiography has increased dramatically since the pioneering seminal work in America in the 1940s of men like Oscar Handlin and Marcus Hansen. The emphasis in this early period was on the assumption of the desirability of assimilation, and most work assumed that migrants could and indeed should adapt relatively quickly to their new environment. The dominant model concerning movement used push–pull factors to explain why migrants left one nation, which was usually taken to be in capital deficit and possessing a surplus of labor, and chose to move to another, which was taken to be capital-rich and short of labor.

In the period between the 1950s and the 1980s, however, there has been an explosion of ethnic-oriented history, which has changed scholars' perspectives on migration. In America and Australia, especially since the 1960s, the political process has produced ethnic-consciousness movements that have accelerated with the ethnic particularism around the world in the 1980s and 1990s. The idea of the legitimacy of multiculturalism has displaced the previous dominance of support for assimilation into the melting pot. The enormous volume of ethnographic work has deepened the knowledge base from which both theoretical and substantive historical issues can be debated, and it has increased knowledge of, and sensitivity to, the complexities of migration history.

Recent American migration work has revealed the old theoretical verities to be too simplistic or, in some areas, entirely inappropriate. Studies have questioned the push–pull model, positing migration patterns in which migrants came neither from poor nations nor from the poorer sections of other nations, and shown that migrants did not always expect to be—in every respect—better off in their adopted nation. Return rates for migrants have always been high, indicating the often temporary nature of much migration. Mobility and economic assimilation have been shown to be a complex function of the skills of migrants, local conditions from the national down to neighborhood level, and the adaptive characteristics in ethnic enclaves to which many migrants belong. Important considerations in the latter issue include cooperation between old and new migrants, family ties, and levels of surplus capital in the enclave. In other words, the characteristics of the recipient nation and its settlement policies have begun to receive more attention than merely the capacity of the migrant to adapt. As discussed above, the old certainties in American historiography on the melting pot theory of American migration history have given way to a recognition of the difficulties of assimilation. This, in turn, has produced widespread evidence of the "unassimilation" of certain ethnic groups, especially among Hispanics, some Asians, and the "internal" migrants from the American South—black Americans—who had initially arrived involuntarily and had been given little opportunity to assimilate, even had they so desired. The emerging picture, therefore, is one that is more exacting and complex, but also increasingly perplexing to the ethnographic historian while being fairer to the migrating people themselves.[3]

Australian ethnographic history has, of course, become an equally dense and methodologically lively field over the past two decades. Here also, ethnic pride and the multicultural debate—particularly since the official embrace of that term in the mid-1970s—has engendered an increase in ethnic studies by historians and social scientists alike. Before embarking on the ethnic history of American migrants, it would be useful to survey this work and place this 1990s survey of the attitudes of American migrants within the Australian historiographic framework.

There is some considerable debate over the use of the terms "ethnic," "ethnicity," and "ethnographic," especially as it applies to English-speaking groups. In its most basic sense "ethnic" simply means "peoplehood" or a sense of collective identity. C. A. Price, using place of birth and peoplehood to define ethnicity, includes Americans among ethnics in his *Ethnic Composition of the Australian People,* but some ethnic organizations do not consider English-speaking migrants as ethnics. "Ethnic" should be an inclusive term that embraces all those people with an identifiable national consciousness and/or some type of organizational structure, such as clubs, sports, churches, and so on—including ethnic organizations. Likewise, ethnicity indicates a certain degree of "other-Australianness," or a general feeling of being collectively "different enough" to be an ethnic. On the basis of these criteria, Americans can be classified as an ethnic group, for they perceive themselves to be—and are construed by the general Australian community as being—distinguishable by accent, values, behavior, and national origin. Americans belong, therefore, by both composition and experience, to a legitimate part of Australian ethnographic history.[4] Nonetheless, it is a mark of the uniqueness of the American migrants' experience that they are perceived as different enough to be ethnics by Anglo–Celtic Australians but not sufficiently so by other non-English-speaking migrant communities.

Australian ethnic historiography is, of course, the result of the cumulative process of historical inquiry. Each study builds upon the corpus of knowledge already existing in both methodological and substantive historical areas. Early scholars in the field, men such as C. A. Price, W. D. Borrie, and James Jupp, began without those advantages, and—in W. D. Borrie's words in 1954 about his work on Italians and Germans—undertook "pioneer background study in a field which . . . [had] been virtually ignored by Australian historians."[5] Over the next four decades, the historiography would expand dramatically, with major studies appearing on Scandinavians (in the late 1930s); Germans (1940s); Italians (1950s); southern Europeans, British, Asians, Jews, and Chinese (1960s); Greeks (1970s), and Vietnamese, Scots, Irish, and Swiss (1980s), to name but a sampling of ethnic studies.[6] American migrants would also begin to receive attention, with a historical study by the American–Australian journalist Ray Aitchison in 1986 and several studies by American sociologists Jan Deanicis (1977), Dennis Cuddy (1977), Bernard and Ada Finifter (1980), J. and D. Bardo (1980s), and Arnold Dashefsky (1992).[7] In addition to this work, there also appeared a large body of research by demographers, sociologists, and geographers on all aspects of the migration experience in post–World War II Australia, with special attention to mobility, assimilation, and multiculturalism. By the 1990s, the historiography had become multifaceted, with the entire spectrum of models on migration and ideological positions fully represented.[8]

In the 1950s much Australian ethnic history centered around theories similar to those pursued by their American counterparts, like Oscar Handlin's push–pull factors in migration and optimism about assimilation. This perspective was well illustrated by W. D. Borrie's subtitle, *A Study of Assimilation*, of his book on Italians and Germans. Research methodologies tended to be discipline-specific, and the cross-fertilization of historical and social sciences was relatively limited. As the volume of work increased, however, the scope of ethnic history widened, and, as in America, the data suggested broader patterns of unassimilation, ethnic conflict, and, especially after the late 1960s, greater emphasis on the hostility of Australians to non-Anglo–Celtic migrants and to any people of non-Caucasian physiognomies. By the 1990s ethnographic research was quite similar to that in North America, and political and ideological issues in American-speak made this area not only complex and lively, but a veritable minefield of ethnic and political sensitivities. Indeed, it was one of the sources of the accusation that scholarship and academics were attempting to impose a particular view of a number of issues on the population at large—an accusation that led to the term "politically correct" being applied to these efforts. In general, they were said to be insisting on a new left-wing cultural agenda, which would see migration from the viewpoint of the benefit of multiculturalism, race relations from the perspective of people of color, gender issues from the female viewpoint, and international relations from the nonstatist perspective of the "marginalized."

The social tensions of multiethnic societies are writ large in human history and provide a major theme of the twentieth century. Without venturing into the pitfalls of the argument over whether ethnic conflict is environmentally determined or intrinsic to the human species, the 1990s conflicts in South Africa, Ireland, the Middle East, Bosnia, Rwanda, and Sri Lanka all provide continuing evidence of the difficulties of multiculturalism to a generation that has not forgotten the Jewish Holocaust, or the Armenian Holocaust of World War I, for that matter. As one watches the rise of neo-Nazism in Europe and the election of neo-Fascists to government posts in Italy in March 1994, the debate over multiculturalism is given added dimensions and urgency in Australia.[9] This was to be given added poignancy by the apparent backlash against political correctness after the Australian federal election of March 1996 brought to power a Coalition government that had openly campaigned against it and was to be only intensified when the Independent MP, Pauline Hanson, launched her One Nation right-wing political party in 1997 in some measure over this issue.

Ethnic historians in the early 1990s no longer considered Australia to be capable of slipping back to the "bad old days" of the White Australia policy. Gone forever, said most ethnographers, are the 1920s, when, as Michael Tsounis points out, the premier of Western Australia could refer to the Greeks as "that fish-and-chip crowd" in a parliamentary debate; gone also are the days of "anti-dago" riots in the 1930s in the mining towns of Western Australia, the worst in Kalgoorlie in 1934, and after World War II of wholesale racist attitudes about Jews, Asians, and people of Baltic origin.[10] Australia had absorbed, without much violence and with an acceptable level of tension and resistance, millions of extremely diverse peoples. But in the 1990s there have been elements of disquiet. Polls throughout the 1980s showed a diminishing level of support, particularly for immigration, but also for multiculturalism—a pattern similar to that discerned in America.[11] Interestingly, this cut across left–right ideological lines, with opposition coming from clearly racist RSL antediluvians, from economists on various productivity grounds, and from ecological objectors maintaining that further population growth would ruin the already fragile Australian environment.[12]

But the multicultural debate has, in the mid-1990s, been increasingly politicized, and right-wing conservative elements, especially in the National Party, have verged on dividing Australia into left–republican "non-Australians" and conservative–monarchist "true Australians," the latter defending the cultural integrity of the Australian nation.[13] The intellectual respectability of these views derives from the historian Geoffrey Blainey, who in the early 1980s sparked a debate on the impact of Asian immigration on the Australian identity.[14] Nancy Viviani, in her book on the Vietnamese, who have frequently been targets of racists, sounded an ominous warning in the mid-1980s: "The foundation of attitudes which underpinned the walls of White Australia are still in good order and the experience of living with Asians (or rather the community's perception of this) can have the effect in practice of increasing pressure for some implicit reestablishment of the White Australia policy. This cannot be explicit, because of foreign relations, but the battle for and against it is being fought now."[15]

In the 1990s, ethnic groups and their defenders believe that the time has come—as ethnic writers in America like Michael Novak have stressed—for Australian society fully to accept migrant traditions and contributions. The last word on this goes to Eva Isaacs, who summarizes the case in her book on the Greeks: "it is the Australians' turn to make a move in learning to tolerate foreign idiosyncrasies and recognizing that something can be learned from living beside them."[16]

In the mid-1990s the temperature has unquestionably been raised on the issues of immigration, neo-Fascism, racism, and multiculturalism. This has sprung from a number of sources. The actions of racist groups, like National Action, which have existed for some time, were reactivated in the late 1980s. There have also been a number of conflicts between different ethnic communities, particularly as Yugoslavia disintegrated, Serbs opposed Croatians, and Greeks opposed Macedonians. The wide publicity associated with the film *Schindler's List* (1994)—itself based on a book by an Australian—and its Academy Award nominations and multiple awards only intensified interest in the persecution of the Jews, and this was fueled by the banning of the controversial Holocaust-denying British historian, David Irving, from Australia. The long-standing hostility toward immigration by a minority of the Australian community, especially toward Asians, was also encouraged from the right by One Nation and from the left by Australians Against Further Immigration. These have all produced incidents of conflict and violence. A recent Ph.D. dissertation by Rolade Berthier still found "deeply ingrained anti-Asian attitudes."

In sleepy Adelaide, a neo-Nazi gang went on a rampage in March 1994, in the major CBD pedestrian precinct Rundle Mall, in which nearly a dozen people were terrorized and several bashed, and in July 1995 over 70 graves were destroyed in the Jewish section of the West Terrace Cemetery. In a string of by-elections in 1994, the anti-immigration party, Australians Against Further Immigration, received between 6.8 and 13.7 percent of votes in by-elections held in Bonython (SA), Werriwa (NSW), Mackellar (NSW), and Warringah (NSW). A spokesman for the party, Denis McCormack, declared: "I quite like Asians, but that doesn't mean I want them all here." In April 1994, the then Labour minister for immigration, Nick Bolkus, himself a Greek born in Cyprus, was attacked and spat upon by Macedonian demonstrators protesting against the government's policy to refer to them as "slavo-Macedonians." This policy resulted from pressure on the part the Greek government, acting through the hundreds of thousands of Greek Australians with the vote, directed toward preventing Australia from recognizing the former Yugoslav republic of Macedonia by that name because a northern Greek province already used it.

In the 1990s particularism increased around the world as economic tensions rose with unemployment. In many countries this was reflected in the growth of ultra–right-wing movements, since the collapse of the Soviet Union and the Tiananmen Square massacre in China had discredited the socialism of the Far Left. Fascist parties increased their strength in Europe, and the civilian militias grew in the United States and engaged in several armed clashes with the government, including Waco, Texas, and the bombing of the Federal Government office building in Oklahoma City. The racial tensions in Australia needed to be closely and officially monitored and the racism of the past and present resisted. The forces ranged against multiculturalism and immigration, however, had already affected Labour government policy, and the intakes of migrants planned for the rest of the century were in the 60–70,000-per-annum range, 50 percent less than in the late 1980s, as announced in May 1994 by the minister for immigration, Nick Bolkus. This reduction in migration numbers was confirmed by the Liberal minister for immigration, Philip Ruddock, when the new Coalition policy was announced in July 1996, with the intake of migrants down by 10,000 and a decrease in the emphasis on family reunion in favor of more business migrants.[17] Then, in 1997, under pressure from the anti-immigration policies of MP Pauline Hanson's One Nation Party and broader public sentiment, the Howard government again reduced the immigration quota, cutting it by 20 percent overall since assuming office in March 1996.[18]

The election in March, 1996, brought a Liberal–National Coalition government into office in a landslide victory. The campaign of 1996 exacerbated the fears of a racist revival in Australia on the issues of migration, reconciliation between Aborigines and whites, and the complex question of land rights and native title for Aboriginal people. Racist comments were made by National Party candidates in Queensland, by the Liberal candidate Pauline Hanson and a Labour Party maverick, Graeme Campbell, both of whom were disendorsed for this, and by independents.

Four candidates who received the most publicity and were elected with very large swings in their favor were Graeme Campbell in the Western Australian mining seat of Kalgoorlie, arguably the largest electorate in the world, Pauline Hanson in Oxley, centered on the regional town of Ipswich (both ran as independents after being disendorsed by the ALP and Liberals, respectively), and National Party candidates Bob Katter in Kennedy and Bob Burgess in Leichardt.[19] Katter and Burgess merely took their places in the governing parties' caucus rooms in Parliament and sniped at government policy from inside the regime. In 1997 they were joined by a Liberal senator from Western Australia, Ross Lightfoot, who had described the Aboriginal people as being the lowest form of human civilization and repeated this claim in the Senate until forced to apologize by the prime minister. Campbell became more serious and, building on the very heated pro- and antigun frenzy that emerged out of the April, 1996, massacre in Port Arthur, Tasmania, when 36 people were shot dead by a lone gunman, announced the formation of a progun, antimulticulturalist, anti-immigration, national party aligned with extreme-right-wing groups like the League of Rights and the Citizens Initiated Referenda (CIR) movement. This echoed American-style NRA, militia-movement, far-right politics.[20]

In the second half of 1996, Pauline Hanson, one of the independents elected in the former ALP-held safe seat of Oxley, near Brisbane, first created a national storm of debate with her White Australia, anti-immigration, anti-Asian, antimulticulturalist views. Even though her views had an immediate impact in a decrease in applications from Asian students for education in Australia and threatened to damage Australia's trade with Asia, the divisive debate continued strongly into 1997, and in April 1997 she formed a modestly neo-Fascist party called the One Nation Party. Views that she espoused on excessive social welfare payments to Aboriginals, Australia being swamped by Asians, and against multiculturalism were in fact widely shared by the Australian population, of whom up to 10 percent said they would vote for her.[21] These were concentrated among the Australian-born residents of Queensland and Western Australia and among older people.[22] These predictions were borne out by the huge electoral success of her party in the mid-1998 Queensland state elections, in which it won 24 percent of the popular vote and 11 seats in the Parliament of '89—a development that threatens to turn Australian politics in a sharp right trajectory on social issues and left on economic issues. Her curious blend of right-wing populism on race and immigration and left-wing populism against globalization is pushing the government Liberal–National Coalition conservatives to the right and pressuring the ALP from the left on the evils of economic rationalism. The upcoming federal election will reflect these pressures from the novice party on all the major parties in Australia. In the general social climate of the 1990s, racial issues in Australia and globally are clearly back on the political agenda.

THE MOTIVES OF MIGRANTS

The answer to the question presented at the outset—why people migrate—is, therefore, one that is immensely difficult and emotive for ethnographers. One can see, with the range of themes that emerged from modern Australian ethnic history, a framework in which one should pursue the broadest study of an ethnic community. Themes running through ethnic historiography are alienation from the country of origin, the prospects for work and opportunities for one's family in Australia, the challenge of language and hostility in a new culture, the persistence of enclavism as a reaction to adaptation and tensions in a multiethnic society, stress of second-generation Australians struggling with their hybrid identities ("hyphenated" migrants in American English), and the extraordinary diversity between, and within, migrant communities divided into religious, regional, racial, ideological, dialect, class, and gender subgroups. Given the complexity of the situation with all its ramifications, generalizations must only be made with great humility and caution. With American migrants, one has the additional methodological problems of a dispersed group without a community focus around a church, synagogue, or mosque.[23]

The postwar migrant experience is one that is incredibly rich in variety and texture. Displaced persons came from the European horrors of World War II; many in the Baltic communities—people from Estonia, Latvia, and Lithuania—had fled across Europe, in some cases first before the Germans and then before the Russians. Many Poles migrated through Africa; their experiences are recorded in the film *Silver City,* made by the Polish Australian Sophia Turkiewitz. Italians came mostly from small villages, many of them from Calabria, Macedonians from the mountains of south-eastern Europe, Jews escaping the Nazi imperium, British people fed up with the English weather and class structure, Vietnamese boat people, and Yanks from Chicago, refugees from the American urban crisis. All attempted to find a bit of territory in Australia where, with human dignity, they could find their place in the sun. The story of post–World War II American migration presented in the next chapter attempts to work within the most syncretistic theoretical framework that does not push or shove the data into any preconceived interpretive model. The experience of Americans in Australia must be presented in a manner that shows all the variegated patterns of both the individual migrants and the collective experience of the ethnic group, with all the cultural and historical baggage that they bring to Australian society.

NOTES

1. See William H. McNeill and Ruth S. Adams, *Human Migration: Patterns and Policies* (Bloomington, IN, 1978).

2. For a recent discussion, see Mary Kritz et al., eds., *International Migration Systems* (Oxford, 1992), pp. 15, 133–149.

3. Morawska, "Immigration," pp. 187, 193, 195, 203, 212–213.

4. Even groups that appear homogeneous, like the Greeks, are not easy to define because of their historical diversity: see C. A. Price, *Greeks in Australia* (Canberra, 1975), pp. 4–15. In Price's book on Jews he defines an ethnic group as "a collection of persons who, for physical, geographic, political, religious, linguistic, or other reasons, feel themselves, or are felt by others, to constitute a separate people." *Jewish Settlers in Australia* (Canberra, 1964), p. 1, fn.

5. Borrie, *Italians and Germans*, p. xix.

6. R. T. Appleyard, *British Emigration to Australia* (Canberra, 1964); W. D. Borrie, *Italians and Germans in Australia: A Study of Assimilation* (Melbourne, 1954); G. Bottomley, *After the Odyssey: A Study of Greek Australians* (St. Lucia, 1979); C. Cronin, *The Sting of Change: Sicilians in Sicily and America* (Chicago, 1970); R. Huber, *From Pasta to Pavlova* (Sydney, 1977); Arthur Huck, *The Chinese in Australia* (Melbourne, 1968); Christine Inglis, *Asians in Australia* (Singapore, 1992); Eva Isaacs, *Greek Children in Sydney* (Canberra, 1976); M. De Lepervanche, *Indians in a White Australia* (Sydney, 1984); J. Lyng, *Non-Britishers in Australia* (Melbourne, 1935); J. Lyng, *The Scandinavians in Australia, New Zealand and the Western Pacific* (Melbourne, 1939); Oliver MacDonagh, *The Sharing of the Green: A Modern Irish History for Australians* (Sydney, 1996); Ilma O'Brien, *Australia's Italians: 1788–1988* (Carlton, 1989); P. O'Farrell, *The Irish in Australia* (Sydney, 1986); M. P. Prentis, *The Scots in Australia: A Study of New South Wales, Victoria and Queensland, 1788–1900* (Sydney, 1984); C. A. Price, *The Ethnic Composition of the Australian People* (North Fitzroy, 1981); C. A. Price, *German Settlers in South Australia* (Melbourne, 1945); C. A. Price, *Greeks in Australia* (Canberra, 1975); C. A. Price, *Jewish Settlers in Australia* (Canberra, 1964); C. A. Price, *Southern Europeans in Australia* (Melbourne, 1963); Alan Richardson, *British Immigrants and Australia* (Canberra, 1974); H. L. Rubinstein, *The Jews in Australia* (Melbourne, 1991); Suzanne Rutland, *Edge of the Diaspora, Two Centuries of Jewish Settlement in Australia* (Sydney, 1988); S. L. Thompson, *Australia Through Italian Eyes: A Study of Settlers Returning from Australia to Italy* (Melbourne, 1980); M. Tsounis, "Greek Communities in Australia," unpublished Ph.D. dissertation (University of Adelaide, 1972); N. Viviani, *The Long Journey: Vietnamese Migration and Settlement in Australia* (Melbourne, 1984); Helen Ware, *A Profile of the Italian Community in Australia* (Canberra, 1981); Suzanne Wegmann, *The Swiss in Australia* (Grusch, Switzerland, 1989); A. T. Yarwood, *Asian Migration to Australia* (Melbourne, 1964); A. T. Yarwood and M. J.

Knowling, *Race Relations in Australia* (North Ryde, 1983); in addition, the Australian Ethnic Heritage Series, under the general editorship of Michael Cigler, has published a wide range of titles in the 1980s. See also Jim Bennett and Ian Fry, *Canadians in Australia* (Canberra, 1996).

7. Ray Aitchison, *The Americans in Australia* (Melbourne, 1986); Jan Deamicis, "It Just Happened: American Migration to Australia," Unpublished Ph.D. dissertation (University of Massachusetts, 1977); Dennis Cuddy, *The Yanks Are Coming: American Migration to Australia* (San Francisco, 1977); Bernard and Ada Finifter, "Party Identification and Political Adaptation of American Migrants in Australia," *Journal of Politics*, 51 (1989), pp. 599–629; J. and D. Bardo, "American Migrants in Australia: An Exploratory Study of Adjustment," *Sociological Focus*, 14 (1981), pp. 46–56; Arnold Dashefsky, *Americans Abroad: A Comparative Study of Emigrants from the United States* (New York, 1992). Further titles appear in the Bibliography.

8. Writing in the early 1980s on Italians, Helen Ware summarizes: "Assimilationist studies of immigrants in Australia are now being replaced by genuinely multicultural studies," in Helen Ware, *A Profile of the Italian Community in Australia* (Canberra, 1981), p. 20.

9. The neo-Fascists in Europe have counterparts in Britain and America, and U.S. groups, such as the Ku Klux Klan, have a great deal of financial backing and are increasingly active in forging ties across the Atlantic: *The Australian*, 17 January 1994, p. 6. These global ties with neo-Fascism have been well publicized in Australia with respect to the One Nation Party of MP for Oxley Pauline Hanson; *The Australian*, 19 June 1997, pp. 1, 4.

10. Michael Tsounis, "Greek Communities in Australia," Unpublished Ph.D. dissertation (University of Adelaide, 1972), p. 126; C. A. Price, *Southern Europeans in Australia* (Canberra, 1975), pp. 207, 209. A 1948 poll showed that 58 percent of Australians did not want Jewish DPs: quoted in Arthur Huck, *The Chinese in Australia* (Melbourne, 1968), p. 3.

11. As in Australia, the American conservatives have campaigned strongly against left-wing programs on multiculturalism and bilingualism, especially in the south-western states: *The Australian* 3 January 1994, p. 9 as discussed by Alan Wolfe, sociologist at Boston University. Nathan Glazer, one of the key figures in migration historiography, writing in *The New Republic*, warns that this may lead to closing the door on mass migration in America, as was done in the 1920s: *The Australian*, 11 January 1994, p. 9.

12. In 1981, 45 percent thought migration levels were "too high," and 48 percent thought that too many Asians were entering Australia; in 1982, 31 percent opted for "no immigration at all" as the best migration policy; quoted in Nancy Viviani, *The Long Journey: Vietnamese Migration and Settlement in Australia* (Melbourne, 1984), p. 270. For a general discussion, see James Jupp, *Immigration* (Sydney, 1991), pp. 108–121.

13. Stephen Castles, "Australian Multiculturalism: Social Policy and Identity in a Changing Society," in James Jupp and Gary P. Freeman, eds., *Nations of Immigrants* (Melbourne, 1992), pp. 184–201, and James Jupp and Gary P. Freeman, eds., *Mistaken Identity, Multiculturalism and the Demise of Nationalism in Australia* (Sydney, 1990); Andrew Jakubowitz, "Ethnicity, Multiculturalism and Neo-Conservatism," in Gill Bottomley and Marie de Lepervanche, eds., *Ethnicity, Class and Gender in Australia* (Sydney, 1984), pp. 28–48; Raymond Sestito, *The Politics of Multiculturalism*, C.I.S., 1982. One sees this trend in the strident 1994 "I Am an Australian" television campaign, in which mono-culturalism is presented as the "true Australian way" by the I am Australian Foundation, which is funded by conservative Australian corporations. The economist Helen Hughes has strongly attacked multiculturalism: see *The Australian*, 23 February 1995, p. 1, and 23 February 1995, p. 9, for her increasingly strident opposition to multiculturalist policies.

14. G. Blainey, *All For Australia* (Sydney, 1984).

15. Viviani, *Vietnamese*, p. 274.

16. Eva Isaacs, *Greek Children in Sydney* (Canberra, 1976), p. 108. Perhaps one should heed the warnings of the controversial film *Romper Stomper* (1994) about the potential for ethnic violence, especially when, in January 1994, one reads of nine youths facing charges in Melbourne over a gang battle between Greeks and Asians: *The Australian*, 3 January 1994, p. 3.

17. *The Australian*, 20 March 1994, p. 11; 26 March 1994, p. 24; 28 March 1994, p. 2; 11 April 1994, p. 2; *The Advertiser*, 28 March 1994, p. 1, 8 July 1995, p. 1; Australians still consider "Asians" the most threatening image: see Philip Bell, *Multicultural Australia in the Media* (Canberra, 1992), p. 62; *The Australian*, 6 May 1994, p. 1, 10 June 1994, p. 1. *The Australian*, 4 July 1996, also reveals an overall drop in population growth, partly due to falls in immigration.

18. *The Australian*, 22 May 1997, p. 1.

19. *The Australian*, 20 April 1996, p. 23.

20. *The Australian*, 3 June 1996, pp. 1, 4, 16 September 1996, p. 2, 8 October 1996, p. 12.

21. See contributions by Bob Catley and Murray Goot, "Is Hanson Right?" *Current Affairs Bulletin*, December 1996–January 1997.

22. Bob Catley, "The Hanson Phenomenon," *Current Affairs Bulletin* (June–July 1997), pp. 29–30.

23. This is even true for English-speaking migrants, as is discussed in Chapter 8; see also John O'Grady, *Aussie English* (Sydney, 1965). Many respondents in the 1993 study reported difficulty in communicating, something they had not anticipated in going from one English-speaking country to another.

5

American Migration to Australia: World War II to the 1990s

WHAT IS A "MIGRANT"?

Any study of migration must begin with a definition of the term "migrant," which, like "ethnic," is a term of some complexity and even ideological import. "Migrant" in our 1990s study of the attitudes of Americans in Australia simply means no more nor less than a permanent settler in Australia. No pejorative connotations are intended or implied. In some quarters, especially in popular culture, it has been construed as a term of opprobrium, and numerous respondents in the study claimed that they were not migrants, even with 20 years of residence, on the grounds that "migrant" implied a person of low socioeconomic status, someone who had arrived on assisted passage (low status again), and, as is particularly crucial for Americans—and a rejection of the Motherland and/or a kind of cultural treason to one's nationality.[1]

Migrant is also employed in the phrase "migrant community," embracing a much broader meaning than just a group of permanent settlers. Migrant organizations as well as some ethnographers and demographers include in the migrant community sojourners (temporary residents), children of migrants (even if born in Australia or raised here), and for social and cultural purposes everyone who perceives him/herself as belonging to the migrant community, ranging from second- and third-generation residents to miscellaneous temporary ones.[2] There is, however, no real objection to the use of the term "migrant community" in a broad sense and with the meaning it has in America, along with "immigrant community" and "ethnics," which are also broadly inclusive.[3]

THE 1993 SAMPLE

Most sociological work on American migration has divided the subject into numerous categories based upon the legal status of the various groups, some of them consisting of composite samples of migrants, sojourners, other types of temporary residents (transients), and various types of "status changers" (from temporary to permanent residence and/or from American citizenship to Australian citizenship). In some circumstances these taxonomic divisions are helpful, but we have found it less confusing in the 1990s attitudes study on which this book is based only to use the category "migrant" and to define a migrant as a permanent resident who intends to remain in Australia. Individuals on temporary fixed-term contracts and migrants who professed no intention to remain in Australia were not included in the study. This method has proven to be less confusing in the presentation of data, and although some taxonomies seem useful as an empirical device, we have found that treating migrants as one category revealed more about husbands, wives, and the progeny of migrants and about subtle patterns of attitudes based upon ideology, class, gender, and race.[4]

All samples, however, have their strengths and limitations, and the 1993 sample—based upon the results of 302 respondents to questionnaires—is no exception. These respondents represent a community sample with some longevity in Australia: 72 percent had lived there for more than 10 years, and 83 percent had more than 5 years of residence. Nearly 50 pervent had lived in Australia for more than 20 years and thus had experienced the massive social and economic changes that had affected the Australian community since the 1970s. The collective social experience and length of residence provided data from the respondents that were comprehensive empirically and contained a wealth of anecdotal data about all aspects of life in Australia.

The sample also, of course, had some inherent limitations. Americans lack community structures and organizations, and consequently the accumulation of respondents' names relied heavily on the opportunistic and "snowballing" techniques of collecting names from referrals by respondents of other potential respondents.[5] Some biases resulted from these techniques, especially in the occupational status of respondents. The 1993 sample contains 73 percent in the professional categories, whereas the known percentage for all American migrants in the professional categories is around 60 percent.[6] The proportion of academics is also considerably higher, at 42 percent, than among the American migrant community as a whole, where the figure is 3–4 percent.[7] Academics are represented in considerably larger numbers because they were easily identifiable from university calendars, they were more likely to respond to a questionnaire as fellow academics, and they were more likely to be interested in cooperating with research efforts that, in many cases were akin to their own work as scholars. Even though academics are statistically overrepresented, they were, as articulate and highly trained observers, extremely prolific sources of anecdotal data.

These major caveats aside, the 1993 attitudes study represents a microcosm of the American community as a whole. Geographically, the 1993 sample is spread throughout Australia, in roughly the same proportions in all the six states and the two territories as the community of resident Americans overall. The gender distribution, educational profile, years of residence, place or region of origin, rates of citizenship, and most attitudinal characteristics correspond very closely to known data from other research and census data from 1981, 1986, and 1991. It is to a detailed analysis of this data that one must now turn with these qualifications and apologies in mind.

THE SIZE OF THE AMERICAN MIGRANT COMMUNITY

As has already been discussed, the American presence in Australia dates from the very beginnings of colonial Australian society, when, in November 1792, the merchant vessel, the *Philadelphia,* sailed into Sydney Harbor. Throughout the nineteenth century and until the 1960s—as, indeed, is evident from Table 5.1— the population of American-born migrants was relatively small; in the twentieth century, it did not match that of the hundreds of thousands of Germans, Greeks, Italians, and other Europeans who entered Australia in the post–World War II wave of mass migration. The American economy in the period between 1945 and the early 1960s was expanding rapidly, and levels of emigration from the

TABLE 5.1:   American-Born in Australia, 1891–1991

Census Year	Number
1891	7,472
1901	7,448
1911	6,642
1921	6,604
1933	6,066
1947	6,232
1954	8,289
1961	10,810
1966	17,412
1971	30,035
1976	30,514
1981	32,620
1986	42,382
1991	50,561

Based on Baum, *Exchange of Migrants*, Table 1, and ABS, 1994; in John Goldlust et al., BIMPR. *Community Profiles. 1991 Census. United States of America Born* (Canberra, 1995), p. 7. The 1991 census figure of American-born of 43,783 excludes overseas visitors.

United States were correspondingly low. In this period of immense American influence on Australian economic life, culture, and society, the direct impact of the American migrant community was negligible; however, before examining the nature of this community and the causes for its expansion after the mid-1960s, one must first have an overview of postwar emigration from America in general, and that to Australia in particular.

U.S. EMIGRATION: GENERAL PATTERNS

As shown in Table 5.2, there was a rise in emigration from the United States in the late 1960s and early 1970s. This small-scale exodus was coterminous with the heightening of social tensions in America. The nation experienced, in less than a decade, the shocks of multiple political assassinations, urban riots, stagflation, and a growing sense that the United States, bogged down in and losing the war in Vietnam, had lost its way. This process of political and psychological disorientation culminated in the Watergate crisis in 1972–74, and Americans, left-wing, right-wing, and apolitical, viewed with apprehension and despair this reduction in the status of and trust in the office of the presidency. Americans, always reluctant to emigrate from a nation historically exuberant in its chauvinism, had, however, an established pattern of movement across the continent and interstate in a search of a better life. Australia, often perceived—incorrectly, as is discussed below—as being like another U.S. state, was therefore an obvious destination, though possibly not permanently, for many Americans, as a nation in which a new life could be created. Indeed, Australia started to emerge as a migration destination for Americans in the popular culture of the period, including such movies as *Butch Cassidy and the Sundance Kid* and *Support Your Local Sheriff*. The increase in emigration to Australia was, therefore, part of a larger process of physical mobility, disillusionment within the United States, and

TABLE 5.2: Emigration from the United States, 1940s–1970s

Decade	Total	Average Annual Emigration to Selected Recipient Nations, 1960–1976	
1940s	281,000	Mexico	64,600
1950s	425,000	Germany	24,800
1960s	900,000	Canada	21,900
1970s	1,176,000	United Kingdom	20,900
		Australia	8,500
		Israel	3,898
Total	2,782,000		

Based on Dashefsky, *Americans Abroad*, pp. 17, 18.

emigration to many countries, including Canada, Israel, and the United Kingdom.

However, one must not overstate this increase in emigration, nor necessarily conclude that it had an ideological cause. Americans remained reluctant, relative to comparable Western nations, to emigrate, and those who did were more often pursuing more mundane objectives—employment being the most significant— than many sociologists and demographers originally postulated. After all, in the early 1970s, following the abandoning of the fixed exchange rates regime of the Bretton Woods financial system and the energy price boom that followed shortly thereafter, the energy-flushed Australian dollar rose against the deficit-wracked U.S. dollar until by 1975 it was worth U.S. $1.53. It is more accurate to place this bulge in emigration within the context of a long-term post–World War II trend toward interstate movement associated with rapid suburbanization. Between 1970 and 1974, 72,500,000 Americans changed their place of residence within the United States—truly an astonishing pattern of physical mobility.[8] Americans—as noted by nineteenth-century observers like De Tocqueville— were permanently restless and always on the search for increased life opportunities.

American emigration in the second half of the twentieth century has been modest by global standards. The studies over the last two decades show that the levels of emigration have never reached the proportions of a mass migration, and the motivational parameters have been very specific: employment opportunities to countries with higher pay rates, which, for academics, included Australia, especially in the 1970s, ideological factors in movements to particular countries like Israel for Jewish Americans, draft resisters going to Canada and Sweden, and a search for adventure by a generation raised in an age of affluence and increasingly globalized transport systems. American emigrants, therefore, in the post–World War II decades do not just represent a tidal wave of dissatisfaction but are a relatively small percentage of the population seeking, mostly on a temporary basis, a change in environment and employment. The major exceptions to this generalization were those evading the draft laws or settling in nations with a specific ideological/religious profile—Jews going to Israel, Muslims to Iran, Buddhists to Japan, Hindus to India.[9] Very few Americans came to Australia for such reasons.

U.S. EMIGRATION TO AUSTRALIA

The growth in emigration from America in the early 1970s is replicated in the migration figures for Australia, as shown in Table 5.3. In the late 1960s and early 1970s the volume of migration increased significantly, and, as shown in Table 5.1, this would result in an increase in U.S.-born residents in Australia from the 17,412 in the 1966 census to 30,514 in the 1976 census, after which the level of American migration remained relatively steady throughout the 1970s and early 1980s. The details of decadal variations and causes for the changing

TABLE 5.3:   U.S.-Born Migrant Arrivals and Departures in Australia, 1960–92

Decade	Arrivals	Departures
1960s	45,783	20,262
1970s*	75,731	51,072
1980s	59,167	34,249
1990s (to 1992)	1,687	669
Totals	182,368	106,252

* Peak years: 1971 = 12,068, 1972 = 10,035 (29 percent of the 1970s).
Based on Baum, *Exchange of Migrants*, Table 2, and BIR, *Emigration, 1991–1992*, Table 8.

levels of migration are discussed below, but first one must elucidate the characteristics of American migration to Australia in general, and their influences on the 1993 sample in particular. American migrants, as shown in the departure figures in Table 5.3, present a variety of curious patterns. This is especially the case with the particularly high rate of return, and this phenomenon is also addressed in detail below.

U.S. EMIGRATION TO AUSTRALIA: THE 1993 SAMPLE

Almost one-half of the 1993 sample arrived in Australia in their mid-20s in the peak decade of post–World War II American migration in the 1970s (see also Table 5.9), and consequently the average age of respondents (46) is in the mid-40s. They are people, therefore, in the early stages of middle age, with a good deal of experience with living in Australia. The distribution by sex in the sample is very close to the known data for Americans as a whole, since the 1991 census shows males at 52 percent and females at 48 percent.[10] As with many migrant groups in Australia—especially southern Europeans—there are more males than females, reflecting the greater propensity of physically mobile males to seek work in international labor markets.[11] (See Table 5.4.)

TABLE 5.4:   Age and Sex of 1993 Sample

Age	%	Sex	%
20–40	21	Male	55
41–60	70	Female	45
60+	9		

N = 302 throughout.
Note: Figures have been rounded up or down, and totals may therefore be slightly above or below 100 throughout.

TABLE 5.5:   **Marital Status and Place of Birth of Progeny**

Married	%	Progeny	%
Yes	77	Born in Australia	34
No	23	Born elsewhere	37
		No progeny	29

Most American migrants are in conventional family units, with a major motivational cause for migration being to establish stability and prosperity for the future of their families. As is discussed in greater detail in Chapter 6, one of the most persistent causes for settling and remaining in Australia is to enable their children to be raised, educated, and employed in the Australian environment, which is perceived as safer, cleaner, less drug-ridden, and offering greater employment security through the welfare state than the equivalent U.S. structures. (See Table 5.5.) Of course, there is some irony here in that the U.S. unemployment rate of the mid-1990s was actually lower than that in Australia—in 1997, it was under 5 percent, as against 8.5 percent. All of the consequent problems of assimilation and alienation are examined in later chapters.

Historically, since the gold rushes in California and Australia in the 1850s, it was assumed that Americans came to Australia primarily from the West Coast in general, and from California in particular. This was based upon geographic propinquity and common cultural patterns, especially between Southern California and New South Wales. The term "Californian" was often used interchangeably for "American" in the gold rush period. While the ties between New South Wales and California are indeed strong, the 1993 sample shows a much greater geographic spread of migrants, reflecting the strong American urban base (76 percent) from which American migrants came and in which most of them now live (see Table 5.6). The majority come from the urban concentrations of both the East and West Coasts, as well as from the large industrial cities of the Midwest, such as Chicago, Detroit, and Minneapolis. As shown in previous studies, therefore, the prototypical American migrant comes from an urban area, mainly the big metropolitan centers; relatively few come from rural areas, especially from the least populous areas of America, such as the Southern and Rocky Mountain regions.[12]

The educational level of American migrants in general, as shown in Table 5.7, and of the 1993 sample, is considerably higher than that of either the American or the Australian populations considered as a whole. In the United States in the 1970s and 1980s, approximately 20–25 percent of males and 12–15 percent of females achieved a tertiary degree or higher, compared to 94 percent and 85 percent, respectively, for the 1993 sample (Table 5.7).[13] The contrast between American migrants and indigenous Australians is similar: in the 1991 census

TABLE 5.6: Place and Region of Birth

Place of Birth	%		Region	%
Metropolitan area[a]	51 ⎫		West Coast[d]	20
City[b]	25 ⎬ 76 urban		Rocky Mountains[e]	10
Rural[c]	22		Midwest[f]	32
			South[g]	10
			East Coast[h]	30

[a] *Metropolitan area*: over 100,000.

[b] *City*: 10,000–100,000.

[c] *Rural*: under 10,000.

[d] *West Coast* (5 states): Alaska, California, Hawaii, Oregon, Washington.

[e] *Rocky Mountains* (8 states): Arizona, Colorado, Idaho, Montana, Nevada, New Mexico, Wyoming, Utah.

[f] *Midwest* (12 states): Illinois, Indiana, Iowa, Kansas, Michigan, Minnesota, Nebraska, North Dakota, Ohio, Oklahoma, South Dakota, Wisconsin.

[g] *South* (15 states): Alabama, Arkansas, Florida, Georgia, Kentucky, Louisiana, Maryland, Mississippi, Missouri, North Carolina, South Carolina, Tennessee, Texas, Virginia, West Virginia.

[h] *East Coast* (10 states): Connecticut, Delaware, Maine, Massachusetts, New Hampshire, New Jersey, New York, Pennsylvania, Rhode Island, Vermont.

approximately 39 percent of Americans had attained postsecondary qualifications, whereas the comparable figure for Australians is 13 percent.[14] The 1993 sample, as discussed above, has a very large component of academics and other professionals, thereby raising the quantum of tertiary-educated to 90 percent, contrasted with 35 percent of the U.S.-born as a whole. Most Americans have attended public (government-funded) secondary schools and received public postgraduate training, and this is reflected in Table 5.7 with the figures 80 percent and 62 percent, respectively; at the undergraduate level, however, the large private sector is represented by a 54 percent public to 46 percent private

TABLE 5.7: Education

Highest Level Attained	%	BA or Higher	%
BA	37	Men	94
MA	19	Women	85
Ph.D	34		

Level of Education	Public (%)	Private (%)
High school	80	21
University	54	46
Postgraduate	62	39

TABLE 5.8:   Employment: Respondents and Spouses

Respondent	Occupational Category	%	
1	Executive	10	⎫
2	Professional	21	⎬ 73 percent professional
3	Academic	42	⎭
4	Technical	0.3	
5	Sales	2	
6	Clerical	8	
7	Service	6	
8	Farming	1	
9	Crafts	0.3	
10	Operators	0.3	
11	Home Duties	2	
12	Student	0.7	
	Other	6	
Spouse			
1–3		49	
4–12		51	

split—that is, almost one-half attending private universities. As is examined in greater detail later when looking at academics separately as a group, American migrants have a high level of elite—often private—educational participation and preference.

As shown in Table 5.8, American migrants are largely professional people and are married to professional people or individuals from the upper levels of semiprofessional occupations. Again, the proportion of professionals in the 1993 sample is somewhat higher than that in the American-born population as a whole, due to sampling techniques. But studies in the 1970s by D. Cuddy and J. Deamicis, and census data in the 1980s analyzed by S. Baum, also all show American migrants to be mainly professional people, in proportions ranging from 55 to 70 percent, depending on the method of occupational classification, with income levels considerably higher than the Australian average.[15] Contrasted sharply with most migrant groups, Americans are professional people who had not emigrated because of poverty or persecution but are voluntary migrants, with considerably higher levels of education, skills, and organizational abilities than either the population of the country of origin or the country of destination.

As shown in Tables 5.1 and 5.3, the bulge in migration of Americans to Australia came in the late 1960s and early 1970s. The 1991 census revealed roughly 50 percent of Americans having arrived shortly before and after 1980.

This pattern is clearly shown in the 1993 sample, with nearly one-half of the respondents having entered Australia in the 1970s, the period of greatest political and social upheaval in the United States and of the highest exchange rate of the Australian dollar (see Table 5.9). The majority of these came without assistance—that is, either Commonwealth government–assisted passage or some other form of assistance—something that politically conservative respondents often commented upon with great pride and even bravado. This "antisocialist" or "rugged individualist" theme is taken up in a later chapter.[16]

Decadal variations in the levels of American migration reveal a fascinating blend of historical, social, and demographic changes, both in America and in Australia: a microcosm of the changing relationship between the two nations and internal changes to both societies. In the immediate aftermath of World War II Americans had, of course, increased their ties and experience in the South Pacific region. Almost one million Americans had served in Australia, and several thousand remained after World War II to settle permanently with Australian spouses. The minister for immigration, Arthur Calwell—who also had sentimental ties, his grandfather having been American—was enthusiastic about Americans (white!) settling in Australia, and in 1947 the first group of Americans sailed to Australia on the *Marine Phoenix* under Commonwealth government assistance. Through the 1950s, the small community of American-born began to grow—8,289 in 1954, 10,810 in 1961—with the greatest concentrations in major eastern state cities such as Sydney, Melbourne, and Brisbane, but with smaller communities also to be found in the Victorian country towns of Ballarat and Bendigo. Though the cultural impact of American society and technology was immense at the start of the globalization process in the 1950s, this did not result in any large-scale migration of Americans to Australia.[17]

In the 1960s, however, as social tensions increased in American society, there was a commensurate rise in the American interest in migrating to Australia. The crucial watershed year was 1968, with the worldwide student upheavals led by movements in Europe and North America. In the United States, the assassinations of Martin Luther King and Robert Kennedy shocked the nation, especially when coupled with large-scale urban riots, the impact of rising political and

TABLE 5.9: Decade of Arrival and Assistance

Decade	%	Assistance	%
1950s	2	Yes	35
1960s	13	No	59
1970s	45	Other	6
1980s	30		
1990s	11		

social demands among African Americans, the dramatic and violent police action at the Democratic National Convention in Chicago, and national anti–Vietnam War protests. The phone lines to Australian consulates in America began to run hot, and interest in Australia would remain high for several years. In 1967–68 there were 66,261 inquiries about migration to Australian consulates in America; in 1969–70 there were 100,961, and they peaked at 126,468 in 1970–71. It was not until the mid-1970s, after the Watergate crisis, that the number dropped again, to 60,705 in 1975.

Thousands of Yanks would travel across the Pacific and increase the American-born numbers to 30,514 by 1976.[18] As is discussed in greater detail in later chapters, this included a wide spectrum of migrants crossing class and ideological lines; there were left-wing migrants disillusioned about Vietnam War, as well conservatives disenchanted by the Nixon years. One migrant was Angela Buchanan, the sister of Pat Buchanan, then speech-writer for President Nixon, the Republican opponent of President George Bush in the 1992 primaries, and later candidate for president in 1996. One migrant eloquently summarizes the feelings of those years: "To a war, assassination and injustice-weary Yank, Australia seemed like the most advanced society on earth: a sort of Garden of Eden, with plenty for all, gentle climate, a gentle society."[19] This may have not been far from the truth, as Australia enjoyed the final days of its social democratic and egalitarian rapture before the onset of globalization and market-driven efficiencies.

The Vietnam War, like World War II, saw thousands of American service personnel pass through and spend rest and recreation leave in Australia: close to 300,000 came to Australia as part of their Asian war service, and approximately 1,000 married Australian nationals. As with World War II marriages, most of these couples returned to America, but many stayed on as migrant settlers. Encouraged by the stridently pro-American policies of the then Liberal government, most clearly exemplified by Johnson's triumphant visit at the behest of Harold Holt in 1966, and in spite of antiwar activity in Australia, American service personnel could feel that Australia was more hospitable than America itself in the late 1960s and early 1970s. In the 1970s, of course, Australia did not wish to accept just any type of American migrant: blacks, hippies, or extremists such as members of the Ku Klux Klan were not welcome, but good solid American veterans were certainly acceptable.[20]

In the 1980s and 1990s, migration from America dropped by about 25 percent, compared to the peak period between 1968 and 1975—a rate a little slower than the fall in the value of the Australian dollar. As is discussed in detail in later chapters, the transcendent motivations, even through the tumultuous 1970s, for migration from America were the search for employment and perhaps adventure, and in the final decades of the twentieth century this would continue. But as in the 1970s with general social alienation, the late 1980s and early 1990s saw an increase in migrants departing to escape crime, alienation, and the urban

TABLE 5.10: Place of Australian Residence

State/Territory	%	
New South Wales	29 ⎫	
Victoria	16 ⎬ 45	
South Australia	29	
Queensland	5	
Tasmania	5	
Western Australia	3	
Northern Territory	1	
Australian Capital Territory	12	

crisis. The empirical data supporting this hypothesis and the anecdotal data illustrating these changes are taken up in subsequent discussion.

The 1993 American migrants, like most Australians, lived in urban areas, with a near-majority in Victoria and New South Wales (see Table 5.10). The actual proportion in the two largest states (55 percent in 1991) was 5–10 percent higher than the 1993 sample, because the sampling techniques produced a bias toward South Australia (the authors' resident state) and the ACT (with a large number of academic respondents from the Australian National University). Americans in the 1993 sample had emigrated mainly from urban areas in the United States, and the lifestyle and employment opportunities would naturally direct them toward the major metropolitan centers of Sydney, Melbourne, Newcastle, and Brisbane. In contradistinction to many migrant groups who took up employment in agricultural occupations or large-scale manufacturing and development industries in rural and regional areas, Americans are urban, professional, middle-class new settlers, with two-thirds of the total community living in the eight capital cities, including 25 percent in Sydney and 17 percent in Melbourne. Sydney also has 78 percent of the American-born in New South Wales, and Melbourne has 81 percent of those in Victoria. Americans are concentrated in the medium- to high-status suburbs in the harborside and coastal suburbs of Sydney, the eastern suburbs of Melbourne, the western and northern suburbs near the city center of Brisbane, the inner suburbs of Perth, the eastern suburbs and beach suburbs of Adelaide, and the high-status suburbs east and south of the city center along the Derwent River in Hobart. They also reside in the new housing areas of all capital cities, which reflects their relatively recent arrival in Australia compared with other migrant groups.[21]

The prototypical American migrant in the 1993 sample corresponds very closely to known data from previous studies and census data: white, married, well-educated, concentrated in the professional occupations, and born in, and now resident in, urban areas (see Table 5.11). Why do they come to Australia, and how do they adapt to the new culture?

TABLE 5.11: Summary of Key Characteristics of the 1993 Sample of American Migrants

	Characteristic	Table	Description
1	Age	5.4	Average age in the mid-40s (46)
2	Sex	5.4	Males 55%, females 45%
3	Marital status	5.5	77% married
4	Progeny	5.5	71% have children
5	Place of birth	5.6	76% born in urban areas
6	Region of birth	5.6	The majority born in large coastal cities and manufacturing centers of the Midwest
7	Education	5.7	Highly educated by both American and Australian standards
8	Employment	5.8	Reflecting educational levels, the majority are in the professional classes
9	Decadal pattern (1940s–90s)	5.9	Steady migration seeking employment but social factors in late 1960s and mid-1980s prominent
10	Place of residence	5.10	As with Australians in general, they are concentrated in the cities of the eastern states

NOTES

The comments of the 1993 respondents and those of migrants cited from other sources are referenced as follows:

Q: 1–319 (302 were used for data analysis) = 1993 sample
R: 1–22 = 1993-sample returnees
A: (page number) = Aitchison, *Americans*
C: (page number) = Cuddy, *Yanks*
Da: (page number) = Dashefsky, *Americans Abroad*
De: (page number) = Deamicis, "It Just Happens"
The original spelling has been retained in respondents' comments.

1. Eva Isaacs makes the same point, *Greek,* p. ix.
2. See Tsounis, "Greeks," pp. 10–11.
3. Not all terms are easily transferred across Anglo-Saxon cultures; for example, "Anglo–Celtic" would not, for obvious historical reasons, be used in an American or English context.
4. See Cuddy, *Yanks*; Deamicis, "It Just Happens"; B. and A. Finifter, "Report to Respondents: Survey of Americans in Australia" (private publication prepared at Michigan State University, East Lansing, 1980), pp. 1–12. Deamicis also found respondents with migrant visas (five years) to be, in many cases, only planning a short-term residence in Australia because it was more convenient to obtain a migrant visa than a temporary one that had to be renewed, thus reinforcing the need to include intentionality in the 1993 criteria for selection: "It Just Happens," pp. 37–38.

5. For discussion of the snowballing technique, see Dashefsky, *Americans Abroad*, p. 22, fn.; Deamicis, "It Just Happens," p. 29; P. Biernacki and D. Waldorf, "Snowball Sampling," *Sociological Methods and Research,* 10 (1981), pp. 141–163. All previous researchers in this area have experienced the same problems: Deamicis, "It Just Happens," p. 8.

6. Various research studies and the Census employ different categories for professional occupations, and this estimate is based upon occupational and educational qualifications: Department of Immigration and Ethnic Affairs, *Profile '81, 1981 Census on Persons Born in USA,* pp. 17, 19; Sam Baum and Christabel Young, *Exchange of Migrants,* Table 19; Deamicis, "It Just Happens," p. 223; B. and A. Finifter, "Americans," p. 7; Australian Bureau of Statistics, *1991 Census of Population and Housing, Ethnic Communities Package–Product 2, Birthplace Profile* (Adelaide, 1994).

7. In the 1986 Census there were 42,382 persons who were U.S.-born. Those between the ages of 20 and 65 were approximately 87 percent of the total, or 36,872; it is known that there were 1,104 academics from North America in 1991, and thus 3–4 percent of total possible adults would be academics. These estimates are based on Baum, *Exchange of Migrants,* p. 15 and Table 1; data on academics from Judith Sloan et al., *The Role of Immigration in the Australian Higher Education Labour Market* (Canberra, 1993), pp. 7, 14, Table 2.4.

8. Cuddy, *Yanks,* p. 32.

9. Dashefsky, *Americans Abroad, passim.*

10. *ABS,* 1994.

11. C. A. Price, *Southern Europeans in Australia* (Melbourne, 1963), pp. 93, 145, 170–171.

12. Potts and Potts, *Gold,* p. 189; B. and A. Finifter, "Americans," pp. 3–4; Cuddy, *Yanks,* p. xvii. Observers have often noted the striking cultural and physical similarities between Sydney, San Francisco, and Los Angeles, with lifestyles revolving around wine production, water sports, sun, and surf. Especially in the post–World War II period, the exchange of ideas and people between California and New South Wales has been strong in education, technology, entertainment, and consumption styles, and one now even speaks of a "Pacific Rim" cuisine common to California and south-east Australia.

13. B. and A. Finifter, "Americans," p. 4.

14. Goldlust, *U.S.-Born, 1991,* p. 22.

15. Cuddy, *Yanks,* p. xviii; Deamicis, "It Just Happens," p. 223; Baum, *Exchange of Migrants,* Table 19. *ABS,* 1994, shows professionals to be 50–60 percent of Americans as a group. Goldlust, *U.S.-Born, 1991,* p. 32

16. Goldlust, *U.S.-Born, 1991,* p. 16.

17. Baum, *Exchange of Migrants,* pp. 8–9; Cuddy, *Yanks,* pp. 17–19; *ADB,* p. 341.

18. Cuddy, *Yanks,* pp. 19–24; Deamicis, "It Just Happens," p. 6.

19. C: 84.

20. Baum, *Exchange of Migrants,* p. 9; Cuddy, *Yanks,* pp. 10, 52.

21. Baum, *Exchange of Migrants,* p. 14; Graeme Hugo, *Atlas of the Australian People* (Canberra, 1992): "NSW," p. 128, 130; "Victoria," pp. 121, 122; "Queensland," p. 107; "Western Australia," p. 112; "South Australia," p. 90; "Tasmania," p. 95.

6

Why Do the Americans Come to Australia?

The friendship between our two countries rests, I believe, upon the many things we have in common. Our countries are both young and richly endowed with natural resources. Our political systems are both free and democratic. We are both melting pots, with peoples drawn from many lands. We have both attained a standard of living undreamed of when our nations were founded. We share a distinctive historical background: the pioneering of vast open spaces and the hard task of hammering out a federal union.

As a result of these similarities in national experience, we are today the same kind of people—self-reliant but neighborly, idealistic but pragmatic, peaceful but always ready to stand up for what is right. Most of all, our peoples share the conviction that the future will be better than the present, and that we have an obligation to make it so.

It is because we have so much in common that we are close partners in world affairs. We have often been comrades-in-arms but we also work closely together in peace. There is a flourishing trade between us. We co-operate in scientific research and in economic aid to the developing nations of Asia. As pioneer nations, we are today co-operating especially closely on mankind's newest frontier—the exploration of outer space.

Since the Battle of the Coral Sea, our partnership has grown into a vital force for peace, progress and freedom in the Pacific. One of the major aims of my administration has been to strengthen it still further.[1]

Lyndon B. Johnson, President

Thus spoke the big man from Texas at the peak of his power and about to be defrocked, in a preface to *Pacific Orbit* (1968), a collection of pieces about

American–Australian relations, edited by Norman Harper and published by the Australian–American Association. Lyndon B. Johnson (or, more accurately, his speech-writer) reflected the Americans' general view of Australia in the 1960s: as free, democratic, affluent society sharing a common optimism about the future. Their combined efforts had not yet lost them the Vietnam War. In general, Americans who migrated had these images of Australia in mind as they organized their legal documents, packed their bags, and sailed—or, increasingly, flew—to the Southern Hemisphere. This chapter considers the theoretical, practical, and motivational aspects of this decision-making process and the multiplicity of sources and images upon which it was based.

WHAT DO THE ACADEMICS SAY?

The literature on American migration to Australia contains a robust level of debate on the theoretical question of why people emigrate in general and to Australia in particular. Beginning in the mid-1970s with B. and A. Finifter, the hypotheses have reflected the complexity of the subject, the ideological propensities of the researchers/observers, and the dominant cultural mood of the times. The Finifters, for example, observing the increase in emigration in the turbulent late 1960s and early 1970s, believed that Americans were emigrating because of political and social alienation, and they particularly structured their research to test that hypothesis. They found employment, ultimately, to be most significant motivation at a time when the U.S. economy was ending its post-1945 full-employment boom and the dollar was under continuing pressure.[2] Jan Deamicis, researching a University of Massachusetts Ph.D. in the late 1970s, found— probably to his disappointment, since he appeared to be hoping for something more exotic—that "mundane" causes such as employment and adventure were paramount in the minds of American migrants.[3] Dennis Cuddy, also working in the late 1970s, produced data that supported Deamicis' findings, and Arnold Dashefsky, a University of Connecticut sociologist who took an overview of American emigration in 1992, concurs that Americans migrating to Australia are still motivated by a search for employment and adventure. Dashefsky rejects theories of alienation and concludes that this trans-Pacific migration pattern does not indicate Americans to be in a state of Durkheimian anomie.[4]

In formulating a methodological framework for pursuing this issue, it is often tempting to postulate a causal model that is interesting, fashionable, and consonant with prevailing intellectual modes of thought and practice. No researcher, as Jan Deamicis points out, wishes to produce results that are "mundane," but one must let the results speak for themselves. The conclusions must emerge from the empirical data rather than be coaxed along by attractive but ideologically biased models of explanation.[5]

Graeme Hugo, in his recent survey of emigration from Australia, cautions against many traditional models of migration on the grounds that they tend to oversimplify a complex multivariate phenomenon. Problems in evaluating the data, the varying motivations of migrants, and a number of statistical differences in data collection between nations all contribute to the difficulties of elaborating an inclusive model for migration. In the 1993 sample of Americans, therefore, it is best to go directly to what the evidence, both empirical and anecdotal, seems to reveal, and from this data base one may then try to draw conclusions.[6]

WHAT DO AMERICAN MIGRANTS SAY?

The respondents in the 1993 sample indicated their reasons for emigrating from America and for deciding on Australia, on a four-point scale, and Tables 6.1 and 6.2 show the percentage ranking each reason in the highest two categories. The text of the questionnaire has been included as an Appendix. The results are quite clear: the majority of American migrants throughout the period between the 1950s and the 1990s emigrated to Australia in search of employment opportunities and adventure.

The respondents were not overtly hostile to the United States (17 percent), and this is reflected in the high rate of return to America, as shown in Table 5.3 (and examined further in a later chapter), and, as is discussed in Chapter 7, the relatively low rate of taking up Australian citizenship. American migrants, therefore, are neither rejecting their own nation nor joyfully embracing another; primarily, they are seeking enhanced life opportunities for themselves and their families—not an exotic motivational framework, but one that is consistent with previous studies of American emigration and with the ethnographic studies of migration to Australia in general on the part of British, Italian, Greek, and other migrant groups from around the globe.[7] Only a small proportion of about one in six, in fact, said that hostility to the United States had motivated their departure.

TABLE 6.1:   Reasons for Emigrating from America

Reason	*Medium to High Importance*	*%*
1	Employment	61
2	Adventure	60
3	Environment	38
4	Following spouse/partner	32
5	Materialism	19
6	Other	18
7	Hostility to U.S.	17
8	Crime	17
9	General economy	16
10	Racial conflict	11
11	Family reunion	7
12	Family conflict	6

TABLE 6.2: Reasons for Choosing Australia

	Reason	*Medium to High Importance (%)*
1	employment	58
2	adventure	51
3	environment	44
4	general lifestyle	42
5	climate	39
6	other	29
7	social harmony	23
8	general economy	21
9	low crime	20
10	family reunion	10

There are, however, more subtle variations in the decadal ups and downs in migration numbers and motivations of migrants over time. This requires a more complex analysis of the social and political attitudes of Americans and Australians about the attributes of each nation and the (alleged) representative national characteristics and stereotypes of each culture. In pursuing this subject, considerable terminological confusion can result in any comparative sociopolitical study of America and Australia. In America, "liberal" means left-of-center, and it is a pejorative term when used by conservatives in adversarial political debate. In Australia, of course, the conservatives are in the Liberal Party, whereas in the United States they are generally to be found in the Republican Party. The Democratic Party in America is center/left, whereas the Democrat Party of Australia started off in 1976 as center/right, although this varied by the issue, and they finished their first two decades as a center/left party. They tend to be antiunion but are on the left on social and fiscal issues and on the environment. U.S. Republicans are conservatives but still republicans in constitutional terms; conservatives in Australia are often monarchists and distrust American republicanism; and in the 1990s the Democrats in Australia are often open republicans. The U.S. political spectrum has historically been to the right of Australia, but this conservative gap has decreased with the rightist economic rationalism of the Hawke–Keating ALP and Hewson–Downer–Howard-led Liberal Party (Downer after May, 1994; Howard after January, 1995).

To avoid confusion, we propose to cut this terminological Gordian knot by using the following classification scheme for political ideology:

- *Social Democrat*: the center/left of the political spectrum of both nations, including the Australian Labour Party and the Democratic Party of America.
- *Conservative*: the center/right, including Republicans and the Liberal Party.

- *Hyperconservatives*:   the right wing of the Republican and Liberal parties and most of the National Party, including both extreme economic rationalists and "moral majority"/Festival of Light/One Nation interventionist conservatives.

This classification system will help to identify cultural and political values in a cross-cultural discussion of attitudes of Americans to Australia, and of Australians to America and to American migrants living in Australia.

Table 6.3 is based upon anecdotal data from the 1993 sample and provides a framework for the remainder of the study in order to give the subsequent analysis some theoretical and social context. The American migrant is depicted at four points: when deciding to leave America, when deciding to come to Australia, while reacting to living in Australia, and ultimately when considering whether to stay or to return to America, within a specific cultural and political universe. The values of American culture, a product of a finite and concrete historical experience, are carried with the person and used to interpret the experience of being a migrant in Australia. Table 6.3 is intended to itemize this American consciousness, at least in an abbreviated form, in order to provide some structure of the American world view. Only by comprehending the nature of this world view can one fully understand how, over time, Americans have emigrated from the United States, made their judgments about Australian life, and, as the majority tend to do, returned to North America.

The data in Table 6.4 show the consistency of employment and adventure as the primary reasons for emigration but also illustrate decadal variations corresponding to changing politico–social environments in both nations. Even in the 1970s, when political turmoil was high in America, employment was the main reason for emigrating; indeed, the 1993 sample, with a high proportion of academics, reflects the pressures of the post–Vietnam War recession and the severe contraction of the academic job market. But social alienation in the 1960s/70s is reflected in the rise in the percentage hostile to the United States, a jump from 6 percent in the 1960s to 21 percent in the 1970s. Likewise, the 1980s figures show a marked rise on the question of the environment, with 50 percent ranking it among the top two reasons, compared to 38 percent for the total sample. This is even more pronounced in the 1985–89 figures, where the environment is among the top two reasons at 62 percent. These late-1980s "eco-migrants" also expressed greater concern over crime (25 percent, compared to 20 percent overall) and were much stronger in their reasons for selecting Australia by registering 30 percent on social harmony (compared to 23 percent overall) and 60 percent for general lifestyle (compared to 42 percent overall). In a "Fourth of July Special" in *The Australian* in 1994, many American migrants interviewed echoed these 1990s concerns about crime and environmental decay.[8] American migration since World War II, therefore, shows a transcendent pattern of motivation centered around employment and adventure, but decadal variations reflect both changing conditions in the United States and expectations/images about Australia.

TABLE 6.3: Matrix of Migrant Political Ideology and Miscellaneous Sociocultural Attitudes toward the United States and Australia

Ideology	#	Topic	Sociocultural Attitudes
Social Democrat	1	United States	A highly flawed hypercapitalist society that has lost its way.
	2	Australia	Australia a desirable and equitable society but needs more reform.
	3	Welfare	Welfare state a desirable feature of a civilized society.
	4	Unions	A necessary and desirable force in a democratic society.
	5	Race	Tolerance and equity should prevail in a multicultural society.
	6	Monarchy	Republicanism should be the immediate goal.
	7	Peace	Cooperation and negotiation the way to peace.
	8	Health	A large public sector the best system.
	9	Education	State education should promote social equity.
	10	Feminism	Women need more state intervention to achieve equity.
	11	Gays	Protection of their rights necessary and desirable.
	12	Cold War	Now over and equal culpability to U.S. and Soviets.
	13	Social regulation	Sex and morality a private matter; keep state out.
	14	Aussies	Friendly and decent people, but provincial and ethnocentric.
	15	Immigration	Contributed greatly to Australian society and economy.
	16	Economy	Public sector must be used to increase employment and social equity.
	17	Gun control	Must be expanded with greater controls.
Conservative	1	United States	U.S. was a near perfect capitalist society but now drifting toward socialism.
	2	Australia	Australia not a bad place, but dangerously socialistic and union-dominated.
	3	Welfare	The welfare state should only be for most marginal people.
	4	Unions	Unions are a necessary evil to be resisted; they depress incomes.
	5	Race	Racial equality desirable but in a monocultural society.
	6	Monarchy	Republic desirable in the future.
	7	Peace	A strong defense policy needed.
	8	Health	A mixed public and private system the best.

(continued)

TABLE 6.3: *(continued)*

Ideology	#	Topic	Sociocultural Attitudes
	9	Education	Australian state schools inferior to private.
	10	Feminism	Men and women can achieve equality without state intervention.
	11	Gays	Homosexuality should not be encouraged.
	12	Cold War	Soviets caused it and must still be watched carefully.
	13	Social regulation	Sexual morality a private matter but pornography, drugs, etc. must be controlled.
	14	Aussies	Friendly people but lazy and obsequious to authority.
	15	Immigration	OK in the past but numbers must now be cut.
	16	Economy	Reduce public sector and let free market reign.
	17	Gun control	Possibly needs to be extended.
Hyper-conservative	1	United States	U.S. was a near-perfect capitalist society but is now drifting toward socialism.
	2	Australia	Australia almost beyond redemption with a socialistic, authoritarian society.
	3	Welfare	The welfare state should be essentially eliminated.
	4	Unions	Unions are a reactionary force; they should be replaced by contracts.
	5	Race	Monocultural societies superior and U.S. becoming a mongrel culture.
	6	Monarchy	Republicanism best system (disagree with Australian hyperconservatives).
	7	Peace	Peace only through strength.
	8	Health	Essentially private system except for poor.
	9	Education	Private education vastly superior to state.
	10	Feminism	Most women do not want equality and state should stay out of area.
	11	Gays	Homosexuality "unnatural" and should be discouraged.
	12	Cold War	Possibly now in a new phase and extreme alertness needed.
	13	Social regulation	Christian hyperconservatives desire control of "moral" areas.
	14	Aussies	A friendly but backward people who are too slavish to authority.
	15	Immigration	OK in the past but now must be cut, monoculturalism emphasized, and troublemakers sent home.
	16	Economy	Public sector only bare minimum; allow free market forces to work for benefit of all.
	17	Gun control	Minimum controls so citizen can defend himself.

TABLE 6.4: Decadal Variations in Reasons for Emigrating to Australia

	Medium to High Importance (%)			
Decade	*Employment*	*Adventure*	*Environment*	*Hostile to U.S.*
1950s	100	30	0	—
1960s	35	60	30	6
1970s	77	60	35	21
1980s	63	58	50	10
1990s	53	66	37	8
Overall (total sample)	61	60	38	17

HOW DO AMERICANS VIEW AUSTRALIA BEFORE EMIGRATING THERE?

The process of deciding to leave one's country of origin is complex and highly specific to historical and social conditions. The myriad reasons can range from the trivial—"what can one lose by a couple of years in Australia?"—to the thoughtful—"after 5 years of planning we decided to leave"—and to the dramatic on the part of Vietnamese boat people or refugees from war and famine in East Africa. For American migrants, however, very favorable conditions exist in which to ponder the decision to migrate. They usually have time, money, official compliance to depart, ease of transport, and the knowledge that, in most cases, they can return to America. Like most things in the modern American "throwaway" society, migration, just like marriage, jobs, and choice of residence, is not necessarily an irreversible decision.

What information, however, do prospective American migrants actually possess prior to migrating to Australia, and, given their very high return rate, how much do they know about social realities in Australia and how much do they comprehend—that is, do they return to America partly because they were unaware of the cultural and other differences, or had they only ever intended a short stay in Australia, regardless of whether or not they later adapted well? One can answer part of this question by an analysis of how American migrants construct their image of Australia and the sophistication, or lack of it, of their decisionmaking process for the trans-Pacific journey.

"Image" has become a much-maligned phrase in the post–World War II era of global domination by Madison Avenue advertising techniques and values. The implication when talking about the image of a person or nation is that there is something inherently false about the projected image. What often gets overwhelmed in this analysis is whether the image is in fact true, or which dimensions of the image reflect underlying objective reality. Postmodernist attacks on the use and misuse of language have accentuated the difficulties in analyzing images by questioning or deconstructing the existence of any underlying objective reality; but this is little more than a fruitless and self-defeating exercise in semantic and nihilistic terrorism. There may be no objective overall reality of a society for one individual, but some things are far less subjective than others: per capita income, life expectancy, air pollution—that is, a whole range of data about a society—can be examined. The issue for American migrants, however, is from what sources and in what form they obtain information about Australia in the process of emigrating, and how inclusive and accurate the data are about their prospective new homeland.

We begin this analysis by first establishing what was "real" about Australia in the period between the 1930s and the 1990s. In this period, any multivariate analysis of Australia, whether by the OECD or other international sources, reveals several incontrovertible facts: Australia is a rich nation, with great natural resources; it has very high levels of health and education provision, long life expectancy, an extensive welfare system, and a per capita income comparable to that in the United States. It has relatively low levels of crime, pollution, infant mortality, and social and political alienation. But in the 1990s, while these national traits have been maintained relative to other OECD-type nations and the United States, that wealth is increasingly unequally distributed when adjusted for class, race, and gender (most notably for Aborigines). According to a 1993 survey by *The Economist*, Australia is solidly in the top 10 nations of the world when ranked according to an exhaustive range of indicators, and a United Nations multivariate study, the "Human Development Index," ranked Australia in 1994 as seventh in the world, just ahead of the United States, the Netherlands, and Great Britain.[9] Other surveys that rank nations according to their wealth per capita, including natural resources and land, regularly grade Australia as first in the world, contested usually only by Canada. These, then, are the facts about Australia—facts that do not preclude major societal flaws or projections about future problems inexorably looming in Australia's next millennium in the fields of pollution, unemployment, or social conflict. This information is readily available from the nearest Australian consulate or any decent library.

Prospective American migrants, therefore, are not so much victimized by a false image of Australia as they are by a partial image of Australia caused by, in order of importance, limited sources of information, simple lack of acquired knowledge due to lack of effort and ethnocentrism, or, to put it in simpleminded layperson's language, just plain stupidity. A wide range of material is available from which to draw data: popular periodicals; travel literature; fiction and non-fiction, with Australian settings or focus; personal experiences conveyed by friends and relatives who have traveled in Australia; and, especially in the postwar era, films and television, especially documentaries, and lately the Wold Wide Web. The data about Australia, therefore, circulates in American culture, but what do Americans assimilate from these sources, and how do they interpret it within the framework of American values?

THE 1950s

American perceptions of post–World War II Australia reflect both nostalgia for the (mythical) American past and images portrayed in popular culture of the Land Down Under. As postwar U.S. society became increasingly concentrated in rather frenzied and sometimes enormous metropolitan centers, and social tensions rose, Americans looked to Australia as a nation in which those quintessential American ideals still existed: an egalitarian society, with an open frontier, hard-working Anglo-Saxon people, a kind of new frontier like the old American West. Images of the healthy bronzed Aussie sportsperson, the tan bodies at Bondi beach, and the mystique of the outback reinforced this idealized projection of what America used to be in combination with what Australia was thought still to be in this hectic modern world. When Ava Gardner said that Melbourne was the appropriate place to film the end of the world—*On the Beach*—there were at least two possible meanings for the statement.

World War II was the first period in which large numbers of Americans gained direct experience of life in Australia. Although, as already described, there were frictions, and even violence, between U.S. and Australian troops stationed in Australia, Americans married Australian nationals, and many remained in Australia. Well over one million Americans served in the Pacific theater and visited Australia, and they returned to America with war stories and memories. For the victorious survivors war can be, of course, a fondly remembered occasion. Many respondents reported that their earliest thoughts about Australia were derived from the war reminiscences of GI parents, and many migrants in the 1970s and 1980s date the genesis of migration from these early impressions of Australia. In the late 1940s, therefore, the major source of information about Australia was from the direct experiences of World War II and not from material appearing in the mass media. During this period America was an insular and ethnocentric culture, with little coverage or interest in the South Pacific—a judgment that many would extend to the entire period under scrutiny about the American mass media and public.

This ignorance about Australia by Americans—including by elite opinion-makers—has long been noted by Australian-based scholars on the subject. Joe Siracusa, a University of Queensland (U.S.-born) historian, among others, has frequently pointed out the difficulties encountered by both Americans and Australians who are concerned with promoting trade and diplomatic ties between the two nations, given the problems of American knowledge deficits (tending toward no knowledge at all) about Australia. In 1940, the first Australian ambassador to Washington, Richard Casey, commissioned a New York public relations firm to find out what Americans knew about Australia and found that it was essentially nothing. In 1962 Frank Hopkins, the U.S. consul-general in Melbourne, wrote a secret report on Australia and (among many contentious judgments about the Australian character) revealed an extraordinarily superficial analysis of the country, especially for a senior career diplomat.[10]

In the 1950s, therefore, Australia was still perceived by most Americans as a distant and exotic land, although their information base was slowly expanding. Sir Robert Menzies was a staunch Cold War ally of America, and the Korean War would again see Australians and Americans join against a common enemy. The camaraderie of the war against Communism would enhance the bonds of World War II, and thousands of Americans would again travel to Australia as part of their rest and recreation. The depiction of Australia in the 1950s American popular press—the *National Geographic* and other travel literature—however, was superficial and limited, without a detailed analysis of the social and political order. Australia was simply a land of interest and opportunity, and the prospects for capital investment were increasingly recognized by the American business community then experiencing the greatest economic boom in American history.

A perusal of indexes to newspapers and the periodical press in America, such as the *New York Times Index* and the *Reader's Guide to Periodical Literature*, reveals a paucity of items under the heading "Australia." The few items are concentrated under topics such as the Korean War, travel, and business opportunities. James Michener, the extraordinarily popular writer in the 1950s (and to the present), writes fondly in *Holiday* magazine about his travels; in *Fortune* and *The Rotarian* business opportunities are reported to be expanding; and *The Rotarian* tells Americans that "Australia [is] Running in Top Gear." *The New York Times* extols the virtues of this pristine land in which explorers were still finding new territory. No wonder that one migrant, echoing a continuing theme, would write about Australia: "It's like America in the 1880s. This is what it must've been like when the railroads opened up the West," and an airman, Bill Moran, who stayed in Australia after marrying an Australian, admits that most Americans knew nothing about Australia.[11]

THE 1960s

The 1960s, however, was a "golden age" of coverage and interest in Australia and was coterminous with the boom in migration between the mid-1960s and mid-1970s. Australia was presented as almost a paradise: a lucky country, a booming economy, exotic beaches, fascinating aboriginal peoples, a nation on the move to affluence, with a stable political and social order—in short, like America used to be, before the trouble in the inner cities, African American assertiveness, Vietnam, pollution, and all the ills of the twentieth century: a picture of Australia, therefore, not essentially false, but limited and partial—no warts at all.

An American sampling the literature on Australia in the 1960s would be encouraged to take the plunge. Ian Bevan's book, *The Sunburnt Country*, was typical: "We think of it [Australia] as a wide-open land; wide open for adventure, construction, development; wide open for living. We think of it as a wonderful place—not perfect, but wonderful." Art Linkletter, one of America's most famous television personalities of this period for his explorations of "kids and people-are-funny" programs, was a kind of one-man promotion machine for Australia. He traveled and filmed in Australia at the behest of his "close friend," Prime Minister (1966–67) Harold Holt. In his *Linkletter Down Under*, he told Americans about "the last frontier," inhabited by "friendly people" who were maybe less productive than Americans and drank too much, but Australia was a place in which to live, travel, and, like Linkletter, purchase property for a second home. Australia offered space and freedom, and to a former Arizona rancher who moved to Australia in the 1960s this was crucial: "I felt they were closing in on me. I wanted to get back to the big country."[12]

The Arizona rancher's slightly paranoiac "they" reflected a general dissatisfaction, which would be coupled with the primary motivations for migrating associated with employment and adventure. The social democratic and conservative migrants both express fears about America but, of course, identify different causes for the ailments.

In the late 1960s the conservatives, and especially the hyperconservatives, feared that America was becoming a socialistic and race-mixing culture. Australia, with the White Australia policy still intact, seemed a safer place. These migrants were covered by the Australia press: *The Melbourne Herald* wrote about a migrant under the headline: "U.S. Socialistic, so He'll Migrate." And the American *Los Angeles Times* described Australia under the headline, "Nope, It Isn't L.A. but Australia—Haven for America's Disenchanted: No Hippies, No Smog, and the Working Man is King." One migrant claimed great " disenchantment with our government over there, the socialistic trends that were coming in . . . and the drug problem, like the school our oldest daughter went to had . . . and they were smoking marijuana. And one of the teachers in the junior high school . . . was raped by two black students. They were busing, I think one of the things too that finally broke the camel's back was that." Another migrant, a gallery conservator, believed "a female or a colored person was more likely to be promoted than a White male." This constellation of fears associated with race and government intervention was also coupled with fear of crime: "But fear has been building up. These days many parents are afraid to go out of the house. My kids are big and strong and healthy . . . I had to leave before one of them had a leg blown off at school." American conservatives, therefore, combined fear and alienation in America with a perceived image of Australia as a white man's nation in which capitalism thrived.[13]

Social democratic migrants in the late 1960s and 1970s also believed Australia to be a safe haven, but with a very different set of values from those of their conservative compatriots. The crisis associated with the Vietnam War stimulated alienation among the Left in America. One respondent was "sick of U.S. politics and general blind patriotism." Another was tired of "gross materialism, and Australia was a damn sight better than the U.S." Gerald Stone, the prominent television current affairs specialist and later editor of *The Bulletin*, emigrated to Australia, "because he didn't fancy the Cold War climate of early 1960s America." The Vietnam War draft evaders came to Australia, although one "did not realize the extent to which Australia was involved in the Vietnamese War." Another came because "migrant status was easy to get, no extradition for draft offenses and postgraduate education was available." And, finally, a music teacher provides a detailed and humorous piece on the complex motivational processes for the social democratic–Left migrant:

In 1965, while President Johnson was performing "escalation" on both the Vietnamese and American draft age males and I was in my first year of teaching, I informed my Local Board that I did not consider myself suitable for the draft because of philosophical reasons. I am required by law to inform them of anything which may affect my draft status.

In reply my Local Board ordered me to report for a p3#-induction physical. And re-classified me 1-A. At the physical I had an interview with an examining MD who could not understand why I was there in the first place! Seems the Gov. was not drafting employed teachers.

I explained my background and presented documentation of a history of ophthalmic migraine headaches. The Doctor arranged for me to consult a psychiatrist to determine if the armed services would aggravate the migraines. As a result of my encounter with this sympathetic military doctor I was re-classified 4-F. As time went on, I became more and more disaffected with my country's activities in S.E. Asia as well as domestic unrest at places like Kent State et al. I had long ago burned my draft card and even canceled a life insurance policy with Sun Life because they were investing in Dow Chemical who was one of the major manufacturers on munitions, defoliants and particularly napalm. (A district manager of Sun Life came to visit me from Boston . . . he simply could not understand my action!)

I had arranged teaching jobs just over the border from Houlton (ME) in New Brunswick (Canada), but never followed through with them.

Shortly after I wrote to the New Zealand Embassy in Washington DC to investigate the possibility of emigrating there. I heard nothing from them, but did mysteriously hear from the Australian Embassy. (Apparently my communication to the N.Z. Embassy was passed along to their Ozian counterpart in DC.)

Within a year I had a teaching job with the NSW Department of Education and a landed migrant visa enabling me to stay in Australia.

Probably the one event which convinced me of the correctness of my actions was the re-election of "Tricky Dirty Dick Nixon."

My choice of Australia was threefold:

—Music teachers live in precarious professional existence in the U.S. Your position can vanish in a minute at March Town Meetings when the locals decide on school budget cuts. You could never purchase a home because of this fear of the unknown. Australia offered permanency of employment . . . even for music teachers.

—I had decided long ago that a high priority had to be placed on the franca lingua. It had to be an English-speaking country. Australia fit the bill and provided a sense of adventure at the same time.

—I absolutely loathe snow and ice and extreme cold. I never want to see another snowflake again except under a microscope. (Remember, I come from Maine where we average 120" of snow per year and has been down to 54°F.)[14]

Images of Australia were also penetrating the consciousness of Americans through the mass media and the internationalization of communications systems. Documentaries about Australia in the 1960s were shown to the now universally television-viewing Americans. The great sporting stars of the 1960s/70s became familiar figures to Americans: Rod Laver, John Newcombe, and Evonne Goolagong were among the best tennis players of the period. The popular films *On the Beach* (1959, Ava Gardner, Gregory Peck) and *The Sundowners* (1960, Robert Mitchum, Deborah Kerr) conveyed exotic images of Australia and stimulated interest in the antipodes. The novels of Neville Shute, particularly *A Town Like Alice* (1950, later filmed with Peter Finch), were widely read, and the works of Nobel prize–winner Patrick White, particularly *Voss* (1974), and of Thomas Kennealy and Elizabeth Jolley were known to a growing proportion of the educated classes. By the mid-1970s the picture of Australia was filling out, and it was understood to be a more complex nation than the post–World War II idealized portrayals—although one is reluctant to guess what Americans made of the popular television program "Skippy the Bush Kangaroo": even in the 1990s its popularity has not waned, for it is still seen in re-runs.[15]

THE 1970s

In many respects, the coverage of Australia in the 1970s was an extension of the late 1960s—an idealized vision of the great unspoiled continent. But the scale of reporting, writing, and academic work on Australia was expanding rapidly in the 1970s, and there was a concomitant increase in the complexity and sophistication of the analyses. Social problems were being analyzed, and the stresses and strains of the Vietnam War years were identified. Economic expansion was no longer viewed as without limits, and the overall positive picture was increasingly tempered by considerations of global structural problems in all Western nations, including Australia. The age of innocence about Australia as viewed through American eyes was ending as the domestic environment in Australia also shifted to an era of greater social, economic, and cultural conflict.

Tony Wheeler, writing in the Lonely Planet guide to *Australia* in 1977, set the tone for the way outsiders in the 1970s viewed Australia: "few places on earth with as much variety as Australia, and not just variety in things to see, also in things to do, places to eat, entertainment, activities and good times." Australia had become a more diverse multicultural society and offered more variety as a culture than it had the 1960s. This was now also enhanced by its relatively low level of pollution. In *The Penguin Book of the Bush*, Edward Kynaston hoped that "Australia may still not be too late to halt the destruction of nature which in some other countries may have already assumed an irreversible trend." John

Gunther, America's most prolific and widely read travel writer, described Australia in *Inside Australia and New Zealand* as "a yearning for the equivalent of an earlier America less beset by intractable problems." Gunther, however, reflecting the shifts in opinion in the 1970s, condemned the White Australia policy and the boring suburban lifestyle, and, especially perceptively, predicted that the future for Australia would rest on its coming to terms with Asia. *The New York Times* continued to cover the positive aspects of Australian life, but numerous pieces also discussed serious problems arising from the Vietnam War, social inequalities, Aborigines, immigration, and other divisive social issues. By the 1980s, the world was intruding into Australian social tranquillity, and both the advantages and pitfalls of Australian life were now recognized by the world's press.[16]

THE 1980s AND 1990s

In the 1980s and 1990s the full complexities of Australian culture should have been easily comprehended by Americans. In 1980, a book reviewer declared in *The New York Times*: "Prosperity and casual lifestyles of Australians are described [in a book about Australia]; pessimism about the future even with high living standards; productivity low and unions too strong; the world is catching up with 'the lucky country.'"[17] Images on the screen showed Australians and/or Australia capable of humor, energy, and vitality, as well as forebodings about the future: all of these are contained in Olivia Newton-John's *Grease* (1978), in Mel Gibson's *Road Warrior* (1981) and *Beyond Thunderdome* (1987), and in *Crocodile Dundee* (1986 and 1988).

In the mid-1980s the massively successful government-supported advertising campaign by *Crocodile Dundee* star Paul Hogan projected an idealized image of Australia, and millions of Americans joyfully followed his invitation to "put a few shrimps on the barbie." Colleen McCullough's international best seller, *The Thorn Birds* (1977), showed images of Australia, based upon the novel, on both screen and television. Greg Norman, Robert de Costello, and Pat Cash maintained Australia's sporting reputation, and the winning of the America's Cup (1983) was a defeat for Americans in a sport in which there had been absolute Yankee domination.

The successful international tours by the Australian Ballet and the Sydney Dance Company revealed to Americans a new dimension of Australian life as a sophisticated society, both culturally and intellectually. Academic interest in Australia increased, centers for Australian studies were established in large American universities like the University of Texas, and the American Association of Australian Literary Studies was established in 1985 to promote study of Australian literature.[18] The Australasian Studies Center was also established at Pennsylvania State University in 1982 with the encouragement of Professor Henry Albinski, who had written a number of books about Australian politics, and a Chair of Australian Studies was established at Harvard University, to be filled annually by a visiting distinguished Australian scholar.

Father John Eddy, an Australian Jesuit teaching at Georgetown University in the mid-1990s, found the students "aware of Australian films . . . and literature. They had a warm, fuzzy sense of . . . Australia and wanted to visit. . . . But . . . they were gripped by the sociological comparisons . . . and it was news to them that Germaine Greer was an Australian. . . . shocked by the White Australia Policy [and] took a strong interest in Aboriginal subjects."[19] In the late 1980s Bruce Chatwin's *Songlines*, a somewhat idealized study of pre-European Aboriginal culture, was a national best-seller in the United States. Australian intellectuals—including Robert Hughes (the Arts), Germaine Greer and Anne Summers (feminism), and Dennis Altman (gay culture)—had by then been at the forefront of radical movements in the United States for over a decade. In short, by the 1980s a literate American contemplating migration to Australia had the information available to make an informed decision, but the crucial question is whether or not that information was assimilated.

In spite of the variety of sources of information about Australia available to Americans, throughout most of the post–World War II period the anecdotal and empirical evidence indicates a low level of knowledge by migrants about Australia prior to emigration. In the 1970s, Jan Deamicis devoted considerable effort to examining the knowledge base of his sample of American migrants and found it, to his surprise, to be consistently low. This puzzled him until he realized that there was a logical explanation:

At first it seemed odd for interviewees to repeatedly tell me how little they had known about the country when they had decided to go, and that their ignorance had not caused them much anxiety or fear. The apparent paradox was due to my preliminary research assumptions about migration and decisionmaking. Expecting that migration would be a serious and weighty matter fraught with lifelong consequences, I reasoned that migrants would take pains to inform themselves thoroughly about conditions in the new country in order to minimize the possibility of making decisions they might later regret. Instead I discovered that for most people, decisions were emergent and situated, and consequently information was an irrelevant concern.

Respondents in the 1993 sample expressed similar views about their knowledge of Australia. One academic confessed: "I read two or three books, but overall I actually knew little about Australia." An advertising executive, migrating in the 1980s, admitted having little knowledge about his adopted nation and found furthermore that "most Americans I meet out here don't know a damn thing about Australia." A respondent who came originally as an opponent to the draft perceived, in retrospect, his ignorance of Australia's involvement in Vietnam to be astonishing, considering that he arrived in 1969, years after large troop deployments by Australia had taken place in the Indochinese peninsula. An inventor claimed he had undertaken "wide reading" but still found himself, upon arrival, to be essentially "misinformed." A respondent, even though married to an Australian, still found she "was largely uninformed about most aspects" of Australian life. The knowledge base, therefore, about Australia, in spite of the availability of sources, is relatively thin for most American migrants, but they are not distressed by this because they perceive Australia to be a temporary place of residence that is not that different from any other American state.[20]

The reason for this paradox of Americans leaving for a country about which they appear to know little may be offered by Henry Albinski, the most prominent and perceptive American interpreter of Australian–American relations. He argues that the cumulative impact of a broad range of Australian influences on America—ranging through many sports, culture from literature to movies, and including some mighty individual Australian achievements—has combined with the nature of the Australian identity and diplomacy to create an enormously positive image of the country among the American population.[21] As a result, while they might know little about the detail, Americans believe with some justification that they know enough about the whole.

IS IT HARD FOR AMERICANS TO LEAVE?

For the majority of American migrants, therefore, leaving America is not as traumatic as for other migrant groups. Americans believe the change to be reversible and Australia to be a relatively benign environment. This generalization must not, however, be extended to all migrants, and the social and cultural pressures on an American migrant can be substantial. American culture and history have produced a self-image of a U.S.-centric universe, and to leave the "kingdom of heaven" is incomprehensible to most Americans. One migrant was shocked by the hostility of a relative: "He got very belligerent and he wouldn't understand at all why we felt we could have a better life anywhere but in the United States . . . You wouldn't expect somebody to behave like that, would you? [He thought] . . . we were traitors." The decision by Americans to leave tends not to be ideological, but it is perceived by their fellow nationals to challenge their tribal identity and represent a threat to the prevailing social order.[22]

American migrants must, therefore, often cope with social opprobrium before their departure, but they are generally confident in their calculations about Australia. Many are extraordinarily practical and confident: "It was easier for my family to settle here (Wee Wau) than it would have been in the South or New England." Another expressed a similar view of "a constellation of life problems, commitments, opportunities, resources and relationships that almost incidentally led to Australia. As one [views it], it's just like moving to California, isn't it?" Some migrants are very weather-oriented: "Being from Long Island I was sick of the snow, Florida was too boring, California too crowded and Adelaide seemed to have the right climate." Other respondents believed Australia "to be a good idea at the time, at least as a place to be temporarily," and yet another believed "I would stay one year, but then I met my husband and have been here for 23 years."[23]

The prototypical American migrant to Australia since the 1940s is not a desperate individual; he/she has come, by and large, in search of employment and adventure, with secondary motivations involving ideological and social issues that vary over time. They have been exposed to a reasonable level of information before migrating to Australia, but the evidence does not indicate high levels of assimilation of that information. They tend to be confident in their decision to migrate based upon the knowledge that the decision is reversible, a belief that Australia is not too dissimilar from America, and the fact that most have enough capital to return to America if they desire. When they arrive, however, there is no longer a division between image and reality; anticipation of Australia has given way to being surrounded by it physically and culturally. At that point, the question on the mind of every migrant, young and old, is universal: "Will I like Australia?"

NOTES

1. Quoted in Harper, *Pacific Orbit*, p. ix.

2. B. and A. Finifter, "Americans," p. 7.

3. Deamicis, "It Just Happens," pp. 9, 56, 91.

4. Cuddy, *Yanks,* p. 39; Dashefsky, *Americans Abroad*, pp. 26, 145–146.

5. Deamicis, "It Just Happens," pp. 18–21, 23.

6. Graeme Hugo, *The Economic Implications of Emigration from Australia* (Canberra, 1994), pp. 7–12; see also Mary M. Kritz et al., eds., *International Migration Systems* (Oxford, 1992), pp. 15, 133–149.

7. R. T. Appleyard, *British Emigration to Australia* (Canberra, 1964), p. 165; W. D. Borrie, *Italians and Germans in Australia* (Melbourne, 1954), pp. 217–231; Tsounis, "Greeks," *passim.*

8. *The Australian*, 2 July 1994, p. 3.

9. Printed in *The Australian*, 1 January 1994, p. 16, and 2 June 1994, p. 8.

10. The Melbourne *Age*, 25 October 1994, p. 4; The Melbourne *Age*, 10 January 1985, p. 7. We are indebted to Joe Siracusa for a copy of the Hopkins document and for alerting us to this material; see also Siracusa's "The American Image of Australia: An Historical Perspective," in Don Grant and Graham Seal, eds., *Australia in the World* (Perth, 1994), pp. 167–172; "In Search of the Australian Character," *World Review*, 23 (1984), pp. 4–30.

11. *Holiday,* November 1950, pp. 98–109; *Fortune,* September 1950, pp. 84–91; *The Rotarian*, June 1949, pp. 22–26; *New York Times*, 3 November 1950, p. 26; C: 66; "Tales from a Suitcase," SBS TV, 20 April 1997.

12. Ian Bevan, *The Sunburnt Country* (London, 1955), p. 15; Art Linkletter, *Linkletter Down Under* (Englewood Cliffs, NJ, 1968), pp. 1, 5, 6, 89 150, 215–216; C: 45.

13. Newspapers quoted in Deamicis, "It Just Happens," p. 10; De: 87; A: 6; C: 47–48.

14. Q: 70, 192, 199, 221; *The Australian*, 25 June 1994, p. 3.

15. For a bizarre anti-Australian diatribe by a U.S. temporary resident in Australia, see Ethel Sloan, *Kangaroo in My Kitchen* (London, 1979).

16. Tony Wheeler, *Australia* (Sydney, 1977), p. 7; Edward Kynaston, *The Penguin Book of the Bush* (New York, 1977), p. ii; John Gunther, *Inside Australia and New Zealand*

(London, 1972), pp. 2–3, 5, 350; *New York Times,* 1 June 1970, p. 8, 8 June 1970, p. 10, 2 August 1970, p. 1.

17. *New York Times*, 22 October 1980, p. 2.

18. *The Australian,* 13 May 1995, p. 9. The 1995 conference in Tulsa, Oklahoma, was attended by 200 delegates.

19. *The Australian*, 27 April 1994, p. 25.

20. Deamicis, "It Just Happens," p. 89; Q: 16; De: 77; Q: 199; C: 125–126; Q: 268; Deamicis found that 53 percent of his respondents considered it "easy" to leave America, and 47 percent found it "hard": "It Just Happens," p. 117. Dennis Cuddy, also working in the 1970s, found a similar pattern in that migrants from America made quick decisions and were generally impulsive, *Yanks*, p. 54.

21. Henry Albinski, "Australia in America: Visibility, Reception and Influence," paper provided by author and short version published as "Australia and America: Images and Effects," in Don Grant and Graham Seal, eds., *Australia and the World: Perceptions and Possibilities* (Perth, 1994).

22. De: 105.

23. C: 33; De: 127; C: 143; Q: 153, 159.

7

Do the Americans Like Australia?

IS AUSTRALIA DIFFERENT?

Regardless of the reasons for Americans migrating to Australia and the data upon which they have based their decision, once they disembark from the ship or plane, they must face reality: they are there. They must immediately confront and adapt to the style of language, institutions, driving habits, food, and sports of a new culture. They will learn very quickly that Australia is not just another U.S. state but a different culture, with a set of values and behavior patterns to which an American migrant must adapt. The capacity of American migrants to do so and the resultant decision whether to remain or return from whence they came occupies much of the remainder of this study.

It is often believed that Americans with a common language and culture have an enormous advantage in adapting to Australia when contrasted with non-English-speaking migrants. It would be foolish to question this judgment, but it should not be overstated. The American Barbara Brewster's book of travels, *Down Under All Over* (1991), provided for her American readers a glossary of peculiarly Australian terms and phrases that number almost 100.[1] Australian English not only has its own vocabulary and style, which is different from American English, but many words have an opposite, or even embarrassing, meaning for the uninitiated. In America, a "precocious" child is the bright offspring of proud parents, but in Australia it can have the pejorative connotations of "smart-assed"; a "purple patch" in America is a bad patch, but in Australia it is a run of good luck or a sudden burst of scoring or good fortune in sports such as Australian Rules football or yacht racing.

Two of the words that most commonly cause problems for Americans are "rubber", which is an eraser for an Australian but a condom for an American, and the use of the verb "rooting," which for an American is cheering (barracking) for one's sports team, but for an Australian it means copulating. This gets even worse with the American "rooting squad"—cheer squad in Australia and cheering section in America. The American style of spoken English is also quite different from the Australian, being characterized by a louder voice, more emotive structures, faster speech that is highly wordy or loquacious, and generally using language for the quite un-Australian purpose of self-promotion. Most American migrants, therefore, fully accept that the similarity in language is a major advantage and generally not a significant problem of adaptation, but there are still problems in communicating effectively, although not to the degree expressed in Churchill's bon mot that the English and Americans are divided by a common language. More significantly—as discussed in detail later in this chapter—the American accent demarcates Americans as aliens and provides an ethnic differentiation—almost as effective as skin color—that immediately and forever makes American migrants feel outsiders, since they are perceived as non-Australian as soon as they open their mouths (something that most Americans are not reluctant to do). Indeed, in the politically correct climate of Australia in the early 1990s, prejudice against Americans—and the English—may well have been the only socially acceptable form of ethnic bias.

Most serious problems of adaptation result from cultural differences that are only understood vaguely if at all by the new American resident in Australia. Generally not well prepared by comprehensive or thoughtful reading, the American migrant will encounter cross-cultural differences at virtually every social interaction. Writing in the late 1970s, the sociologist D. Phillips summarized the process:

The point is that the United States and Australia, despite certain obvious historical and cultural similarities, are in fact two quite different societies. When they reach Australia most American migrants are a relatively privileged group with clear advantages derived from their relative affluence, education, skills and command of the language. But they are underprivileged and on dangerous ground when it comes to their preconceptions about life in Australia. Many of them arrive expecting a "little America down under" and most of their initial impressions confirm this view. Gradually, as they begin to realize the enormous and highly complex differences between the two societies, they often develop a sense of betrayal, as if Australia had somehow let them down.[2]

The problem of adaptation becomes, therefore, an extremely complex question of social analysis: to what must the American migrant adapt? What social attributes are most central to adaptability and maladaptability? How do adaptation characteristics differ by race, gender, class, and ideological persuasion? Do Americans suffer discrimination, and if they do, what kind of legal protection is sought and/or available? How do Americans decide whether to stay in Australia or return to America? What kinds of pressure do their children feel as they straddle two cultures? Finally—in the end, do they feel satisfied with life in Australia?

DO THEY LIKE AUSTRALIA?

One can deal first with the good news. As illustrated clearly in Table 7.1, the vast majority of the 302 migrants in the 1993 sample are satisfied with life in Australia. Almost one-fourth, however, expressed some level of dissatisfaction, and one must explore in detail the nature of both the satisfied (well-adapted?) and dissatisfied (maladaptive?) migrants in order to comprehend fully the cultural processes of adaptation. Not only must these elements be dissected into the various levels and components of satisfaction and dissatisfaction, but the more subtle and varied problems of American migrant subgroups must be examined and defined. First, however: what do American migrants find they must adapt to—that is, what is the cultural context in which they finds themselves?

HOW DOES THE AMERICAN MIGRANT PERCEIVE AUSTRALIAN SOCIETY, AND HOW DO AUSTRALIANS PERCEIVE AMERICA AND AMERICANS?

Table 7.2 shows (as also reflected in Table 7.1) that those who feel substantial elements of discrimination in Australia represent approximately one-fourth of the total 1993 sample, and those who are dissatisfied are roughly equal in number to those who feel some level of serious discrimination. It would seem to be a truism that people who are rejected will be dissatisfied; generally this is true for American migrants, but the pattern is somewhat more complex when considered in terms of subtle variations. However, of the 1993 sample, among those who feel serious discrimination, 65 percent are still satisfied with life in Australia (11 percent less than the total group), whereas those who do not feel any substantial discrimination are more likely to be satisfied (86 percent) than the

TABLE 7.1: Level of Satisfaction with Australia (Percentages)

Very satisfied	48	⎫ 76
Satisfied	28	⎭
Mixed feelings	21	⎫
Dissatisfied	2	⎬ 23
Very dissatisfied	0	⎭

TABLE 7.2:   Perceived Levels of Discrimination (Percentages)

Feel discriminated against	Yes	40
	No	60
Level of discrimination:		
The "yes" group	Trivial[a]	38
	Medium[b]	35 } 62 (24% of total 1993 sample)
	High[c]	27

[a] Trivial: jokes, sneers, negative body language, odd remarks—not affecting life opportunities.
[b] Medium: persistent pattern of discrimination, belief that it affects life opportunities.
[c] High: overt job discrimination, refusal of a job or promotion, trauma, factor in leaving Australia.

group as a whole (76 percent). The great majority of American migrants, there-fore, are both satisfied and feel free of discrimination in Australia. There is a sizable minority, however, who consider their host culture to be one in which they feel uncomfortable and uneasy. Why do American migrants, on the whole, like Australia, and what are the constituent elements of dissatisfaction and dis-crimination that the rather large minority feel and perceive?

WHY AMERICANS LIKE AUSTRALIA

As one would expect from Tables 7.1 and 7.2, the great bulk of anecdotal data from the 1993 sample of American migrants indicates high levels of adaptation to Australian society. The majority are quite comfortable with their position in life and the decision to remain in Australia. Although it is tempting to assume that length of stay in Australia automatically indicates approbation, it is neither true that all long-term residents like Australian life, nor that all returnees have rejected Australia as a nation by the specific act of returning to America. Those who remain, however, generally find Australian society a civilized place in which to live, raise children, travel, and retire. They find environmental condi-tions superior to those in America and express a strong attachment to the regions in which they live. Most prefer what they believe to be the Australian slower pace of life and the egalitarianism of the welfare state. They view the future for their children, in terms of educational opportunities, safety, and general environ-mental pollution, to be better than in the United States. In short, they are satis-fied with their decision to emigrate, and they intend to remain in Australia permanently. American migrants, like most people, are sensitive to their imme-diate environment—the city in which they live, the schools, the workplace—it is the conditions in these to which they must respond and adapt on a daily basis. Respondents in the 1993 sample were especially sensitive to the advantages of the region in which they lived, and most provided details of why they preferred Australia by reference to the geographical environment to which they had

migrated. An ecologically-minded dentist in Tasmania loves, somewhat paradoxically, the "hunting, fishing, open space, access to outdoor activities and the
fewer people than the U.S." A South Australian declared that "Adelaide is a
wonderful place to live; the lifestyle is much more humane, less consumerism,
less fear in society." Another South Australian also appreciates the lifestyle and
the wine country near Adelaide:

Yes, I am very happy here in Australia. I have a whole new scope of interests that I
did not even know existed in the States. I have developed an educated (semi) taste
for wine and thoroughly enjoy the gourmet weekends available in S.A. The food in
restaurants is superb. In most cases the restaurant is first or second generation and I
feel this gives the food a more authentic taste. In comparison to the American
assembly line this is a refreshing difference. I enjoy living close to the city and we
try to go to the theater, night clubs and other shows in town. Also we are only
minutes from the beach. I could go on and on, but I won't.

   I would like to add I have met several other women from America on "a year or
two exchange" program. I must say I found their attitudes very depressing. Without
exception, they were all counting the days to go home. It did not matter how many
sights I told them about, the proximity of the beaches, the free things to do etc.
Suffice it to say, if you are happy, you can be happy anywhere and if you are
unhappy there are varying degrees of unhappiness depending on your location. This
is my opinion.

The Northern Territory is also appreciated for its outdoor beauty and ameni-
ties: "I traveled in 1978 and retired in Darwin; I met my current wife there and
fell in love with the area as well. I've been here ever since and don't intend to
leave." Another respondent in Darwin states, "we have no anxieties here, our
lifestyle is superb and it is hard to imagine more preferable alternatives review-
ing the world situation." And some find the entire nation a delight; for example,
one migrant prefers "the good light in Australia" as superb for an artist.[3]
   Urban centers, where most Americans live, are also appreciated, even though
the population densities are comparable to U.S. metropolitan centers, as is the
case with Sydney and Melbourne. The latter is described as "a big city, but still
safer and more pleasant than Cleveland." Perth is "better living than almost any
other city in the world. I go back to the U.S. every year and it is a great country
but Australia is the best place to live in the civilized world. Never a regret about
moving here." The Australian Capital Territory has very strong supporters, who
believe "Canberra has been a wonderful place to work, live and raise a family."
Another sees Canberra as an "ideal place to live, good schools and a high
standard of living." Another agrees that "Canberra is socially, economically and
intellectually the best place in the world for me. Now that I have retired [from
academic life] I find I enjoy life here even more."[4]
   These judgments about Australia are often made within the context of com-
paring Australia to the United States in general and to the specific area in the
United States where the migrant lived at the time of departure or from which he/

she originated in particular. These comments frequently use the catch-all American phrase "lifestyle," which is inclusive but often vague and too all-encompassing. As is also shown by previous research in the 1970s, the 1993 respondents often were not just satisfied with Australia but found it superior to the United States in terms of lifestyle.[5] For respondents, this included an enormous range of attributes about Australia: the standard of living; clean environment; red wine; the bush; "better than life in Texas"; good restaurants; "better light for painting"; better health care/social security system; less of a drug problem; less crime; a cleaner environment; greater job opportunities—these are a few of the areas in which the Australian lifestyle was deemed superior by respondents.[6]

Lifestyle is often placed within an ideological framework (as outlined in the classification system in Table 6.3). Social democratic migrants focus on attributes of the United States associated with its weak welfare system, inadequate health care, violence, and general conservative social and economic structures. Some respondents, therefore, not only reject America because it is too far to the right, but they embrace Australia for its more social democratic society. One respondent "came because of the 1975 Labor Government"; several migrated because of the Vietnam War; some objected to the "U.S. military–industrial complex and a society in which the rich dominate"; and many considered Australia to be a more equitable and just society.[7]

Conservatives and hyperconservatives, however, were generally critical of Australia; they are considered in greater detail in Chapter 10, which deals with those who are dissatisfied with life in Australia. The hyperconservatives generally reject America for being too socialistic and for being a rapidly declining society. They hope that Australia will be an improvement, although it is often difficult to see upon what data they base their judgment. Once in Australia, of course, they see the same problems, but even in a more advanced and deplorable state within the context of their hyperconservative view of the world. Hence most of their comments are listed in the section on criticisms of Australia later in this chapter. However, one respondent clearly summarizes why the hyperconservative rejects America:

I came out with an American husband and two children, ages 10 and 13, as part of the exodus from [Midwestern state] when the following happened:

1. bussing was about to be instigated by a few "do-gooders" at the local school,
2. race riots in Michigan were pretty scary,
3. dope had reached the 7th grade where my son was supposed to go,
4. the churches were practicing birth control, which at that time horrified me,
5. the police force and courts had been rendered helpless,
6. the progressive schooling system lacked all discipline, and
7. boy scouts had turned into a shambles.

So my husband applied for a job which he found being advertised for in one of his professional journals. His resume arrived in Adelaide too late, and they hired someone else. However, someone on the board of directors there was also on the board of directors for . . . and felt that he was too good a catch to let go. They wrote back and offered him a job. They also offered assisted passage if we remained in Adelaide for three years. It took us one year to get here from the time we first read the ad.

I later, upon his instigation, took up further studies, and became the first (and still the only) American Land Broker in the state.

This was the end of my marriage, as he ran, unable to cope, professional jealousy being paramount. I'll fill you in on this as well if you wish.

You asked about why I haven't become an Australian. Until the dual citizenship came in about 2 years ago, I couldn't handle the negative way others felt when they gave up their citizenship. I also felt that I would consider it when I became embarrassed about being an American. I am quite patriotic. I don't like the idea of being forced to vote. I enjoy my "Bill of Rights" and Constitution, and still recoil at communism as it used to be and at the current socialism going on.

If Australia became a democracy and if I could relate to those things which were part of my development, and see free enterprise succeeding, I would feel good about being an Australian citizen.[8]

Approbation of life in Australia is often related to very specific problems that were perceived as especially acute in America but absent or in a much less acute form in Australia. In the 1990s the American public has shifted its focus to these social issues—drugs, crime, gangs, guns—as the most critical issues in American life, surpassing areas such as jobs, health, education, and even the economy. This is reflected clearly in the views of respondents about their preference for life in Australia.

Drugs and crime are coupled together as the two great scourges of modern American life, and often this is code language for antagonism toward blacks and Hispanics, who are viewed as primarily responsible for both problems. Conservatives and hyperconservatives often couch their racial views in code language understood within the American community in phrases like "law and order," and a "drug-free environment." However, these issues are considered significant by Americans in general, regardless of class, race, gender, or ideology. Respondents describe "Australia as a relatively safe, drug-free country in which to raise a family. The latter reason was brought home to us since we've had children, not when we emigrated initially." Another respondent, a big-city emigrant, appreciates "the lower threat of crime in Australia," and yet another likes "a society which is in general easy-going, tolerant and relatively free of crime. I especially appreciate the lack of gun ownership and accompanying violent acts. What I do miss is a sense of history and strong community/national ties."[9] Christina Thompson, the American-born editor of *Meanjin*, greatly worries that Australia will become like America, with high rates of crime and street people—the absence of which in Australia she wishes to maintain.[10]

The criticism by many American migrants that the United States is "ahead" of a "backward" Australia (see below) is viewed very differently by those satisfied with life in Australia. They view the alleged "backwardness" to be a virtue, especially if "forward-looking" includes drugs and crime levels in the United

States. One respondent expresses this: "I enjoy being in Australia because it is 5 to 15 years behind the U.S. and I don't mind that"; another will regret it "if Australia goes the way of the U.S."; and a third "does not like the sociological changes that are appearing in Australia—drugs, unemployment, crime, rich and poor, etc." Respondents want Australia to retain its positive attributes and not become "another Los Angeles, with large gaps between rich and poor where one does not want to raise kids."[11]

Most Americans have come to Australia for employment opportunities, and they view Australia favorably within the context of a desirable work environment. They regard their jobs as a source of income, status, mobility, and satisfaction, and they intend to remain in Australia largely because of job satisfaction. One respondent believed he "would not have been as successful, and achieved as high a standard of living, if I had stayed in America"; another has "opportunities I would not have matched [as an academic] in the U.S."; and a psychologist "with a MS in counselor education can practice as a clinical psychologist in Australia whereas in the U.S. I would have needed a Ph.D." An academic appreciates his career in Australia, but also has some difficulties:

In response to your last question about being satisfied with my life in Australia, I found it a difficult question to respond to as there are many ways to approach the answer. I have an excellent job and my career as a University lecturer in this country has advanced much quicker than I would have anticipated it doing in California. My higher degree qualifications initially got me further than they would have in applying for a position in the California State University or University system. Tenure is something that is still more or less "handed" out early here and therefore I feel that I had a much more secure position much earlier than I would have had in the US. Also to pursue my Ph.D., which I am planning to do, is an easier and less costly path than would be possible in the US. So overall, when I look at career security and growth, I feel that there are far greater opportunities for me in Australia than would be immediately possible in the US.

Personally I find things a bit harder here. Some of that is due to being very far away from family and friends, something that is new to me. I am not unhappy with my choice, but at times find it very difficult. Trips to California are costly so it means yearly or longer for overseas holidays to visit family. I have also found that in general the Australian people are more reserved than what I am used to and I have had difficulty developing the types of close friendships that I was accustomed to. Although one of the main reasons for my migration was to continue a relationship, it does not make up for the lack of close friendships that I have not been able to develop in the past 2½ years.

And, finally, a nurse believes that Australia will offer her greater opportunities for social and occupational mobility:

I feel my employment prospects were greater in Australia than in the US. In my profession (nursing) in the mid 1980s there were few nurses with baccalaureate. Although my BS was not in Nursing, it was still considered an advanced degree and provided me with job opportunities above my Australian colleagues. If I had been in the US, I don't think I would have been provided with the same opportunities.[12]

These American migrants, then, find Australia a favorable environment in which to live. This majority of American migrants (in spite of considerable anti-Americanism in Australian culture—a subject considered in the next section, on those dissatisfied with Australia) believe Australia to be hospitable and living there as generally equal or superior to living in America. Some even find being American in Australia an advantage: one "finds discrimination has been generally *in favor of me* rather than against"; a black basketball player says, "Australians actually prefer Americans"; a nurse says discrimination "if anything has been the opposite, especially from older World War II veteran male patients"; and another nurse also "finds being a Yank has been an advantage. Patients, particularly older male patients, often spent time in the military, or fought with Americans, or met them on R & R leave from Vietnam and they found Americans to be great people, and my accent would 'break the ice' with them." Most American migrants, even though in a strange environment and adapting to a new culture, have succeeded in achieving job satisfaction and favorable prospects for their families, and regrets about leaving America have been maintained at acceptable levels of emotional pain. This satisfied majority one can view as a success story for Australian culture, but the dissatisfied minority should not be ignored, for they also provide insights to the nature, attitudes, and prejudices of Australian society.[13]

THE BAD NEWS: WHY SOME AMERICANS DO NOT LIKE AUSTRALIA

We [American migrants] are more likely to be "loners" who get lost in the crowd and attract little attention to ourselves—which can be a good thing whenever the Yanks are blamed for what they do and damned for what they don't do.

—a retired research scientist

I now feel displaced, if not stateless. It seems I will never be warmly received here, yet I couldn't live in the U.S. again. I like and prefer nearly everything about Australia *except* this hostility towards Americans. I like governments here but I could never share an unqualified enthusiasm for all things Australian to the point of rejecting all American history and cultural institutions, or accept the basically racist idea that Americans are evil, stupid, venal or greedy to a degree absent in Australia. I don't accept the idea that Australians are better than Americans, or that my pride in my personal background, accomplishments or social group is pretension. I refuse to be ashamed of being American, and I will keep my accent even though a U.S. accent (in Australia) rubs me the wrong way, too.

—a lawyer

I have lived in Australia for 20 years. I have experienced what I consider barbarically unfair treatment. I have also lived and worked in other non-American countries (Germany, France, Switzerland, Australia, Belgium), and I can say that—despite contempt for American culture there, too—I was never personally subjected to such childishly and cruelly obsessive anti-American treatment as I have been in Australia ... It is caused by a rankling and deep-seated sense of personal and cultural inferiority.

—a retired academic[14]

Dissatisfaction with Australia by American migrants has two dimensions to it. First, it results from objections to Australian life that are often a function of American values and expectations brought with them from the North American culture. Second, it results from some form of rejection of the migrants by Australians or some institutional pattern in Australian society that appears to the American migrants to be intrinsically hostile to their presence in Australia. In the 1990s, hostility to America and Americans has become something of a leitmotif in Australian culture in all social classes and ideological groups and in everyday political and social discourse. Since World War II, anti-Americanism has had its historical roots in the social democratic–nationalist critique of America, but it also has older, deeper, and broader historical sources, running back into the nineteenth century. It has always been intertwined with the question of an Australian national identity, and it requires a detailed historical analysis to comprehend fully its impact on how American migrants adapt to Australian culture. Only once this process is completed can one analyze the criticisms American migrants have about Australia, the dissatisfaction and discrimination that a minority perceive, and the elements of dissatisfaction that are peculiar to subgroups of American migrants by class, race, gender, and ideology. This will then provide a holistic framework in which to make final judgments on the adaptability of U.S. migrants and an understanding of those who give up, pack their bags, and, as the more crude and ardent anti-Americans would wish, "go home back to Yankeeland."

As illustrated in Table 7.3, anti-Americanism is not a single attitudinal, cultural, or ideological phenomenon. It takes an enormous variety of forms, and in the 1990s it can be identified in areas as diverse as politics, economics, popular culture, television, sport, education, health, and general cultural values. In an extreme form it entails total rejection of the national collectivity of America and individual Americans in an atmosphere in which Australians and Americans eye each other with mutual (and growing) antagonism and suspicion that sometimes merges into contempt. Before the varieties of anti-Americanism are explored, however, one must first examine its historical etiology.

To summarize and pick up the threads of the argument begun in Chapter 1, the ambivalence about each other and the frictions between Americans and Australians date from their earliest contacts in the nineteenth century. They have always viewed each other with suspicion and fears about economic competition in the Asian–Pacific region. American visitors and settlers in Australia—whalers, sealers, miners, businesspeople, architects, politicians, entertainers, soldiers, sports

TABLE 7.3: Matrix of Political Ideology and Australian Anti-Americanism

Ideology	*Anti-Americanism—Short Summary*
Social democrat	America is the source of international capitalist and imperialist global structures. Throughout the Cold War period the United States employed tactics of strategic hegemony to cover capital penetration of world markets. Domestically the U.S. has a dangerously gun-happy polarized society in which a large underclass is increasingly marginalized. Cultural imperialism from the U.S. must be resisted in order to create a truly independent Australian culture. The American model of social equity is not instructive for Australia, for it does not protect weak, handicapped, or less well educated sections of society. In general, individual Americans range from tolerable to obnoxious.
Conservative	America is our great historical ally, but much of American culture and politics should be avoided in Australia. The American presidential system is not a model to be followed, nor should Australia pursue the mass education (public) policies found in the U.S. Increasing distrust of other American models: multiculturalism, bilingualism (in schools) and a generally "open" society. The U.S. *laissez faire* economic model, however, is still and perhaps increasingly the norm to be emulated, but Asian labor markets must set the standard in order to increase Australian exports to them.
Hyperconservative	Concurs with most conservative views but has a strong emphasis on monarchist position and historical (Tory) distrust of U.S. presidential system, mass democracy, and "vulgar" society. Christian hyper-conservatives are suspicious of American-style open society, especially on issues of pornography, drugs, gays, and other "morality" issues. Rural hyperconservatives increasingly restive on issues affecting rural exports and arrangements in GATT. Monoculturalism increasingly stressed in a contradistinction to multicultural America.

people, and academics—have been given a mixed reception. Sometimes admired but often feared, sometimes encouraged to come and then rejected, the American migrant has solid grounds for suspecting that most Australians do not have uniformly favorable attitudes toward America and/or Americans. In the twentieth century, America as the source of the global model of modernization commands, simultaneously, universal mimicry and hostility; it is the inspiration for the technologically latest system in almost every area in modern society but also for the "horrors of the future in the present," associated with junk television, fast food, crime, violence, and a large marginalized underclass without hope.

Many Australians watch the deterioration in America and desperately hope (without real conviction) that it will not inexorably (as it may) be an adumbration of things to come in Australia.

The parameters of anti-Americanism in the 1990s, shown in an abbreviated form in Table 7.3, of course simplify its ideological varieties. The social democratic anti-American, a product of the Marxist historical antagonism to the great bourgeois imperialist behemoth, has also argued for many of the positive aspects of U.S. society. Left-wing critics do acknowledge, among many areas, that there are things to admire in America: many ecological advances, especially in recycling; a Bill of Rights in the U.S. Constitution; freedom of information legislation; air bags in cars; libel laws that allow greater freedom to criticize public figures; land rights for the indigenous population that have been granted, however imperfectly, for nearly two hundred years—these are a few areas in which Australian Social Democrats see America as a civilized society. Consequently, even though the main thrust of Australian anti-Americanism since World War II comes from the left, the views of America from the social democratic standpoint are by no means monolithic, nor entirely antagonistic to the United States.

Australian conservatives and hyperconservatives have, of course, been great admirers of most aspects of America. The Cold War alliance, emerging out of World War II, cemented traditional ties between the conservative political and social elites in both nations. The United States was viewed as the bastion of resistance to Communism and the leader of the world capitalist system. Domestic policies in America were to be emulated, especially with respect to antiunion legislation (the so-called "right to work" laws), low taxes, and general technological efficiency. It is only in the last decade that anti-Americanism has begun to appear in the conservative political parties, although some of it has drawn upon an older English-derived historical Tory dislike of American culture and republican institutions. The conservatives have come closer to the social democratic nationalist view of America, and one must examine 1990s anti-Americanism in detail in order to comprehend this convergence of ideological groups around anti-Americanism.

ANTI-AMERICANISM IN THE 1990s: "THE YANKEE PERSONALITY"

Table 7.4 lists the most frequently used words and phrases encountered by American migrants by which they are described by Australians. As is evident, the negative stereotypical perceptions are communicated more often and with greater complexity than the positive ones. Many are epithets intended as terms of opprobrium, and the volume and frequency of these negative stereotypical descriptive judgments seem to have increased in the 1980s and 1990s. As researchers on Australian attitudes, like Jonathan Kelley in the late 1980s and 1990s, have shown, the average Australian feels at best ambivalent about America, and the

TABLE 7.4: The Most Commonly Used Stereotypical Language in the 1993 Sample of Anecdotal Data by Australians to Describe Americans

Negative	rude; crude; vulgar; arrogant; loud; garrulous; chauvinistic; jingoistic; egotistic; greedy; materialistic; ethnocentric; emotional; poorly educated; naïve; brash; overconfident; superficial; gullible; sentimental; fools; aggressive; big-headed; boring; "full of themselves"; violent; gun-happy; oversensitive to criticism, especially about the U.S.; too rich; racist; war mongers; pushy; too religious; cheat at sports.
Positive	efficient; articulate; hard-working; progressive; tolerant; egalitarian; optimistic; "can-do" attitudes; technologically creative; competitive; friendly; hospitable; idealistic.

trend is toward a persistent antagonism to America and American cultural forms coexisting with a massive American presence in Australian popular cultural life.[15]

The popular image of America and Americans, therefore, is generally a negative one in the 1990s, but one riddled with contradictions. Respondents frequently comment on subtle but persistent messages: the raised eyebrow and/or knowing smirk of the television newsreader after one of those "only in America" stories: "Those crazy Yanks are at it again." The main character of the popular Logie-winning television show, *Police Rescue*, claims that Americans are innately garrulous and "have talking in their blood. They can talk under wet cement." After each Buffalo-pat-throwing contest, chicken-clucking contest, rattlesnake round-up, especially gruesome mass murder, or the Tonya Harding ice-skating scandal in the 1994 Winter Olympics, the message, through body language and commentary, is frequently that this is what we would expect— America and Americans are slightly, if not totally, deranged and unpredictable.[16]

The intensity and frequency of these observations has increased commensurate with the growing physicality of American culture in Australia. On the streets of Australia, on the campuses of universities, and in the homes of millions of families, U.S. symbols have spread. U.S. college and professional sports teams and symbols adorn hats, T-shirts, shoes, and windcheaters (sweatshirts); Levi Strauss jeans, Reebok shoes, and the latest U.S. fashions dominate the dress of most people between the ages of 10 and 40; and one is surrounded by a cacophony of music and noise, from 1950s rock to the adversarial rap of the 1990s. As Australian parents watch their children in Dallas Cowboy T-shirts watching reruns of "Happy Days" on television while they read the latest gossip about Michael Jackson or Michael Jordan, the question must arise as to where the line between Australian and American cultures can actually be drawn. Anti-Americanism in the 1990s, therefore, is a generalized fear by Australians about the possibility of the detribalization of an Australian society, to be replaced by an American–Australian hybrid identity.

This process, of course, is not unique to Australia. The global spread of American models has also produced a world-wide reaction against transnational pressures: particularism and cultural nationalism have burst out throughout Europe, the Middle East, and in the Asian–Pacific region. One sees resistance to Americanization in French particularism in Quebec; in Muslim fundamentalism in Iran, Egypt, and Algeria; and in nationalist (cultural) revivals in Ireland, Wales, and elsewhere in the Celtic world. The thread that runs through all of these social and political movements is a resentment of global homogenization—the same reaction that one finds in Australia—that one's culture is being coopted by global Americanization. What are the many and varied elements that make up Australian anti-Americanism in the 1990s?[17]

ANTI-AMERICANISM IN POLITICS
AND FOREIGN POLICY

Antagonism toward American foreign policy and America in general has been entrenched in the Australian political Left for several decades, especially since the Vietnam War heightened the already strong objections to U.S. global policies. The left-wing intellectual critique of U.S. foreign policy centered on the assertion that it protected American capitalist penetration of world markets by supporting procapitalist governments and movements around the world, regardless of their human rights behavior. The election of Gough Whitlam in 1972 witnessed a spread of these views to the general population, and even in the 1980s conservative pro-American years of Malcolm Fraser and Bob Hawke, American politicians like Ronald Reagan drew attention to anti-Americanism in Australia (although one could never claim Reagan to be well-informed).[18] In the 1990s, all political parties have cooled in their ardor for America, and the tendency to distance themselves from America has also been extended to a critical analysis of U.S. political institutions.

The Left in Australian politics views the pro-American foreign policy of the Hawke–Keating ALP, exemplified by Hawke's excessive zeal in his support for George Bush in the 1991 Gulf War, as being unnecessarily responsive to U.S. global policy needs. Continuing pressure exists on the part of the Left against the presence of U.S. communications bases in Australia and the growing need for Australia to formulate its own strategies in the Asian–Pacific region. As Australia moves toward greater integration with Asian economies, the Left continues to argue for a more independent foreign policy to reflect the realities of the future.[19]

Not just the Left, however, has raised misgivings about subordination to U.S. foreign policy objectives. Increasingly, conservatives and hyperconservatives, especially in the National Farmers Federation and the National Party, aroused by trade conflicts, U.S. protection of its domestic market against agricultural imports, particularly of beef, and Australian export markets being threatened by subsidized American exports (most often through the Export Enhancement Program—EEP) have speculated loudly what kind of ally the United States may be, that rewards a half-century of conservative (obsequious?) loyalty by dumping commodities on markets served by the rural sector in Australia. With enormous irony, the conservatives have threatened to use the U.S. bases as a bargaining chip with America—a threat that was greeted with derision and charges of treason when voiced by the Left during the Cold War decades. Much of the spectrum of the Australian political scene, therefore, has in the post–Cold War years drifted toward relatively higher levels of antagonism toward U.S. domination of Australian strategic foreign policy requirements. The principal exception has been the Liberal Party, in office in 1949–72 and 1975–83, and reelected in March 1996.

Social democrats and conservatives have also adopted anti-American rhetoric as part of Australian political debate. All parties seem to wish to distance themselves from American-style politics and institutions in the belief that this goes down well with the Australian public. Paul Keating, at the National Press Club during the 1993 national election campaign, attacked John Hewson for "American-style" campaigning, which he called un-Australian. He accused Hewson of using U.S. advisers, American-style rallies and razzmatazz, and slavish obeisance to Friedmanite monetarism (economic rationalism), and of having a "dog-eat-dog" vision for Australia. Keating warned that the Australian public would reject these unwanted imports. In the subsequent federal election the ALP candidate in the South Australian seat of Hindmarsh, John Rau, brought legal action against some Housing Industry Association material on the grounds that it was unfair and inaccurate. In a radio interview he argued that this type of "American lobby politics" had no place in the Australian political system, for it was undemocratic and against Australian traditions of a "fair go."

Frequent fears are voiced against American "shock jocks"—extreme right-wing radio presenters like Rush Limbaugh, who have their counterparts in Australia in immensely popular broadcasters like John Laws and Alan Jones in Sydney, Howard Sattler in Melbourne, and Jeremy Cordeaux in Adelaide who present very similar if not quite such strident views. And these political judgments are replicated in popular culture and protest, as shown by protesters at the American base at Nurrungar blending anti-Americanism with republicanism and by the zany film star Yahoo Serious merging Australian anti-British nationalism with anti-Americanism in his film, *Reckless Kelly* (1993), on bush ranger Ned Kelly, the Australian equivalent of Jesse James.[20]

In 1995 the ALP and the general Australian media loudly condemned the use of "push-polling" in the Northern Territory elections and a by-election in the ACT in March, in which the ALP suffered a huge defeat. Push-polling was universally condemned as an "American-style" technique, which, in the guise of information polling, actually intends to promote a bias against an opposition candidate. A senior Liberal said, "some things we pick up in America should be left there"; Paul Keating called it "Republican thuggery"; and Mike Steketee, the leading political writer for *The Australian,* saw it (on the front page) as part of a general, undesirable drift toward U.S. political tactics: "Both the Liberals and the ALP, but particularly the former, have borrowed campaigning techniques from the United States, where winning elections is such a ruthlessly professional operation that the end justifies any available means and the truth is relevant only if it happens to fit in with the strategy."[21] This is, to the certain knowledge and experience of one of the authors, perfectly true of all major Australian political parties and, it may be ventured, perfectly understandable in a democracy.

The conservatives are not free of this anti-American mood in political circles, in spite of the historical ties between conservative political forces across the Pacific. The loss of the 1993 election by John Hewson produced Liberal scapegoating for the loss that the Queensland Leader, Joan Sheldon, rather imaginatively blamed on American influences. She attacked her party's adver tising campaign and advisers, including U.S. Republican Party imports Larry Cirignauno and Bruce Blakeman, saying it was time to say, "Yankee, go home. I know the Republican advisers meant well, but what passes for communication expertise on an American college campus does not travel well to suburban Australia, or to a Queensland pub or shopping center." Ms Sheldon broadened her attack by advising her fellow Liberals (at a State conference) that "Republican advisers of late had not been [successful] even in the U.S. We should remember that after the Gulf War . . . George Bush was so far ahead in the polls he was out of sight—even further ahead than the Coalition was at the same time. . . . I believe we must . . . trust our own gut feelings, rather than going further down the Republican track of blind faith in the computer."

The republican debate has revived the hyperconservatives' old Tory instincts about American democracy. In 1993 the leading Perth Queens Counsel and then Shadow Liberal Attorney General Daryl Williams (attorney general, 1996), in voicing Western Australian anticentralization views, also drew attention to the dangers of American republicanism: Australians would reject the Americanization of Australia, and "few would vote for a republic which abolished the states or set up an American-style presidency." The funding of the Australian Shooters Party by the National Rifle Association (NRA), the hyperconservative pro-gun lobby group in America, is viewed with suspicion by Australian conservatives for importing American obsessions with guns and direct-mail high-pressure lobbying. And on the hyperconservative lunatic fringe the fear of America takes on a metaphysical dimension, with one antirepublic sign in the crowd that greeted the 1994 tour by Prince Charles claiming that the republican push was an American conspiracy led by the devil, the proof of which was the fact that the official U.S. seal was the "seal of Satan."[22]

From the serious to the not-so-serious, the anti-American anxieties in Australian political culture have grown. The message is a general suspicion of U.S. politics and institutions, as revealed in a "Dateline" item on SBS (multicultural) television: the presenter, the highly respected Paul Murphy, concluded a piece on Colonel Oliver North's (of Iran–Contra fame) successful 1994 campaign for the senatorial nomination in Virginia for the Republican Party (which he lost in the mid-term election) by saying "that is politics, American-style," followed by chuckling. That is, American politics are amusing, unstable, and replete with born-again Christian loonies. A similar warning was sounded by John Howard in the 1996 federal election campaign when he charged that Paul Keating's policy launch was replete with "imported and alien character assassination from U.S. political culture."

Across popular culture and political lines, the traditional antagonism of the social democratic Left has flowed to more sections of the political spectrum. Partly this is a consequence of the resistance to U.S. cultural models, but it also results from concomitant problems in the areas of trade and economic relations. In trade, political perceptions of America as a somewhat rapacious and feckless ally are combined with the very immediate and pressing needs of an Australian economy in recession for much of the early 1990s.[23] It should be added that with the defeat of the Soviet Union the common purpose that had united the American and Australian right wing—the fear of communism—had disappeared, and they were free to pursue their own discrete interests, unencumbered by a common enemy.

THE ECONOMY, TRADE AND COMMERCE

In no areas in the 1990s have bilateral relations between Australia and the United States come under greater pressure than in economic and trade relations. The economies of the two nations are competitors in the production of primary products, especially of crucial export commodities such as wheat, wool, beef, and other agricultural foodstuffs. The protectionist mood of the U.S. Congress in the early 1990s, in response to the maintenance of the European Common Agricultural policy of barrier protection, resulted in more aggressive trade policies in the Asian–Pacific region, and not only were Australian exports hit by American competition, but the U.S. market became—in spite of the impending conclusion of the Uruguay Round of the GATT talks in 1993—more difficult for Australian goods to penetrate. Back and forth across the Pacific, an endless stream of delegations from the Australian government and rural industries has tried to plead a better deal for Australian exports, only to meet an apparent brick wall. The tensions between the two nations have, of course, risen accordingly, and the friction has transcended traditional party lines. But in fact the United States did successfully support agriculture being included in the WTO deal of the mid-1990s partly as a result of Australian pleading.

The areas of conflict cover almost the entire Australian economy, from primary products to manufactured goods and from tourism to banking and finance. The level of disputation was particularly high in the early 1990s. In February 1993, the public imagination was captured by Campbell Soup's takeover of the "true-blue" Aussie biscuit company, Arnotts. When the AMP (Australian Mutual Provident Society) insurance company tipped the scales in favor of the takeover, the leader of the family shareholders, Ms Alice Oppen-Arnott, proclaimed her shock and disappointment at this betrayal of a great Australian company. To add insult to injury, Campbell's CEO, David Johnson, was an expatriate Australian, which probably explained his interest in the purchase. Instead of viewing this takeover as a useful injection of capital and expertise into a clearly under-performing Australian company—which would not have been vulnerable otherwise—the politicians became outraged patriots. In the federal election campaign, a Democratic advertisement continued the rage by attacking the takeover and bemoaning that it was now "a cookie company" (economic *and* linguistic imperialism).

By the mid-1993, the commodities in dispute included bananas, skimmed milk, wheat, zinc-coated steel, sugar, and coal. An "air war" broke out over routes between Australia, the United States, and Tokyo, and Qantas was battling to protect itself from the U.S. giant Northwest Airlines. The newspapers and politicians screamed for action: Greg Sheridan, the normally quite conservative foreign editor of *The Australian*, wrote, under the front-page headline, "U.S. steps up assault on our markets," an article with the title, "Era of friendship is rapidly coming to a close." His colleague, the normally pro-U.S. conservative Paddy McGuiness, in his usual pugnacious style, viewed the Americans as the "bully boys of GATT." And the "bustard of the bush" even got into the act from the cartoon panels by complaining about the Yanks and parodying the anti-American World War II refrain "Bloody Yanks—over-bearing, over-subsidized, and over here."

In Canberra the National Party leader Tim Fischer attacked the United States for adopting "a baseball bat approach in the air war." In July the then shadow treasurer, Alexander Downer (later Liberal leader in May, 1994, and after March 1996 foreign minister), took the fight to New York City, where he warned an American business audience that Australians were losing patience with Americans, and the American alliance was in jeopardy. Downer rejected a linkage between trade and security issues but admitted that it was hard to maintain conservative solidarity with the United States under this protectionist onslaught. When the new U.S. ambassador, Edward Perkins, arrived in Australia in November—a distinguished career diplomat, to the relief of Australians, after a string of Republican political fund-raisers had been sent to Canberra—he took it upon himself to hose down the bad feelings between the two trading nations. By the end of the year John Hewson and Paul Keating were "born-again" economic nationalists, and 1994, with a looming trade war between the United States and

Japan as a possibility, did not seem to promise an end to economic and trade conflict.

In the event, of course, the GATT Uruguay Round was successfully concluded in late 1993 and created, in 1994, the World Trade Organization. This has done much to abate the fear of U.S. protectionism in Australia with its promise of a liberalization of world trade and the inclusion of agricultural products in the new regime. But despite Washington's support for Australian policy, the more general issue of the domination of the United States remains.

One letter-writer to the *Adelaide Review*, however, was sanguine about Australia's resistance to U.S. power: "We don't have a democratic government that has served us for ten years, just to let the U.S. walk over us [after GATT]." In mid-1994 the war of words continued with a major trade report in America critical of barriers to trade with Australia. The Australian government responded angrily, pointing out the 2/1 trade surplus enjoyed by the United States with Australia and the continuing problems that Australian commodities like sugar and steel had in entering U.S. markets protected by a range of trade barriers. In September 1994 another icon of Australian industry, Aeroplane Jelly, was taken over by a U.S. multinational, and the process of U.S. economic aggrandizement seemed unstoppable. With the statement by U.S. Agriculture Secretary Mike Espy in November that the United States may fill export markets lost by Australia due to the drought, insult was added to injury.[24] In point of fact Australia enjoyed a balance of payments surplus with all its Asian trading partners and ran up an overall deficit largely because of its continuing and large deficit with the United States and to a lesser extent the European Union, from which much of its agricultural production was excluded.

Australians were also alarmed by the new crop of American CEOs coming in to run Australian companies in the context of liberalization and globalization—a situation with which American corporate bosses have had more experience. Historically these high-profile positions were held by Australians or possibly by Britons, and Americans were only visible as CEOs of the automobile companies. In the 1990s, however, American accents were more and more being heard in board rooms and over the media, and warnings were sounded about these rapacious Yankee interlopers. "Hatchet-men" were brought in to shake up Channel 10, and the infamous "chainsaw" Al Dunlap was hired by Kerry Packer with a five-year contract (he was fired after two years) to "rip into" Australian Consolidated Holdings. *The Australian*, under the headline "GUNS FOR HIRE," suggested to the Australian public that the Yankee invasion had just begun: "In the global market place you will find nationality an increasingly irrelevant consideration." Robert Joss, from Wells Fargo Bank in California, had come in to run (save?) Westpac; Frank Blount was head of the corporatized public utility that was soon to be privatized, Telstra; Sam Coates had been brought in to run the already one-time loser airline Compass (which became a two-time loser); and George Trumbull had been appointed CEO at AMP in the nearly deregulated

finance sector. The influence of American economic might appeared to be ubiquitous: commerce, trade, advertising, travel, management, and electronics all
subject to the global power of the Yankee dollar.[25] This was a reflection of its
status as a hegemonic power.

In March 1996 the election of the conservative Howard government opened
another front in the debate over American models of society and the influence of
American business in Australia. The new Coalition government proposed to sell
part of Telstra (the old renamed Telecom) to fund its environmental program,
and this caused a storm of protest from the opposition parties. The mildly left-
wing leader of the Australian Democrats, Cheryl Kernot, attacked the proposal
as economic vandalism of a public asset, and when the American-born CEO of
Telstra, Frank Blount, went public in favor of the sale, she suggested that his
"corporate U.S. culture" was not desired in Australia. The new senator from
Tasmania (elected in March 1996), Bob Brown—the famous environmentalist
turned Green left-wing federal politician—also attacked Blount and charged that
Australia must resist at all costs going down the American road to "a U.S.-style
society here in Australia" with a great gap between rich and poor. The message
to the Australian people was a familiar one: the U.S. model of society is un-
Australian and is based on a dog-eat-dog philosophy that is incompatible with
the Australian traditions of egalitarianism and fairness.[26]

In one area of U.S. economic imperialism this anti-American consensus does
not seem to apply: all major political parties in Australia have embraced Ameri-
can-inspired Friedmanite free-market economic theory, or economic rationalism,
as it is called in Australia. All except a minority of economic theorists, left-
wing intellectuals, and a sprinkling of old-fashioned atavistic Country Party
McEwenite agrarian socialists seem to have adopted the precepts of economic
rationalism. John Hewson (Liberal leader to May, 1994 when he was replaced in
a party-room challenge by Alexander Downer), a former economics professor
trained in liberal economic doctrines (monetarism) in the United States, and Paul
Keating, as treasurer and prime minister, both accepted the general propositions
developed by the Chicago School of Milton Friedman and his associates on the
overall principles of economic management. As Michael Pusey, in his *Economic
Rationalism in Canberra*, and others have argued, these ideas have established a
vice-like grip on both parties, the bureaucracy in Canberra, and the majority of
economists in the 36 Australian universities. Only a few prominent intellectuals,
such as Hugh Stretton, have stood up against the tide of conservative theoretical
hegemony.[27]

The critics of economic rationalism rejected it as a viable set of economic
principles for long-term sustainable development in Australia, and the theme of
anti-Americanism can again be seen to run through their critiques. This import,
even though it came with admixtures of British Thatcherism, is seen by the
critics as another unwanted product of a much stronger anti-union, anti-inter-
ventionist American tradition. It is considered to be inappropriate for Australian
conditions and inadvisable, given the past state interventionist policies in Aus-

tralia and the continuing successes of interventionist state policies in Japan, Germany, and the Scandinavian states. The anti-monetarist argument, therefore, rests upon traditional anti-Americanism as well as the questioning of the economic theories upon which monetarism is based. Since these liberal economic doctrines have been strongly supported by Washington-based institutions, including the World Bank, the International Monetary Fund, and the U.S. government—to the degree, indeed, where they have been termed the "Washington Consensus"—it is hardly surprising that left-wing critics should conflate their anti-Americanism with their anti-market attitudes. By the mid-1990s the American economy was outperforming most others in terms of output growth, job generation, and technological innovation—an uncomfortable demonstrative effect for its critics.

As Philip and Roger Bell have argued in *Implicated, the United States in Australia*, the spread of economic rationalism to Australia in the 1980s was part of the general process of global Americanization. The intellectual tradition in Australia in favor of public sector intervention—led by the ALP Left, the public sector employees, and protected industry unions, and social democratic academics like Ted Wheelwright and Joseph Camilleri—was overrun by the onslaught of Reaganomics and Thatcherism.[28] In America the Left was still living off the intellectual capital of the New Deal, but in Australia and America the conservative offensive in economic theory triumphed. In the universities, the public sector, business, and at all levels of the economy and society, the pattern was one of linguistic and economic imperialism: "down-sizing," "efficiencies," "becoming more competitive in the international market"—American jargon and American policies. As the old New Deal doyen of liberal economists, the Canadian J. K. Galbraith, has suggested for several decades, when all the rhetoric is discounted, the ideas of his antagonist Milton Friedman are as old as capitalism itself: reduce the power of the unions, deregulate wages, and thus increase profits.[29] It is ironic, therefore, in the 1990s, as anti-Americanism has increased on cultural and political issues, that, except for a minority on the left, American ideas on economic management have so effectively dominated political and economic debate in Australia.

The left-wing critique of American models of industrial relations in general, and collective bargaining in particular, strongly argues for the line that Australia must resist imported American paradigms. The American "free" collective bargaining system (here called "enterprise bargaining") is perceived by the Left in Australia as a method that inevitably reduces union power and membership, lowers wages, favors powerful male-dominated unions, and is particularly inimical to the interests of lower-paid workers who are disproportionately female and from non-English-speaking backgrounds (NESB). Claire Williams warns that the American model will widen social friction in Australia, and Mark Bray, in a detailed survey of the literature on U.S. collective bargaining, concludes that in the United States "decentralized bargaining [is] a method for protecting their [employers'] interests" that "allows employers to avoid unions and exclude them from representing large sections of the economy." Bray warns also that it will inevitably lead to a society "of great inequity" if these prescriptions are followed in Australia.[30]

In economic theory and practice, therefore, America is generally perceived as a threat to Australian interests and traditional Australian egalitarianism. American models in economic organization would, most argue, reduce equity in Australian society and replicate the enormous social tensions of North America. In a major symposium on U.S.–Australian relations in *The Australian*, Kim Beazley, minister for finance (1994), and the other participants concur that friction will continue between the two nations on geopolitical and trade issues for the foreseeable future.[31]

In the late 1990s, the international pressures of global capital markets continue to heighten issues of national sovereignty, and small economies like Australia perceive ever greater threats to their autonomy in world trade. Hence, while American migrants to Australia are greatly advantaged by their possession of the English language and similar culture, they are, nonetheless, exposed to a level of prejudice and anti-Americanism that, although it derives from hostility to the hegemonic character of the U.S. state, meets with a public acceptability that would be intolerable in Australia were it leveled at, say, Arabs or Chinese.

NOTES

1. Barbara Brewster, *Down Under All Over* (Portland, 1991), pp. 221–223.

2. D. Phillips, *The Australian American Connection* (North Ryde, 1977), pp. 1–2.

3. Q: 111, 73, 138, 178, 139; A: 153.

4. Q: 72, 102, 118, 164, 207, 189.

5. Cuddy, *Yanks*, found that 26 percent believed Australia to be better than the United States, and 56.5 percent were satisfied with life in Australia: pp. 100, 101, 105–106, 109.

6. Q: 74, 132, 255; A: 153–155.

7. Q: 160, 236, 78.

8. Q: 260.

9. Q: 35, 5, 52.

10. *The Australian*, 22 May 1997, p. 11.

11. Q: 20, 23, 116.

12. Q: 134, 248, 281, 290, 285.

13. Q: 168, 92, 133, 274.

14. Q: 287; private correspondence, 21 November 1994, 29 October 1994.

15. Jonathan Kelley and Clive Bean, eds., *Australian Attitudes* (Sydney, 1988), p. 41.

16. "Police Rescue," ABC TV, 4 February 1993.

17. In September 1994, the Parti Quebecois swept to victory in Quebec provincial elections on a pledge to fight "a sea of Anglophones, 270 million of them in North America," *The Australian*, 17 September 1994, p. 30. In November 1995, they came within 1% of passing a referendum for a sovereign Quebec.

18. Aitchison, *Americans*, p. 139.

19. For a recent left-wing rejection of "American models" by faction leader Lindsay Tanner of the Federal Labour Left, see *The Australian*, 26 December 1994, p. 9.

20. ABC TV, 11 March 1993; "Keith Conlon Show" 5AN, ABC Radio, 10 March 1994; *The Australian*, 17 April 1995, p. 11, and 12 April 1993, p. 6.

21. *The Australian Financial Review*, 1 March 1995, p. 3; *The Australian*, 1 March 1995, p. 1; "PM," ABC Radio, 27 February 1995; *The Australian*, 25 March 1995, p. 1.

22. *The Australian*, 29 March 1993, p. 2, 10 April 1993, p. 1; "Sunday" program, Channel 9, 13 February 1994; "AM," ABC Radio, 25 January 1994.

23. "Dateline," SBS, 8 April 1994; "PM," ABC Radio, 14 February 1996.

24. *The Australian*, 5 February 1993, p. 1; election advertisement, 8 March 1993; *The Australian*, 2 June 1993, p. 3, 4 June 1993, p. 1, 16 December 1993, p. 13, 5 June 1994, p. 25, 2 August 1993, p. 5, 27 April 1993, p. 2, 4 August 1993, p. 2; *The Adelaide Review* (April 1994), p. 2; "AM," ABC Radio, 10 May 1994; *The Australian*, 22 October 1994, p. 2. Tim Fischer was so aroused in October 1995, that he declared that the American intention to dump wheat in traditional Australian Asian markets was "a declaration of war" against Australia; ABC TV News, 2 October 1995.

25. *The Australian*, 13 February 1993, p. 22. Al Dunlap bounced back to earn 100 million dollars in 1995 for shaking up the Scott Paper Company: *The Australian Financial Review*, 16 October 1995, pp. 1, 16. He published a book on these victories in 1996, entitled *Mean Business*; see *The Australian*, 5 October 1996, p. 5.

26. "PM," ABC Radio, 21 June 1996; "Meet the Press," Channel 10, 23 June 1996.

27. For a growing literature on American imperialism in conservative economic theory, see John Carroll and Robert Manne, eds., *Shutdown, the Failure of Economic Rationalism* (Melbourne, 1994), which includes Hugh Stretton's piece "Reconstructing the Financial System," pp. 154–171; Bob Lingard et al., eds., *Schooling Reform in Hard Times* (London, 1993); Simon Marginson, *The Free Market: A Study of Hayek, Friedman and Buchanan and Their Effects on the Public Good* (Kensington, NSW, 1992); Michael Pusey, *Economic Rationalism in Canberra* (Canberra, 1991); Marian Sawer, *Australia and the New Right* (Sydney, 1982); Peter Self, *Government by the Market? The Politics of Public Choice* (Boulder, 1993). See also Brian Toohey in *The Australian*, 1 October 1994, p. 24, where he discusses his book on the subject, *Tumbling Dice* (Port Melbourne, Victoria, 1994), and Will Hutton, *The State We're In* (London, 1995), for an analysis of Thatcherism in Britain. A similar analysis has been made for America: Kevin Phillips, *Arrogant Capital* (New York, 1995). Even the old Right joined the attack on economic rationalism: see John Carroll, "The Middle-Class Quake," *The Australian's Review of Books* (February, 1997), p. 19. A cogent Canadian voice has been added to the debate with the Massey Lectures by John Saul, *Unconscious Civilization* (Ringwood, Victoria, 1997), and a similar note of alarm has been sounded for Australia by Stephen Bell, in *Ungoverning the Economy: The Political Economy of Australian Economic Policy* (Melbourne, 1997). For an explanation of the dominance of the doctrines of economic rationalism, see Bob Catley, *Globalising Australian Capitalism* (Cambridge, 1996).

28. Bell and Bell, *Implicated*, pp. 120–127.

29. John Kenneth Galbraith, *Almost Everyone's Guide to Economics* (Boston, MA, 1978), pp. 86–87; in his eighties, Galbraith continues to believe in the old liberal New Deal values of a pragmatic but effective public sector: see his *The Culture of Contentment* (Boston, MA, 1992).

30. Claire Williams interview on 5AN, ABC Radio, 9 May 1994, and her *Beyond Industrial Sociology* (Sydney, 1992); Mark Bray, "Decentralized Bargaining in North America and Japan," in David Peetz et al., eds., *Workplace Bargaining in the International Context* (Canberra, 1992), pp. 129–130; see also Jenny Stewart, *The Lie of the Level Playing Field* (Melbourne, 1994), who argues that the non-interventionist state invariably leads to concentrations of power and an inequitable society.

31. *The Australian*, 3 September 1994, pp. 12–13.

8

Cultural Relations

"Australia Don't Become America"

—popular song by Cranky, 1995

It is one of the great ironies of Australian popular cultural life that while the broad mass of Australians have embraced American culture with considerable enthusiasm, much of the cultural elite has been very quick to condemn it. This has sprung from a combination of right-wing Anglophile condescension toward American mass culture, left-wing criticism of American cultural imperialism, which was particularly virulent during the Cold War period, and 1990s posturing within the now mass student market in the universities around the themes of postmodernism and identity politics. At the forefront there have been the controversies over cultural studies and political correctness, but in the background has been a generation of Australian intellectuals that became seemingly permanently alienated from the United States during the anti–Vietnam War protest period.

HIGH CULTURE AND POPULAR CULTURE

A transcendent theme in Australian cultural nationalism has been the only partly successful resistance to the continuing inroads of American cultural forms: vaudeville, live theater, film, television, art, architecture have all been art/cultural forms over which the battle for an Australian identity has been fought at one time or another. A strong tradition has opposed American influences, American personnel, and American management of Australian cultural life.

To detail the history of anti-Americanism in cultural terms would require a separate study—quite beyond the scope of this one—but the visibility of Americans in Australian culture has continued to grow over the past decade. Seeing black Americans in Australian sports and advertising has become common, far more so than Aborigines; American forms in commercial radio and television dominate and are used as models for Australian productions; Don Lane, a former comedian, has become prominent as an American football presenter, Chelsea Brown (of the American "Laugh-In" fame in the 1960s) appears on various game shows, and Marcia Hines (who originally came to Australia to star in the rock musical "Hair") is a well-known singer and actress, among others. They and other Americans have become familiar faces in Australian entertainment; but their number is small, and generally Australians have attempted to reserve most areas of popular culture for Australian nationals.

One battle-ground in Australia—indeed around the world—is the resistance to the spread of American English. In the Australian cultural renaissance of the 1960s and 1970s conservative intellectuals like Max Harris as well as left-wing nationalists resented the use of Americanisms in Australia. Max Harris, long a self-proclaimed guardian of linguistic purity, perceived America as "Vulgarland" and lamented that "there [were] few American exports. . . . Australians have resisted [accepting the] tasteless vulgarity of Miami [and] the loud uncouthness of Dallas."[1] In the 1990s, English has become the lingua franca of the world, and unquestionably the American variant will continue in its prominent position in spite of attempts by cultural nationalists like the elders of the Académie Française to ban Franglais from French speech.

One area of American English that has become increasingly common in Australia is the use of Yiddish phrases transmitted into Australian culture through the mass media of television and film (especially Woody Allen films). Recently the former prime minister, Paul Keating, who is rather famous for his robust language, referred to the Liberal leaders in Victoria as "schmucks" [literally a penis, but a general term of opprobrium meaning a fool or idiot].[2] Other Yiddish words now in common use are shown in Table 8.1.

Bill Bryson, writing in an *Australian* "Fourth of July Special," takes special note of Jewish and black American terminology spreading in both American and Australian culture and language, and to the list in Table 8.1 he adds *kibbitz* [chat] (used for an observer at a card game), *nosh* [eat], *schmo* [backward person], *bagel*, *pastrami*, *glitch* [a mistake or slip], and "a raft of expressions without which American English would be very much the poorer: 'I should live so long,' 'I should worry,' 'get lost,' 'I'm coming already,' 'I need it like a hole in the head.'"[3]

Criticism of U.S. language imperialism in Australia in the 1990s is a persistent theme and subject of general debate. Roly Sussex, at the Center for Language Teaching and Research, University of Queensland, is compiling a dictionary of American words adopted into Australian English. He warns Australians that they "shouldn't so easily abandon our language which is so central

TABLE 8.1:   Yiddish Words in Common Use in Australia

Word	Literal Meaning	General Usage
chutzpah	cheeky, daring	same
kosher	conforms to Jewish laws	not crooked, above board
meshugener	crazy person	same
schlemiel	misfit, bungler	fool
schlock	slovenly person	cheeky, cheap goods
schmuck	penis	idiot, fool
shiker	drunkard	same
shlemazel	unlucky man	mix-up, mess
shmalts	animal fat	overly sentimental
shmate	rag	out of style clothes
shmendrik	simple, fool	same
shmerts	pain	*angst*
shnorer	beggar	moocher
shtik	thing, act	"do your own thing"
shyster*	crook, con man	same

* Not actually Yiddish but perceived to be Yiddish; actually after a New York attorney, Schuester, frequently rebuked in court (c. 1840) for pettifoggery (*Webster's,* 1958, p. 785).

to our culture." These views are echoed by Bruce Moore, author of a study entitled "How to Avoid Americanisms," and these scholars see a general detribalization of Australia as the culture loses its distinctive language in the process of Americanization.[4]

Criticism of Americanization in Australian culture takes many forms, ranging from the serious to the jocular and the absurd. Between 1992 and 1995 Telecom Australia ran a series of advertisements in which two American male bimbos, named Bernie and Chucky, were continually amazed by Australian telecommunications technology. Chucky is even intimidated by a galah [cockatoo] in Karratha, Western Australia, who seems to be more clever than the naive American. Dennis Altman, the gay writer and academic political scientist, complains about the cultural cringe exhibited in a review by McKenzie Wark of his book *Homosexual: Oppression and Liberation*:

I should be used to the fact that the cultural cringe is strong among our cultural critics, and that they are far more likely to quote Americans than Australians. In this they are merely reflecting their journalistic colleagues, who need the visit of an overseas celebrity such as Armistead Maupin before they will write about issues such as outing or gay writing. Even so, it would be at least historically accurate were Wark to recognize that the ideas he associates with the 90s were part of the theoretical discussion of the early gay liberation movement 20 years earlier.[5]

Noel McLachlan, a Melbourne historian, makes a related charge in a review of *Creating a Nation* by Patricia Grimshaw and colleagues, but McLachlan sees his fellow Australians as neglecting to acknowledge American influences *because of* anti-Americanism:

But why, finally, isn't Australian women's profound debt to American feminism more clearly delineated? It's no accident that Lucy Frost, whose wonderful *No Place for a Nervous Lady* (1984) so movingly evoked "voices from the Australian bush," is an American. Her working-class Sarah Davenport summed up the expectations of all New World migrants: "We was all in good hopes that we was coming to better [sic] ourselves." *Creating a Nation* certainly transforms our understanding of how far women have fulfilled those hopes—and the often searing price they paid.[6]

And Peter Craven, writing in *The Australian* on Australia Day, defends the appointment of an American, Christina Thompson, as editor of *Meanjin* from the anti-American criticism that is expected inevitably to follow:

One of the remarkable things about Christina's candidacy is that it was supported by such diverse figures as Mudrooroo and Barry Oakley, the literary editor of this paper. Anyone pondering whether an American can handle the legacy of Australia's most complexly contested cultural ground (everyone thinks they own *Meanjin*) should remember the quality of historical writing about Australia which was produced by the American historian Hartley Grattan [sic].[7]

When Bob Catley was made editor of the *Current Affairs Bulletin* in 1996, in contrast, no criticism of his Welsh/London background was anticipated, and no comment emerged.

In 1993–94, the "I Am Australian" foundation was spending millions to identify and advertise what (on television mainly) it is to be an Australian. In popular culture and intellectual culture in the 1990s, a component of this identity continues to be anti-Americanism. America is perceived as a source of corruption in modern society, and at times the analysis takes absurd forms. In a letter to the Adelaide *Advertiser,* owned by the Australian–American Rupert Murdoch, which takes this conception of America to new heights of paranoia and metaphysical import, the writer argues:

On October 31, I became extremely irate and incensed when young children, nine years and under, came knocking on my door begging for sweetmeats in celebration of Halloween.

A custom which embraces the arrival of darkness and death is hardly a notion which promotes positive development. Ever increasingly these days, the media promotes overseas ideas, products and sports heroes. No wonder there is a growing concern about Australia's lack of national pride in this economic downturn.

Unfortunately, until Australian concepts are endorsed to the same extent as those from overseas, our national pride and spirit will only continue to erode.

Also, I have four children ranging in age from five to 16. My husband and I have gone to great lengths to educate our children about the dangers associated with strangers and playing unsupervised in front yards and on footpaths. I feel a great deal of anger toward the parents who so negligently put innocent children at risk of harm . . . or worse.

Too late, once a child is abducted or molested, they would say that they should never have been allowed to roam the streets unescorted.

It is high time those concerned wake up to which country they live in and take the time to celebrate our wonderful land responsibly, instead of mindlessly adopting the follies of others.[8]

In politics, economics, culture, and now even Halloween, American forms pollute the world. Where will it all end?

In the mid-1990s, Australian sensitivities to American cultural imperialism show no signs of waning; if anything, one senses an increase in the momentum to resist U.S. influences. At the opening of the Sydney Film Festival (1994), many observers, including (then) Shadow Minister for Trade and Industry Dr. John Hewson, expressed disappointment at the American content of the films viewed on the opening night, and all expressed a strong desire for Australian films to be in that position. The director of the new Australian film *Sorrento Hotel* (1994), Richard Franklin (the successful director of *Psycho II*), promotes Australian nationalistic themes in the film, and in an interview he warned of the intrinsic absurdity of aping America: "we must prevent Australia from becoming American, for one can see it is clearly falling apart." And the Adelaide University student newspaper, *On Dit*, took up the issue with fervor as left-wing students condemned "U.S. free-market capitalism," as exhibited by the hype and fever over the suicide of the rock hero Kurt Cobain. Conservative students responded with claims that the "vast majority [of Australians] . . . are not disaffected and therefore content" with American imported culture. The visit of Billy Graham to Australia prompted an ABC radio presenter to ask: "Do we need his brand of U.S. imperialism?" One is hardly surprised that national identity and American cultural imperialism are central themes in two important novels published in the mid-1990s by prominent Australian writers David Malouf (*Remembering Babylon,* 1993) and Peter Carey (*The Unusual Life of Tristam Smith,* 1994).[9] With the growing intensity of the multiculturalism and republic debates, Australian national cultural identity is sure to continue as a subject of discussion at all levels of society.

TELEVISION AND SPORT

Two areas that are central to Australian life—and increasingly tied together—have engendered enormous anti-American heat: sport and television, the two major sources of Australians' leisure activity. They are both extraordinarily sensitive topics that arouse emotion, antagonism, industrial action, and intellectual soul-searching by the entire Australian community—the man and woman on the street, journalists and intellectuals all have had their say on Americanization in these two areas.

The controversial subjects associated with television in general and its American content in particular are almost endless in number: the proportion of U.S.-produced programs on Australian television; the level and consequences of violence on television, especially U.S. police action programs; the effect of the number of hours spent watching television; increased U.S.-produced programming projected for pay television; the effect of American symbols and content in advertising (sexual themes, rap music); and the overall Americanization of Australian life engendered by U.S. content in television. Parents, social scientists, social workers, communication experts, politicians—almost everyone has expressed views, held conferences, made television documentaries in which these issues, in part or *in toto,* are analyzed and dissected.[10]

At the highest level of opposition and abstraction, U.S. television is seen as coterminous with the decline of civilization and as the destroyer of Australian culture. A letter-writer to the *Adelaide Review* finds Australian television replete with "juvenile American *Readers Digest* hyperbolic stuff . . . or news [using] the American format that insists that three minutes is long enough to cover a topic which could well take three hours to investigate . . . In every day and in every way the American Fifth Column seems to be after destroying us with [their] rapid culture." And Foster McTaggart, also writing in the *Adelaide Review,* warns:

In Australian television we are being drawn to the American style of presentation. The Yanks want to "live" with their journalists and anchor-people. They want them in their homes. God help them. Australians and Americans are still from vastly different cultures, yet for some reason the entire local industry is telling us we should see more of our dominant medium presented in their style.

Mike Brady, composer of the unofficial anthem of Australian Rules football, "Up there Cazaly," and ardent cultural nationalist, believes that nothing less than cultural genocide will result from U.S. dominance on Australian television. Brady is "astounded that people won't resist and oppose the increasing desensitizing" to U.S. cultural penetration that has taken place in the post–World War II period. In the same ABC documentary in which Brady appeared, Australian television is portrayed as already transmitting 50 percent foreign content and rising; the most popular shows as coming from the United States; Australian television as now replete with U.S. copycat shows, including, for example, the top-rated *Sixty Minutes*; and the major news bulletins following American formats and taking American wire services. Dire warnings of total U.S. control of Australian television are also voiced by Steven Alomes, author of *Australian Nationalism*. A Melbourne academic, Professor Hedley Beare, issues strong warnings about the pernicious effects of American sitcoms, which are creating "archetypes for telling children about human virtues" and "replacing the portrayal of myths and legends." Television, therefore, is seen as a key arena in which to defend Australian national identity, an area in which most commentators in the 1990s, however, have become increasingly skeptical and disillusioned as American cultural hegemony inexorably tightens its grip.[11]

There are few observers of popular culture, with the possible exception of Cultural Studies purists, who find popular U.S. television an especially edifying medium of entertainment or information, especially in its current phase of game shows, Oprah Winfrey, and down-market drama in shows like "Beverley Hills 90210." The introduction of pay television in America has essentially increased 10 or 12 channels of bad television to 70 or 80 channels of an identical product. Michael Medved, in his *Hollywood Versus America*, has launched the most recent of a host of attacks on the violence, content, and effect of U.S. television and film.[12] He argues, as do the Australian critics of U.S. television, that the medium has become a threat to an orderly and civilized culture. As Australians assess their identity in the Asian–Pacific region, the ever-present cultural influence of the electronic media emanating from America will continue to be a crucial area of disputation and anti-Americanism.

One result of this long-standing concern about foreign and particularly American domination of the Australian media has been the continuing regulation of its ownership. In the 1970s, the final days of the regulated economy, the exclusion of foreign nationals from media ownership meant that it was controlled by four large Australian companies: Rupert Murdoch's News Ltd; Kerry Packer's Consolidated Press; the Melbourne-based Herald and Weekly Times group; and the Sydney-based Fairfax empire, centered on *The Financial Review*, *Sydney Morning Herald*, and the Melbourne *Age*.[13] As the process of economic deregulation opened the media, like other Australian industries, to foreign ownership, so the then dominant Labour Party fiddled with the ownership regulations to produce outcomes favorable to its political fortunes.

In this process it generally adopted a media ownership regime that prevented any company owning a television station and a newspaper in the same metropolitan area and did not permit foreigners to own more than 15 percent of a media company. Coupled with the process of deregulation, this soon led to the Australian media being dominated by the richest man in Australia, Kerry Packer, and the most successful Australian of his generation but now U.S. resident and citizen, Rupert Murdoch. After a general shakeup during the Labour government, Murdoch emerged with most of the nation's newspapers, part of a national television network, and its major pay television system, Foxtel. Kerry Packer retained his television network on Channel Nine and a string of magazines including the influential *Bulletin*, and he harbored the long-held ambition to buy the remnants of the Fairfax empire, which had been destroyed in the early 1990s by its new young American-educated owner. Murdoch had already consumed most of the old Herald and Weekly Times group.

In 1995, after supporting the Labour Party for over a decade, Packer shifted his allegiance to the Liberals in the hope that Prime Minister Howard would change the cross-media ownership laws to enable him to buy the former Fairfax newspapers, with their very profitable and up-market advertising revenues. In addition, Packer and Murdoch became engaged in a series of conflicts over the media/sports industries that involved, at different times, ownership of Rugby League—a sport that they split into two competitions—pay television, and the appropriate media ownership regulatory system. But it should be noted that the two major Australian media bosses were closely connected to the United States: one had become a U.S. citizen in order to develop News Ltd into arguably the most successful media company in the world; the other used American programming techniques and shows in order to keep Channel Nine at the top of the ratings.[14] Ironically, and partly because of the rivalry between them, Packer emerged as one of the major influences against globalization and a promoter of Australian nationalism in the 1990s. But this chiefly related to the promotion of his business interests in a favorable situation with respect to foreign companies and did not extend to the wide range of U.S. cultural products that he promoted on his television network.

Furthermore, by the 1990s the media and sports became inextricably entwined, as they did worldwide; sport often drew the largest free-to-air television ratings, and longer sports broadcasts were required to fill the almost limitless timeslots available on pay television. Australians had to acquire new sporting tastes to satisfy these voracious entertainments.

SPORT

"Kick that American butt."
—sign at Davis Cup tie between United States and Australia, 28 March 1993

How American have we become in an age when every second 16-year-old sports a Chicago Bulls cap with its bill turned backwards, Nike pumps, a U.S. college sweatshirt and a street cred home boy haircut? When we look at American society today, to what extent are we looking at ourselves in a decade's time?
—"Fourth of July Special," *The Australian*, 2 July 1994, p. 1

Now one can really get serious about anti-Americanism—for few areas are more crucial, or involve more Australians, than sports, in the formulation of Australian national identity. There are "safe" and traditional sports such as Aussie Rules, rugby, netball, and cricket—sports in which the Yanks do not participate, or at least only at a very low level. These sports dominate the Australian landscape because of the relative isolation of the country during the period of the development of mass and commercial sporting activities in the late nineteenth and early twentieth centuries. They are a combination of peculiar

British influences—both Rugby codes—but in reverse order of popularity from that elsewhere—cricket, tennis, netball—and local inventions, Australian Rules football. Like America, Australia has its own unique sports profile, which is now being challenged by those particularly American sports, basketball, baseball, and grid-iron—all made in America.

But the tentacles of American cultural imperialism have now extended themselves even in the sporting arena, to Yankee sports on television, Yank sports in Australia directing Australians away from cricket and Aussie Rules to "grid-iron," baseball, basketball, and all of them on television; and the symbols of U.S. college and professional sports everywhere one turns. An outpouring of anguish by sports journalists, television commentators, radio editorialists, and cultural critics has taken place in opposition to this wave of U.S. sporting imperialism. The increasing coverage of gridiron Superbowls, baseball World Series, NBA basketball, and their equivalents in Australia threatens to overwhelm the most sacred sporting dimensions of Australian society. This is a feat not previously achieved by soccer, which had failed to gain a toehold among Australian loyalties before the advent of mass migration in 1945; even into the 1990s, Australian soccer is essentially an ethnic sport, with its national league teams formed from and named after different ethnic communities.

The two most successful and fastest-growing sports imported from America are basketball and baseball. The National Basketball League (NBL) was established in 1979 and has 14 teams, with a huge national following throughout Australia. A "7.30 Report" TV item in 1994 claimed 700,000 participants in Australia, and most are avid watchers of the extensive coverage of both Australian basketball and American NBA on Channel 10 and college basketball on Channel 2. The New South Wales Australian Cricket Board interviewee was alarmed at the drift to basketball, which attracted young Australians by its young hip image, American heroes like Michael Jordan, and general cool rap subculture. The Australian Baseball League (ABL) was established in 1989 and has a national eight-team structure with television coverage. Both sports have quotas on the number of American imports in order to prevent a swamping by American athletes, who would shut out Australians. (It should be noted that this is part of a global sporting phenomenon, which has led the ancient London soccer team, Chelsea, to be able to field an entire team of foreigners for the 1997 season.)

The fear that American basketball imports who become Australian citizens would take places on the national team has received press attention. The flow is mostly of second-level players to Australia at such a rate that the teams are limited to a certain number of imports, although the traffic has now become two-way, with basketball players like Andrew Gaze joining Washington D.C. and Luc Longley playing with Chicago and becoming in 1996 the first Australian to play on an NBA championship team. A few baseballers have also made it into the American major leagues, with the New York Yankees' Mark Hatton being the first Australian to pitch in a major-league game; and in America's professional gridiron league Darren Bennett of the Milwaukee Brewers became in 1995 the first All-Pro of Australian background in the NFL. The overwhelming cultural threat, financial challenge, and preponderance of global coverage of American sport, however, clearly puts the Australian sporting community on the defensive about U.S. sporting imperialism.[15]

The anti-American attack on U.S. sports has deep roots in the Australian psyche. With the 1994 scandal surrounding the U.S. Olympic skater Tonya Harding, it was easy to inflame Australian perceptions about American sport and alleged American sporting behavior. There has long been a belief in Australia that Yanks, when under pressure, will move the goalposts, or—not to put too fine a point on it—cheat. The historical memory runs back to the great Les Darcy, the Australian boxing folk hero, who died suddenly in the United States in 1917, unable to secure a title fight against strong political/sporting opposition in America. His story was made into a television film in the 1980s and perpetuates the legend. There was also the alleged poisoning in 1932 of Australia's great racehorse Phar Lap, whose mysterious death was revived by the film *Phar Lap* in 1983. The circumstances surrounding machinations by the New York Yacht Club in the course of the victorious Australian challenge in the America's Cup in 1983 aroused great antagonism in Australia—although the win probably did more than any other single event to lift Australia's favorable image in the United States. The alleged fixing in 1991 of the fight between Australian champion Jeff Fenech and Azumah Nelson by the larger-than-life fight promoter Don King in Las Vegas, and another controversial decision in Las Vegas against Russian–Australian boxer Kostya Tszyu in 1996 produced extended newspaper outrage in Australia.

Sports presenters frequently reinforce the view that American sports—especially boxing—are bizarre and fixed, as revealed in a recent heavyweight championship bout (1994), when an ABC sports presenter was reduced to such fits of laughter by the winner's behavior that he could not continue broadcasting. In August 1995, at the Pan Pacific International swimming meet in Atlanta, Georgia, the Australian coaches and press reacted with indignation and leveled charges of bias when American officials repeatedly objected to techniques used by Australian swimmers, which included one disqualification of a world-champion swimmer. This incident prompted the ABC TV sports satirists Roy Slaven and H. G. Nelson to attack the United States vehemently for being "the home of cheats" and for cheating the Australians consistently, going back to "the murdering of Phar Lap and Les Darcy." Sport is just another area in which stereotypical Yankee behavior—arrogant, pushy and sneaky—can be demonstrated.[16]

With money, reputations, and careers at stake, many sporting commentators have sounded a clarion call to stop the rot. Peter Roebuk, cricket commentator and former captain of Somerset, although an English foreigner himself, demanded an end to

Yankee Imperialism [in Australian sport]: . . . this predator is . . . insidious . . . for behind the invader is the force of America, or American money, and the new imperialism . . . is driving us all towards some doleful homogeneity. . . . Soon the archetypal sportsman here will not be a gum-chewing digger with green cap pulled down over a dry and skeptical eye; he will be a brazen, elongated and soulless figure whose roots are more Bronx than Broken Hill. . . . We already drink Coca-Cola, listen to rap, wear Levis and feast upon hamburgers and fried chicken; isn't it enough? We must resist at all costs the spread of American sporting culture . . . [or] our minds and our world [will] grow even smaller and even more the slave of imperialist and corporation.

Lance Campbell, the *Advertiser* television and sports writer in Adelaide, focused his attack on the presentation by Don Lane at the 1993 Superbowl, under a headline reading "Don's Party a Bore." Don Lane, now a gridiron presenter on the ABC, has entered Australian anti-American folklore as the former cohost with Australian Bert Newton of a late-night "comedy" program; this lanky Jewish–American comic from New York City is the butt of many jokes as well as the object of ridicule in the common quip, "You're in more trouble than Don Lane at a gag night!" Campbell attacked "gridiron as impossible to watch and part of U.S. content on television which is boring, tedious, excessively emotional and unfit for Australia's public broadcaster, the ABC." The current-affairs "7.30 Report" on the ABC discovered a "new American plot" of sporting imperialism: the flooding of Australia by American sports cards, shutting out the indigenous product of rugby and Aussie Rules cards: Aussie collectors, laments the reporter, now "not only look American with Yank hats and T-shirts but now their cards are mostly American." Sports cards, furthermore, alleged the reporter, promote compulsive gambling and other antisocial behavior. In sport, sport on television, and television generally, the anti-Americanism among Australian critics concentrates on a familiar constellation of fears: the global and corrosive influence of modern American culture on Australian society.[17]

The sporting arena is a crucial area in which many Australians, therefore, resist American control over cultural forms. Ron Barassi, an Aussie Rules icon and legend as a player in Melbourne and coach in 1994 of the Sydney Swans, sees the litigious nature of American sport as a threat to Aussie Rules. When asked whether players should resort to the law over head-high tackles, Barassi states that he "doesn't believe in players going to court; this is the worst side of American life and we don't need it here." Nonetheless, in 1996–97 the courts were used extensively against sporting authorities (of which Barassi was a part), including in football, where the Carlton Football Club failed to get a decision reversed, and in yachting, where an unselected competitor nearly bankrupted the ruling body by a successful appeal to the civil courts, who awarded costs and damages.

With the gaze of the world on Australia for the 2000 Olympics, the search for a chief executive officer is in place, and the head of the search committee shows similar sentiments when arguing that the "head of the Olympics for Sydney must be an Australian"—no imports desired, and especially not from America.[18] There was, of course, a certain irony involved, since the United States had been most important in getting the Games for Sydney by checking the Beijing bid for geopolitical reasons. To resist Americanization of Australian sport has become intrinsic to Australian national identity.

SOCIAL ISSUES: EDUCATION, HEALTH, AND CRIME

In the modern era the United States has long been perceived as a model for social change in many key areas of education, health, civil rights, and freedom of information. However, in Australia, as around the world, there is an ambivalence, a tendency to praise and damn America simultaneously. This ambivalence has shifted in the 1990s toward avoidance: violence in U.S. schools, falling literacy and numeracy, the cost of the American health care system, street violence, and the Clinton administration's admission of crises in all of these areas—these changes have weakened the attractiveness of U.S. models.

Much of the criticism of U.S. education by Australians has English historical roots. The Australian educational establishment has its origins in the English tradition, and, especially at the tertiary level, there has been (and is) a strong Oxbridge (Oxford and Cambridge Universities in Britain) connection. Before 1945, each state had a university that catered for the social elite products mostly of the local private colleges and imitated the British universities. The English elite educational establishment has always had an anti-American streak in it: the alleged superficiality of American scholarship, the "quickie" Ph.D., and the degrees given for "basket-weaving"—this is part of the anti-American folklore of the British academic tradition. In the last decade the Australian intellectual establishment has built on these British impulses by viewing as alarming —also to Americans, not just to Australians—the growth of political correctness, trendiness, and a crisis of confidence in America about literacy and education in general. As a result, Australian educators have become even more ambivalent about accepting American models in education but at the same time continuing to recruit large numbers of American-trained academics and teachers—although in the 1990s, with a surplus in teachers, the latter group is less desired.

In the 1990s, fierce debates have been raging in America over the issues of political correctness (PC), cultural studies, multiculturalism, and various alleged pressures for ideological conformity on university campuses. These debates have been replicated in Australia, but with the additional dimension—as with economic rationalism—that this whole area is depicted, especially by the Left, as a part of an American intellectual debate that Australia could do without. The higher education press, especially *The Australian* weekly "Higher Education Supplement," is replete with debates, polemics, and dire warnings about these

American imports and the disruption they have already caused to American academic life. A former anthropologist from Sydney University, Roger Sondall, warns Australians about the anti-science movement coming from America: "But although higher superstition has evidently gone a good deal further in America than in Australia, experience shows that it's only a matter of time before what happens in the United States is faithfully copied here. The value of Gross and Levitt's book[19] for Australian readers is that it enables us to learn in advance about the anti-Science" movement. Again, the extremes, or alleged extremes, of American society are perceived as a threat to more rational modes of intellectual discourse.[20]

The PC debate has aroused a wide spectrum of antagonism in Australia. The conservatives have taken up the cause against the inroads of the alleged PC left-brigade, but the Left argues that the PC threat is a fraud, trumped up in order to stamp out quite reasonable changes in language and social behavior long needed in Western nations to protect marginal groups along race, class, and gender lines. Feminists, especially, view the anti-PC position as a subterfuge by which to turn back the reform clock; however, some feminists, such as a writer Susan Mitchell, who was then creeping to the right, perceived the PC tendency as a threat to free speech:

Fortunately, we were not settled by Puritan Fathers or Mothers of America. It is ironic that those who teach about the evils of US imperialism are often the first to import its ideological baggage and thus give such satisfaction to their enemies. Surely, the role of the university is to encourage . . . rational discourse and . . . not language that encourages . . . injustice and discrimination.[21]

The PC debate was to play a part in the 1996 defeat of the Labour government, and both the incoming Coalition government and the Pauline Hanson One Nation party were to claim continually that they had extinguished its influence. PC was more consequential in Australia than in the United States because the even newer, much smaller, even thinner, and certainly less confident nature of Australian culture makes it vulnerable to fashionable trends, even bizarre ones, that a more established and confident national intelligentsia would easily resist and dismiss with the contempt it deserves. This probably accounts for the virulence of such shallow anti-American concoctions as postcolonial, postmodern, and deconstuctionist theories among the postsocialist but PC Left in Australia and their belated discovery of passé gurus like Michel Foucault.

Health care in America has undergone a similar transformation in Australian eyes since World War II. In the past, the U.S. system was admired for its training, skill, and general efficiency. In the 1990s this picture has shifted sharply as the American health system is afflicted with massive costs and is now one of the most inefficient among the OECD nations. The U.S. system costs up to 15 percent of the GDP, leaves many Americans without insurance cover, and fails to produce a better health regime or life expectancy. The scheme introduced by the Australian Labour government, Medicare, covers everyone, costs about 8 percent of the GDP, and does the same job. Americans now come to Australia to examine the Australian health system, and the general perception by the Australian public is that the American model is more typical of what not to do in health care. This was illustrated in an unprecedented move by hundreds of Australian doctors who went public in an Australian Medical Association–organized nationally circulated advertisement against contracts between doctors and the private Health Funds, which warned in *The Australian* of the dire consequences "of U.S.-style managed health care," which would make Australians "the next set of victims" of U.S. health policies.[22]

The perception of inadequacies in U.S. health care rests largely in the wide gaps along class and racial lines and the belief that American medicine is too strongly attached to "feel-good" practices and the cash nexus. Many Australian health critics point to the spread of psychoactive drugs like Prozac in America as evidence of a health system overprescribing quick solutions to complex socio-medical problems and of the influence of multinational drug companies. Increasingly, therefore, the health economists and social psychologists in Australia seek to avoid the importation of U.S. solutions to problems in the area of health care, based upon the belief that the U.S. system, which spends some 15 percent of its GDP on health—one of the highest in the OECD—is neither efficient nor equitable.[23]

In many other areas of social policy Australians will select policies that will be praised or damned by invoking Australian anti-Americanism for or against it. In the mid-1990s, hyperconservatives imported numerous policies in the law-and-order area, such as the privatization of prisons and, in Western Australia, military-style boot camps for young offenders. Again, these changes are opposed by the Left as ineffectual but also as imports from America that will produce greater social friction, wider gaps between rich and poor, and a sullen underclass: that is, the U.S. social model is rejected as an ideal for Australian society by social democrats.

Philip Adams, long a left–libertarian critic of America, warns Australians vigorously against America's growing authoritarian policies exemplified in the "three strikes you're out" legislation sweeping America. A conviction for three felonies would bring an automatic life sentence in many states, and this was a feature of Clinton's 1994 Crime Bill. Adams, under the headline "Brain Cells Not Jail Cells, Bill," warns that "Australians have a dreadful habit of looking to the United States for political and cultural inspiration and . . . American presidents have an awful habit of changing the course of Australian history . . . we should be alerted to these grim developments." These sentiments are also echoed by criminologists and radio presenters in recent comments on numerous shootings by Victorian police, with statements like "we don't need trigger-happy police, like in America," "these guys are watching too many TV cop programs from America," and "we don't want our streets to be like America." Tom Uren, the former Whitlam government left-wing minister, sees a similar threat to egalitarian and democratic Australia in American-style enclave high-security housing, which, he maintains, would "create an American underclass and an unwanted Americanization of Australia." John Howard, reelected leader of the Liberal Party in 1995 and prime minister after March 1996, voiced similar fears of televising criminal trials, as in the O. J. Simpson trial in Los Angeles, and of U.S.-style gun proliferation. America is, therefore, perceived as the source of hyperconservative experimentation about which Australians should be gravely skeptical.[24]

In the aftermath of the massacre of 35 people by a lone gunman in Port Arthur, Tasmania, on 28 April 1996, there was an outpouring of vitriol and paranoia against the new Howard government's tighter gun laws, passed *after* the massacre, from pro-gun extremists who argued that a homosexual, urban, one-world plot was being foisted on freedom-loving, God-fearing, gun-owning, true-blue Aussies. The prime minister responded that "it was essential Australia did not make the same mistakes as the United States, where gun ownership was out of control. I would hate to contemplate the future of this country if we went willy-nilly down the American path when it came to gun violence." The polls showed between 80 and 90 percent in favor of the government's new gun laws, and Howard took full advantage of the overwhelming sentiment in Australia against an American model of gun ownership and the obsession with the "right to bear arms," which is based upon Article II of the U.S. Constitution.[25]

Philip Adams took this argument for rejection of American models probably further than any other Australian critic of the United States. He views America as an essentially "unhinged" society: "Americans are the most unstoppable, over-the-toppable, energetic, creative, vibrant, vulgar and friendliest of people. They are also very, very, very violent. And the sooner they're all on Prozac the better."

He views with alarm the deterioration in the American social order and sees it descending into reactionary chaos: "Yet again the United States is going backwards. Just as it's backing back into the ghettos, backing back into discredited politics of prohibition, backing back into Scopes-style trials that attempt to condemn the straight-forward teaching of biology." Since the Republican sweep in 1994 mid-term elections, Adams' apocalyptic warnings have taken a new urgency:

The dawning realization among sane Americans that the Republicans have sold their soul to the likes of Ollie North and the rabid Right [should be noted. Australians are] so very, very lucky to be living in Australia where the faithful might sing *Onward Christian Soldiers*, but don't tote guns.

Adams believes 1990s America to be beyond redemption and totally despairs at the thought that Australia has already been overwhelmed by U.S. cultural imperialism: "But [American] culture is now in every nook and cranny in the synopses between every neuron in every Australian mind. What worries me even more than the Empire State building in the back yard . . . is that so few seem to care."

These attacks prompted an insulted American in Adelaide to question the validity of these "ethnic" attacks in a letter to the editor:

When he says "Americans are . . . too rich, too religious, too self-confident . . . too violent," he is talking about me, my family, my friends and role models. If one were to substitute another nation or ethnic group for "Americans" in that statement, Adams would be labeled a bigot or racist at best.

Can one prevent anti-Americanism in general from attaching itself to individual migrant Americans, asks this letter writer in fear of increasing opprobrium associated with her nationality in Australia.[26]

Anti-Americanism, therefore, takes a wide variety of forms in most areas of Australian culture. It is part of the search for an Australian identity and resistance to transnational American cultural forms. It says to the migrant American "Australia for the Australians" and places substantial pressure on the American to keep his/her head down. As a letter to the *Advertiser* puts it:

Are we now an American State?

Bleary-eyed, I stumbled out of bed on a Saturday morning, flicked on the TV and was assaulted by a barrage of commercials coaxing teenagers to buy Cokes and Big Macs, and to hang out in Nike street gear. I was as much disgusted by the cunning marketing strategies of the multinationals as the blatant Americanism that is forced on to our children. Are we now a State of America?

It would be nice to hear an Australian accent on an advertisement directed at teenagers now and again. Not only are these advertisements aggressive but they are depicted in ghetto-style locations where life probably is very short and they indeed play particularly hard.

As a person involved in the physical education of children, I see the influence of the "life's short, play hard, winning is the only option" type commercials. Our children are being conditioned to be loud, brash, flamboyant and obnoxious in victory. "In your face, Dude." The victors of such simple games as relays celebrate by goading the losers, who, as the advertisements tell them, feel like nobodies. Every day I try unsuccessfully to get children to understand that there is no success without failure.

Many Americans have only vaguely heard of Australia, yet we all sit around at night watching hours of *The Brady Bunch* reruns and such tripe in order to live and act like Americans.

The French have been chastised for acting against the invasion of English into their language. Perhaps that is better than happily sitting back while another country's culture completely engulfs our own.

The response to this on the part of at least a large minority of American migrants has, of course, two dimensions to it: criticism of Australia and perceptions of discrimination. For the most part, these responses are accepted by the

Australian public, although not without some resistance, particularly among the left-inclined intelligentsia. For the individual American this often has the paradoxical impact that, while many Australians will be very familiar with and readily consume U.S. culture, politics, and sport, they also resent Americans.

NOTES

1. Max Harris, *The Angry Eye* (Sydney, 1973), pp. 68–69.
2. ABC TV Evening News, Adelaide, 2 March 1993.
3. For general histories of Yiddish, see Sol Steinmetz, *Yiddish and English* (University, AL, 1986), on the U.S., and Benjamin Harshav, *The Meaning of Yiddish* (Berkeley, CA, 1990), on its future as a language; *The Australian*, 2 July 1994, p. 4; see also Bryson's book *Made in America* (New York, 1994).
4. *The Australian*, 11 March 1995, p. 14; 5AN, ABC Radio 6 March 1995.
5. McKenzie Wark, *Homosexual Oppression and Liberation* (New York, 1993).
6. Noel McLachlan, *Creating a Nation* (Melbourne, 1994).
7. *The Australian*, 10 March 1993, p. 8; *The Australian,* 12 February 1994, p. 5; *The Australian* 26 January 1994, p. 24.
8. *The Advertiser*, 4 November 1993, p. 18.
9. "AM," ABC Radio, 11 June 1994; "7.30 Report," ABC TV, 3 June 1994; *On Dit*, 30 May 1994, p. 7; David Malouf is also an ardent supporter of Australian Studies in the education system to raise national consciousness, *The Australian,* 17 September 1994, p. 29; 5AN, ABC Radio, 13 March 1995; David Malouf, *Remembering Babylon* (Sydney, 1993); Peter Carey, *The Unusual Life of Tristram Smith* (St. Lucia, 1994).
10. For discussion of these issues, see Bell and Bell, *Implicated*, pp. 168 ff.
11. *The Adelaide Review* (October 1993), p. 10 (November 1993), p. 24; "Attitude" program, ABC TV, 7 March 1993; Steven Alomes and Catherine Jones, *Australian Nationalism* (North Ryde, 1991); *The Australian*, 20 August 1994, p. 7.
12. For a review and discussion, see *Australian*, 10 April 1993, p. 1. The coming of the Nickelodeon Pay-TV children's channel to Australia has sparked a sharp debate in the mid-1990s over American cultural imperialism. In a television special on the topic, Paul Keating (prime minister, December 1991–March 1996) expressed his fear that Australia was being swamped by "American bilge"; Barbara Biggins, Australian children's television expert, warned that "Australian children will not dream Australian dreams but American nightmares"; Stuart Cunningham and Toby Miller, in *Contemporary Australian Television* (1995), described Australia inundated by U.S. culture: "Sunday Program," Ch. 9, 19 February 1995; "A Current Affair," Ch. 9, 22 February 1995; *Campus Review,* 28 February 1995, p. 11.
13. See the rather wild Marxist account in Humphrey McQueen, *Australia's Media Monopolies* (Camberwell, Victoria, 1977).
14. See William Shawcross, *Rupert Murdoch: Ringmaster of the Information Circus* (London, 1993); Paul Barry, *The Rise and Rise of Kerry Packer* (Sydney, 1993).
15. Gridiron is played at a club level but has hopes for a national competition: "7.30 Report," ABC TV, 14 April 1994; *NBL Official Guide, 1992* (Melbourne, 1992); private correspondence, ABL, 25 May 1992; *The Australian*, 17 February 1995, p. 23; Adelaide *Sunday Mail*, 31 December 1995, pp. 72–73. Australian pitcher Graham Lloyd was a key man in the New York Yankees' victory in the World Series in 1996; he was the first Australian to play in an American World Series: ABC TV, 27 November 1996.
16. "James Leslie Darcy," *ADB,* pp. 206–207; Michael Wilkinson, *The Phar Lap Story* (Sydney, 1983); *The Australian* throughout June 1991 and January 1997; ABC TV News,

Adelaide, 23 April 1994; ABC Radio News, 13 August 1995; ABC TV, 18 August 1995. A new biography about Les Darcy by Ruth Park and Rafe Champion, *Home Before Dark* (Ringwood, 1995), has been given national attention: see *The Australian Magazine*, 2 October 1995, pp. 13–19.

17. *The Adelaide Review* (December 1992), p. 24; *The Advertiser*, 4 February 1993, pp. 9–10, "7.30 Report," ABC TV, 11 April 1994.

18. Evening News, Adelaide Channel 10, 9 May 1994; "World Today," ABC Radio, 14 June 1994.

19. Paul Gross and Norman Levitt, *Higher Superstition: The Academic Left and Its Quarrels With Science* (Baltimore, MD, 1994).

20. For example, see *The Australian*, 27 April 1994, p. 27, and for America, see Dinesh D'Souza, *Illiberal Education* (New York, 1991). For a conservative view of the debate, see *The Australian*, 6 January 1996, p. 21.

21. *The Australian*, 1 June 1994, pp. 22–23. For a feminist attack on the conservative use of PC, see Carol Bacchi, "Consent or Coercion," *The Australian Universities' Review*, 37 (1994), pp. 55-61, especially p. 58; *The Australian*, 15 April 1995, p. 15. See also John K. Wilson, *The Myth of Political Correctness* (Durham, 1996), and the robust debate in America with Alan Bloom, *The Closing of the American Mind* (New York, 1987), and the response with Lawrence Levine, *The Opening of the American Mind* (Boston, MA, 1996).

22. *The Australian*, 15 January 1996, p. 7.

23. "Sunday" program, Channel 9, 22 May 1994; for detailed discussion of these views, see George Palmer and Stephanie Short, *Public Policy: An Australian Analysis* (Melbourne, 1989). Recent innovations attracting attention in Australia include HMOs (Health Maintenance Organizations), the Oregon (State) Plan, and case mixing, all of which have been adapted, in part or whole, by some Australian states and governments.

24. The Western Australian government has announced plans for American-style boot camps for young offenders, "AM," ABC Radio, 3 May 1994; *The Australian*, 11 June 1994, p. 2. Some reports have already indicated failures of the boot camp programs in America: *The Australian*, 13 June 1994, p. 7; 5AN, ABC Radio, 19 May 1994; "Sunday" program, Channel 9, 3 July 1994. For a rejection of American models in urban development, see Paul Rees in *The Australian*, 26 December 1994, p. 9; "Sunday" Program, Channel 9, 4 June 1995. Cheryl Kernot, then leader of the Australian Democrats, rejected American-style policies on political pork-barreling, user-pays education, and, along with ACTU president, Jenny George, industrial relations policies: "AM," ABC Radio, 16 September 1996.

25. *The Advertiser*, 7 May 1996, p. 1; *The Australian*, 10–17 May 1996, *passim*.

26. *The Australian*, 6 August 1994, p. 2; 15 August 1994, p. 8; 26 November 1994, p. 2; 10 September 1994, p. 2; 9 September 1995, p. 2. Adams almost makes his regular column in *The Weekend Australian*—itself, of course, American-owned—a forum for anti-American hysteria. He confesses his fear of U.S. language, drugs, drug laws, basketball, Reaganomics, election campaign tactics, movies, Christian fundamentalism, fast food, and, on his "Late Night Live" radio show, even acknowledges his hatred for "American synthesized voices on elevators," *The Australian*, 8 April 1995, p. 1 and "Late Night Live," ABC Radio, 22 March 1995. Adams took his crusade to television in 1995 in a panel discussion in which he exchanged insults on American cultural imperialism with Gerald Stone, the newly appointed editor of *The Bulletin* and American-born: SBS TV, 3 December 1995. In May, 1996, Adams was so depressed by the March, 1996, Coalition victory in the Federal election, he devoted his entire—very long—column to a desperate plea for Australians to reject American models, *The Australian*, 25 May 1996, p. 2.

9

The Australia Americans Don't Like

Americans exposed to anti-Americanism in other countries unsurprisingly tend to reciprocate. In the case of Australia, they are dealing with a friendly country with attributes similar to their own, whose citizens tend to excite a combination of bewilderment and reflexive, emotive criticism.

AMERICAN ANTI-AUSTRALIANISM

American hostility to Australia has no global or historical dimension to it, as anti-Americanism does; it is simply a reflection of the experience of American migrants living within Australia; they bring with them generally positive conceptions and images of Australia or none at all, and consequently the anti-Australian observations emerge out of direct contact with Australians and Australian institutions.

Table 9.1 is an extrapolation of general views held by American migrants (as shown in Table 6.3), with a focus on specific objections to Australian society. These criticisms fall into two general categories: (1) general faults perceived in Australian culture, especially where they are perceived to be "inferior" to the United States; (2) criticisms that can be arranged within an ideological framework, as used in Tables 6.3 and 9.1. This is intended to be an explanatory device and is by no means a definitive approach to the social and political attitudes among the one-quarter of migrants who consider themselves dissatisfied (Table 7.1) and/or discriminated against (Table 7.2).

TABLE 9.1:   Common Anti-Australian Stereotypical Language Used by
American Migrants

Ideology	Descriptive terms/phrases
Social democrat	racist, class-ridden, resistant to change, inefficient, prickly, Royalist, xenophobic
Conservative	socialistic, lazy, state schools poor, prickly, Royalist, anti-American
Hyperconservative	not enough freedom for gun ownership, pornography freely available, union-dominated, passive, lazy, poor schools, prickly, Royalist, anti-American

WHAT YANKS DISLIKE ABOUT AUSTRALIA: GOVERNMENT, CLASS, RACE, EDUCATION, AND NATIONAL CHARACTER

The anecdotal data from the 1993 sample provide criticisms of Australian society that range from the thoughtful and ideologically structured to the trivial and even bizarre. Many respondents, especially academics, have thought long and hard about the virtues and shortcomings of Australian society. Others, such as one Adelaide respondent, who is most exercised about the lack of varieties of chili sauce available at Woolworth's (2), compared to the cornucopia of chili sauces (10) in the supermarket in her home town, Tucson, Arizona (to which she is soon to return), are trivial in the extreme.[1] The dislikes and faults cited by the respondents represent, therefore, the entire spectrum of sophistication, bias, ideological orientation, educational level, and class- and gender-based views that we can elicit from a cross-section of the American community in Australia.

The American migrant arrives with a strong, or even obsessive, antistate-intervention historical tradition, which derives initially from the character of the American achievement of independence and has been sustained by two centuries of the application of eighteenth-century ideas about liberty and progress. American "rugged individualism" values represent a transcendent distrust of central government and a persistent lumping together of social democratic ideas with communism or a generalized threat to bourgeois capitalist society. In the eyes of most American migrants, Australia is too far along the spectrum toward central-ized government and intrusion into the private (capitalist) life of the individual. This has remained true even after a decade of what appeared to many Austral-ians to be furious deregulation.

One respondent finds this disappointing, for "this is a very over-regulated and intrusive society—which surprised me [because] I love the people and environ-ment." Another finds that this "weakens" the character of the people: "I also continue to have difficulty with the handout mentality here and general lack of initiative." A recent migrant believed migration would help him escape "social-istic" America but finds "Australia is a wonderful place, too bad that socialism is destroying it, but then that is what is happening in America. Even though it is an unworkable system, people refuse to learn from history. It's a great means of destroying wealth, creativity, productivity and individual freedom." A business-man in the agricultural sector believes "socialistic" values to be the underlying fault with Australian society:

Biggest mistake I ever made. But I am in love with my land I don't give a rat's ass about Australia still love the USA. Ethos/pathos differential still enormous and got a hell of a spot on the planet earth. [. . .] is to Australia what California is to America in many respects. Many creative delightful people down here for a small population. I have no friends but many acquaintances. Motto is "I'm just visiting for 50 years, if I like it I'll stick around." Biggest peeve Aussie government destroying the work ethic. I'm a basic work rule but my motivation here is socialistically being withered.

They've discovered best to not kick my head cause I kick back usually much harder. The insatiable taxual appetite and the idiot tall poppy syndrome are what I loathe most. I'm a dinkum American entrepreneur who can't wait for this country to get their micro-economic act together. They are 25 years or so behind the USA in that respect and 5–7 years behind N.Z. who are more dynamic than their Aussie brethren. What hope for this country, if not—I like bananas.[2]

Many migrants blame big government and big unions for keeping Australia "backward" and "not internationally competitive." The quality of political life is frequently attacked for its "emptiness" and "low quality of federal pollies" who preside over the intrusive Canberra political world. Some feel bitter and resent-ful at the incapacity of politicians to "put things right" and despair for the future of their families: "none of them are worth a f___ for directing society to the 21st century."[3]

Most American migrants had come to Australia to take up or seek employment (as shown in Tables 6.1 and 6.2). They view themselves as independent folk not requiring "handouts" from government. Of those in the 1993 sample, 39 percent received some kind of financial assistance to migrate, whereas 61 percent did not: those replying in the negative were often quite proud of their self-sufficiency, especially the conservative respondents. Not surprisingly, disappointments in employment and low income prospects are two particular areas that cause an-tagonism toward Australia—especially for those American migrants attempting to be free and proud capitalists, independent of the public sector.

One Sydney academic complains that he "feels left behind by my peers financially as academic salaries are so low, especially in Sydney." Another feels that "the standard of living and quality of life are certainly in question due to political, economic and environmental misdirections." A teacher enjoys "coastal lifestyle" but "we aren't well off financially and can't see we will improve in the future." One migrant feels secure, but "economically we have suffered" compared to their previous American standard of living. A comprehensive and thoughtful summary of how financial and professional expectations must be lowered in Australia is provided by an academic:

For the most part I am very satisfied with my life in Australia. I have had an opportunity to pioneer the development of my chosen profession here and have gained much from the work. I miss the involvement in the arts at the level I enjoyed it in the States. There, more population and saturation of the arts in the New York area offered a sharper cutting edge to my arts life. My discipline takes the developmental path of the individual as the grist for the artistic mill. I found the US more accepting and wanting for this type of art. Here art takes a backseat to entertainment, and student work, regardless of the level, is automatically judged as inferior to "professional" work in the field. I most often feel I am creating my art work in a vacuum and sometimes think I should return to the States and re-involve myself there.

When I migrated I hadn't realized that I would be committing professional suicide in the USA as far as remaining involved in the scene there. Eleven years later I am more fully aware of this.

I also know I never feel any of the above consistently enough to be moved to do anything permanent about changing my life as it is now. The family aspects and the freedom to develop one's ideas, the climate—all of these balance the professional imbalance.[4]

In some areas American migrants, regardless of ideological position, share a generalized criticism of Australia. One of these is the perceived "feudal" aspect of Australian society associated with the constitutional monarchy and a class system tied to the large private (compared to America) school sector. Approximately 25 percent of Australian students are in the private sector, much higher than the comparable 10–12 percent in the United States. These views, of course, reflect American historical and social traditions with a bias against monarchy and a 200-year-old commitment to public (state) education. A hostility toward the Queen is the reason often given for not becoming naturalized Australians—a subject considered in greater detail below—and this opposition to "feudal" Australia in general contributes to American migrants' belief that they are maintaining their tribal American value of egalitarianism.

One migrant expresses indignation at the monarchy: "Royalist influence not to my liking . . . this sort of thing galls me!" A Canberra migrant enjoys the lifestyle in the ACT but finds "a very *divided* community, i.e. public and private schools based more on class than in America." Another believes Australia to be egalitarian except "class divisions are social. In America it is mostly financial but [in Australia] it is the school you go to." And one respondent summarizes the class divisions as being central to problems in Australia: "still find combination of 'old school tie' and 'working class' polarization difficult at times and repression of U.S. brand of enthusiasm a nuisance due to Australian cringe at strongly 'Yank' ethnic behavior."[5]

Racism in Australia is perceived to be a problem by many American migrants, but the most frequent criticism of Australia about racism comes from black

American migrants, who are concentrated occupationally in sports and entertainment and constitute a visible element in the migrant American community. Their experiences in Australia are now a substantial subsection of the American migrant story and are dealt with fully in a section below on class, gender, and race. In addition to racism against black Americans, there were complaints from migrants who were startled "to find Australia was such a racist country." Another was "teased at school for being part-Asian," and a Queensland migrant felt alienated first because "I was Jewish" and later "because I became a Sikh." The wife of one basketball player was "discriminated against because they thought I was an Aborigine, but when they realized I was American I was treated better."[6]

One institution with which almost all American migrants have contact is education. Many social democratic migrants express strong support for Australian schools, especially the state system, but conservative migrants in Australia (as they do in America) express strong hostility to Australian state schools. The state sector is perceived by one respondent to "be markedly inferior" and linked to "lack of freedom to speak as in America." One parent worries about their children failing to develop in the state schools, for "Australia lacks the stimulation and involvement of life in the U.S." and "the schools do not make up for it." Tertiary state education is often lumped together with the secondary system: "tertiary education declining like the high schools" was one comment; and one academic resented "the suggestion that U.S. Ph.D.s [are] inferior to those generated in any Commonwealth countries especially when Australian universities are often mediocre."[7] It should be said that most U.S. Ph.D. programs involve a reading course of two years, followed by a dissertation of similar size to that which alone is the requirement in Australian universities, and academic tenure requirements in America are notoriously more difficult than in Australia.

As outlined in Table 9.1, these critiques can be viewed as a general stereotypical image of Australia by those holding negative judgments. The terms most often used in this stereotypical view by a minority of American migrants—although some of these traits would be held by a majority based upon anecdotal data—would be that Australians are xenophobic, prickly, jealous of success, backward, provincial, and lazy, and that the nation, as a whole, is declining. One can, of course, interpret these data in many ways. First, it may be an accurate depiction of some aspects of Australian national character, or at least the views of it held by American migrants. Second, it may be the way Australians behave when confronted by xenophobic, provincial, hyperconservative, backward behavior and comments by American migrants. Finally, it may be a reflection of both the boorish attitudes of Americans and the boorish attitudes of Australians toward their new migrant brothers and sisters—a kind of stereotypical symmetry by people with a common cultural background.

However one ultimately views the American migrant critique of Australia, some themes have dominated in the period since World War II and, indeed, since the nineteenth century: Australians are perceived to be less energetic than Americans and especially sensitive to criticism ("prickly"). The Australian industrial structure is considered overly dominated by "Big Unions and Big Government" and "something must be done" to push this "backward" nation into the twenty-first century. These stereotypical analyses form the core around which the dissatisfied American migrant formulates his/her views; in addition, the complaint is that Australia does not give the migrant from North America "a fair go," and to that complaint we will now turn.

WHY SOME YANKS DO NOT FEEL THEY GET "A FAIR GO"

No problems or objections to Australia were mentioned more often, or with a greater depth of emotion, than the feeling of being alien, of not belonging, of "otherness"—to use the contemporary postmodernist jargon. It seems that no matter what general situation one is in, for an American migrant Australia is not home. The smells, sights, and tribal attachments of one's country of origin are never replicated in the country of migration, and scores of interactions each day impress the fact on one's brain that one is in an alien land. The constellation of emotions and the level of emotional investment that one has in a country of origin is never quite reproduced abroad. To be discriminated, against, therefore, always comes on top of a permanent sensation—for some at quite a low level, for others a source of great *angst*—that "this is not my country, and I don't ever feel I will belong." For most American migrants the inability to blend into the general population, as one could in America, was mentioned as a continuous nuisance or, in a few cases, source of considerable pain and anxiety and even despair.

For the majority of migrants (Table 6.1), discrimination is perceived or judged to be trivial—the odd Yank joke, the jibe at America, the surprise at the accent, the lack of knowledge about cricket—that is, nothing to cause pain or anxiety. But a minority of about one-fourth of the 1993 sample had experienced substantial levels of discrimination (medium to high) involving major problems of alienation, rejection, harassment, truncated employment advancement, inhibition of political careers, or some other major area of perceived discrimination based upon ethnicity.

The American migrant raises interesting questions of discrimination in the Australian community. He/she is not poor, nor non-Caucasian (on the whole), poorly educated, or physically differentiated by some obvious characteristic. But, of course, the accent is unmistakable: with the possible exception of Canadians, no one else speaks like a Yank. In the social environment, therefore, the ethnic differentiation is easy to make, and few Americans are ever quite free of the perception by Australians that this chap/woman is not "one of us." How is that crucial characteristic of spoken English perceived by Americans to determine their careers and social adaptation to Australia, when coupled with the general recognition of their U.S. nationality?

The most generally perceived form of discrimination respondents felt was a pervasive sense of not belonging. Many respondents believe that the Australian personality and temperament excludes Americans, with their peculiar forms of behavior and enthusiasms. One respondent found the cross-cultural experience illuminating but disheartening: "I realize how important early culture, morals, belief systems, etc. are, and my personality doesn't fit here." Another found the American character not suited to Australia, in which he "doesn't see much of a national spirit relative to the U.S. I'm not sure many people give a damn about what happens to their country. Apathy seems to be the rule." A migrant from the South perceived an ironic and double sense of alienation: "Being a Southerner I find being called a 'Yank' extremely offensive." Discrimination perceived toward American migrants in the most pervasive form, therefore, was not direct or overt, but simply the sense of "otherness."[8]

A crucial area of discrimination of a substantive nature, however, is much more direct and affects the most sensitive dimension of life for an American who is primarily in Australia for employment: the securing of a job, promotion, and mobility in the workplace. Like most migrant groups, Americans have some difficulties with securing employment and with the recognition of qualifications brought with them from American institutions of training and/or education. Several respondents found it especially difficult to find a job in nursing. One complained: "the Australians were threatened by my level of education and experience as a nurse and I couldn't get the parity I had in America"; another found "the hierarchy of the [named] hospital seemed biased against American qualifications." Several skilled professionals reported problems with having their experience recognized: "my architecture license was not recognized," and "couldn't get proper recognition for my skills and training in ceramics." Often respondents reported strong suspicions that they were denied a job because they were American, but they lacked any empirical evidence upon which they could make a legal or industrial claim.[9]

Most American migrants do, however, secure employment, and as a group they have lower unemployment rates than Australians as a whole; indeed, in the case of most academics and other professionals, they have secured their employment before arrival. Respondents also believed, however that they were denied advancement and promotion based upon ethnicity once they were gainfully employed.[10] Some academics found that grants were not available to non-Australian citizens; another academic had a growing fear "that promotion would be delayed because I was American." A respondent in museum management felt "that management positions in my area would always go to British and Australian graduates." A nurse was told: "you won't get promoted because so-and-so doesn't like Americans," and two respondents believed that "being non-Australian would inhibit promotion to higher levels" and that "search committees always favor Aussies over Yanks."[11]

These patterns of discrimination persisted in what respondents felt was the "job culture"—that is, a general atmosphere in which a multiplicity of messages indicated that Americans would not get ahead. Their complaints were multifarious and ranged in the academic world from "a British bias against U.S. social science," to a general "hostility at the University of Sydney toward Yanks," ethnocentrism against "imported ideas," and "Americans always having to defend their ideas and are wary to suggest anything. Coworkers resent being told anything by an American." A publisher in Sydney found that she did everything "wrong for I was punctual, hard-working, outspoken, female and all these traits were resented by my colleagues." One migrant believes it is "difficult to voice opinions on issues because I am an outsider and from the 'dominant' culture." A Sydney academic found everyone cordial, but "at staff meetings I had a feeling I was tolerated but my views were ignored whether on departmental or theoretical questions."[12]

An American accent was blamed by many respondents for overt discrimination. The evidence in this area is compelling and raises the most serious legal questions of ethnic bias and equal opportunity. One academic reported that a student review published the comment that: "'X'—why an American? Couldn't she at least put on an Australian accent and pronounce 'Premier' properly?"; another comment went further and questioned why 'X' was employed at all: "'X,' an American teaching Australian legal systems?!!" Accent prevented several respondents from securing employment on air in radio and television: "my accent from dominant culture prohibits me from more active radio work," and another found "my accent denied possibility of work on radio or TV." A teacher was "prevented from teaching Australian history because I had an American accent" and failed as "a guide at the War Memorial because of Americanisms." One migrant, in a position in which he has to communicate to audiences about Australian sport, confesses to continuous embarrassment about his accent: "I don't think even elocution lessons will help me." In a "Current Affairs" (Channel 9) program, an American psychologist claims she was rejected as a compère for a sex education series on the grounds of her accent. A final respondent found the use of language in general preventing her from effectively communicating to Australians:

The hardest part is the subtlety of language. My field is one where I used to talk a lot. All that is out the window and I'm a babe asking basic questions about products, companies and technology. Words that look the same have different meanings. Items have new names and all names are misunderstood. I assumed English is English but it's not. A good education I suppose, but hard to get used to.[13]

The most comprehensive discussion of this type of discrimination was published in the *Canberra Times* by an American migrant, Joyce Sanders. The material is so compelling and detailed that it is reproduced in full:

A Victim of the Hidden Discrimination:
Joyce Sanders Asks Why She Is Finding It So Hard to Get a Job

It is accepted that discrimination in recruitment will not take place in the job marketplace of 1992.

Even if there were not anti-discrimination acts at the federal level as well as supplementary state and ACT laws, it is passé to be racist and sexist. Our social mores have finally embraced the granting of equal rights to those who don't look or speak like us or think the earth was created by the same god or gods. Job advertising included "We are an equal opportunity employer" even before the legislation came into force.

When a Vietnamese walks in for a job interview, an employer might engage in some unspoken positive discrimination as he or she rolls over in his/her mind that this person of Asian descent uses better English than the previous Anglo-Australian applicant and the employer toys with the thought that Asian immigrants have a reputation for more diligent and stable work habits.

When considering the Italian or eastern European applicant, the employer may silently consider how good it may look for his or her staff to appear multicultural, and the employee's name, whether it be Shevchenko, Stavropoulos or Pellegrino, will reflect on him or her as a generous, enlightened and intelligent employer.

There is, of course, a foremost consideration of whether the applicant can do the job well. But once that is settled, the employer uses many unspoken reasons for tipping the balance in favor of the applicant of migrant origin or descent, whereas in the past, the opposite would have applied.

After all, there are deeply embedded sympathies for those who were victims of the world's man-made and natural calamities. To give a job in some way helps to alleviate the guilt or involvement in past wars or for not providing more financial aid to fleeing dislocated peoples the world over. However much one may want overall immigration reduced to maintain the presently perceived "lucky country" lifestyle, this in no way prevents one's giving every consideration to the migrants who are already here.

That is, except for those of one particular national origin. For one special group of migrants, none of the equal opportunity legislation applies. No-one offers this group sympathy in searching for a better life in Australia. No-one concedes that they even have the right to do so. No-one thinks for a moment that it might be racist to suggest that this group return home.

They are never included in the idea of the multicultural Australia. Their dances and songs are never seen in the festivals of multiculturalism celebrated on Australia Day. To deny them jobs in Australia might even be seen in a humorous light.

You won't have guessed the name of the national group of whom I speak. You will laugh with disbelief when I tell you. But I am prepared for that.

As an American—that is, a United States—migrant I am accustomed to having racial (the term is defined legislatively to include national origin) slurs directed at me in social gatherings by middle-class, young Australians who would never dream of making such derogatory comments to the face of a Vietnamese or Italian. I take it as a matter of course that I will be denied jobs because of a faint trace of accent by intelligent, enlightened Australian employers who would be horrified of denying an Asian immigrant a job on the basis of accent.

You still don't believe me. I am not to be taken seriously.

That of course is exactly the problem. The discrimination that a US immigrant faces in Australia (unless applying for a job as blues singer or basketball player) is totally unacknowledged. It is true that thousands of Americans do live and work in Australia (28,000 as of January 1992), but unlike other immigrants, they have for the most part been recruited to fill particularly specialized positions (as the Anthony Hopkins character in the movie *Spotswood*).

Within these positions, the need for their expertise forms the basis of their acceptance in the workplace and in the broader community. But once they leave the recruited position and attempt to move into the general Australian workplace, unlike other migrants who can move freely between positions even granting that the competition is fierce, the American meets a wall of resentment and discrimination.

To the Australian employer, my accent produces no feeling of sympathy as for those who have escaped lives of poverty, war and deprivation in Turkey or Yugoslavia—the US has no official refugee fleeing its McDonald's-laden shores. Escaping crime and freeways hardly has the same urgency about it. At best employers ask wouldn't I rather live in the US with its lower taxes and higher salaries. At worst they give me responsibility for the politics of Nixon, Reagan and Bush, blame me for bad sit-coms and the death of Kennedy.

This would all be comical if it didn't mean that I leave yet another job interview with no hope of acceptance. I understand the attitudes of these employers and I understand my continued lack of success, despite maintaining that it is an unfair and ridiculous situation.

The Australian student radicals of the late 60s and early 70s are now the middle-aged employers in government departments and private companies. They rightly hated Americans for the Vietnam War and the diluting of Australian culture with US music, food and customs while hiding their guilt at the complicity of their own country. Although in 1992 they will buy their clothes from US-owned discount stores and celebrate their children's birthdays at McDonald's, they won't broadcast this around the office or if it is mentioned it will be in the tone of "What can you do?" with shrugged shoulders.

Then when I arrive for an interview (just as guilty as they of cultural racism after my mere 20 migrant years of trying to be more Australian than the Australians, reading only Australian novels, seeing only Australian films and planting only Australian plants) they take out all their guilt and hostility on me.

How could an American work in the Australian War Memorial (though some Asian staff would look good for the Japanese tourists)—it might offend someone. An American couldn't work for the Australian Heritage Commission—it's a contradiction, isn't it, to think that someone not born here could value Australia's heritage.

Certainly no job could be had in Parliament House—how could an American be allowed to explain the Australian parliamentary system to touring Australian school children? It would be scandalous. An American in the National Gallery might devalue the history of Australian art.

In fact, the whole idea of a US cog in the wheel of the Australian Public Service might mean that the wheel might turn in an un-Australian direction.

And so the one with the trace of a US accent walks out of another unsuccessful interview for the job for which she was perfectly qualified in every way except for her place of birth, victim of discrimination that officially doesn't exist.

There's seldom much proof other than that in midstream the line of questioning suddenly changes from where the applicant received tertiary qualifications to where the interviewer spent three weeks of his US holiday—at which stage you know you are being viewed again as just an American rather than as an applicant for this job.[14]

Accent is also a key issue in political participation by Americans in public political life. Only two Americans have ever been elected to the Australian Parliament (excluding King O'Malley, as discussed above, who claimed to be Canadian). One is Norm Sanders, who was elected as a Democrat to the Senate from Tasmania in 1985 and who had gained notoriety in the Tasmanian lower house (elected in 1980) for his strong environmental positions. He was an academic in California who had moved to Tasmania in the 1960s. The other is Bob Charles (a respondent), the only American-born member of the present Parliament (1997), who came to Australia as a businessman in 1969, took out citizenship, and entered Parliament in 1990 as the member for La Trobe in Victoria. In 1994 he gained notoriety as a monarchist, even though he is a descendant of a signer of the Declaration of Independence, and because as an outspoken opponent of the then Liberal leader, John Hewson, gave public support to John Howard on an ABC "Four Corners" program.[15] He was often abused across the Chamber for being a Yank—but then abuse of all sorts is common in the Australian Parliament.

Norm Sanders acknowledges the difficulties American-born politicians encounter in Australia: "Americans have to learn that despite the similarities of language and . . . people . . . Australia is a foreign country." Another American political aspirant who ran in Tasmania found the going very difficult: Maureen Maloy found "as soon as I opened my mouth I offended people. It was my American accent. People seemed to think I was Big Brother telling them what to do." Bob Charles does not believe he has experienced problems as an American but recalls that Keith Wright, then an MHR from Queensland, interjected that he should "go back to Yankeeland"—a comment that he eventually withdrew upon the insistence of Prime Minister Paul Keating, who, while no stranger to abuse himself, did apologize for calling a member a "bald eagle." Many respondents felt they were constantly put in their place on political issues and believed this arena was only for Australians: one complained that the U.S. role in Vietnam meant that Americans should have no say in Australian politics; another received "ethnic slurs and threats of violence" if he voiced political views because of the Vietnam opprobrium; one respondent felt alienated from political debate because Australians "seem to blame me personally for Ronald Reagan, George Bush and all American TV shows." The message to many respondents seems clear: politics is for indigenous Australians, and "Yanks need not apply."[16]

In the 1990s, discrimination against Americans, at least for a minority of the 1993 respondents in this study, appears to be common and to manifest itself in many forms. In equal opportunity cases in Australia it has been established that discrimination based upon accent is clearly illegal under the Commonwealth Racial Discrimination Act (1975) and the related State Acts in all mainland states and territories (relevant Acts from 1977 in New South Wales through to the ACT in 1991). In the case *Fares v. Box Hill College of TAFE and Orrs* (1992) it was reaffirmed that general ethnicity (Hungarian in this case) could not be used as a basis for denying someone a job. In the case *Wilhelmina Lyffyt v.*

Capital Television (1993), ACT Commissioner Balkin cogently argued that accent was implicit in any definition of ethnicity, although in this case the complainant had not demonstrated that her Dutch accent was the *causal agent* for her not securing a newsreader's position in the ACT. The legal question of accent as inherent in ethnicity and covered by the Racial Discrimination Act, therefore, is clear and incontrovertible.[17]

No American is known to have taken legal action based upon ethnic discrimination, nor did any respondents in this study indicate that legal action was anticipated. Most who argued that they experienced discrimination believed that evidence was difficult to obtain, and often they acknowledged that discrimination seemed to be vague or unproven feelings in their employment. This is an area that requires further study in these politically correct times, and more research will undoubtedly reveal discrimination along ethnic lines. The consequences of discrimination for American migrants are crucial in determining how they ultimately adapt to Australian society, for in patterns of adaptation one can judge how well the migrant American adjusts to Australian life, whether all Americans are able to cope equally considering class, race, and gender, and what variables are associated with remaining in Australia or returning to America.[18]

Using the accepted methodologies of social science, it would be difficult to demonstrate that Americans as a group are discriminated against, given that their income and educational levels are higher and their unemployment rates lower than those of either the general population or almost any other individual ethnic group. Nonetheless, it is still quite possible that they are unable to achieve what they regard as their legitimate aspirations in Australia because of discrimination, and that their high level of achievement springs from the characteristics Americans already collectively possess before they migrate. It is clearly the case that many Americans believe that they have been discriminated against in Australia and that most of them put this down to their being, as the words were so often put, "from the dominant culture."

NOTES

1. Q: 187.
2. Q: 269, 69, 54; R: 12.
3. Q: 11, 94, 209
4. Q: 56, 184, 229, 278, 47.
5. Q: 150, 207, 242; A: 8.
6. Q: 25, 26, 181, 89.
7. Q: 109, 206, 312.
8. Q: 79, 99, 138.
9. Q: 313, 239, 69.
10. Americans in general have higher rates of employment than do Australians as a whole: Baum, *Exchange of Migrants,* Tables 14, 23. In *ABS,* 1994, the rate of unemployment is in the 2–4 percent range, depending on which age groups one includes—well below that for Australia as a whole in 1994 (10–11 percent). Goldlust, *U.S.-Born, 1991,* pp. 24–25, 42, places U.S.-born unemployment between 7 and 9 percent.

11. Q: 66, 102, 180, 274, 241, 184.

12. Q: 44, 56, 126, 155, 235, 154.

13. This student publication has been cited, but the reference will not be recorded. Q: 103, 225, 291, 239; *The Australian*, 2 July 1994, p. 4; Channel 9, 28 October 1994.

14. *The Canberra Times*, 18 March 1992, p. 9. Reprinted by permission.

15. Aitchison, *Americans*, p. 17; *The Australian*, 15 May 1993, p. 12.

16. Aitchison, Americans, pp. 17, 144; Q: 90, 143, 9; phone interview with Bob Charles, 10 June 1993.

17. CCH, *Australian and New Zealand Equal Opportunity Law and Practice* (1992), pp. 67, 51; for *Wilhelmina Lyffyt v. Capital Television* (1993), typescript, ACT Human Rights Office.

18. An American brought a case in Perth in 1998 to the Western Australia Equal Opportunity Commission on the grounds that being called a "f___ing Yank" was discriminatory, but the Commissioner ruled that this was not illegal and dismissed the complaint. *Advertiser*, 30 May 1998, p. 5.

10

How Do American Migrants Adapt to Australia?

Theoretical models for predicting the adaptation of migrants, like those for other aspects of migration, have attempted to explain complex and variegated patterns of human behavior. What characteristics of individuals and groups make them more or less adaptable in a particular culture? What characteristics of a culture make it easier for migrants to adapt? Areas of investigation since World War II of macro-community characteristics have included the size of the migrant community, the nature of ghettoization, the strength of religious institutions and other facets of civil society, and the volume and distribution of capital in the community. Focusing on smaller groups and/or individuals, studies have examined family structures, the skill levels of migrants, similarities in values allowing rapid educational mobility of individuals, psychosocial characteristics of individuals, and an enormous range of institutional characteristics of the host nation (government policies, racism, levels of toleration) that may inhibit or accelerate assimilation. The volume of literature in this area, therefore, is enormous. Yet a definitive model has not been constructed and indeed may not be feasible in an area involving so many subjective elements of human behavior, volitional variables, and the simple fact that some groups and individuals seem to adapt more easily than others without a clear and empirically identifiable explanation.

Adaptation in modern America and Australia has also been the subject of intense emotive scrutiny. Throughout the periods of mass migration to both nations, the questions of assimilation have generated violent ideological debate. In the 1990s, in Bosnia, Quebec, Georgia, and Rwanda—indeed, around the globe, including Australia—the multicultural question has become increasingly divisive and often threatens the integrity of the nation-state itself. How do migrants adapt? Should they be "forced" to conform? If they do not adapt—for example, by refusing to become citizens—should they be deported? All of these questions are hotly debated in Australia and provide the context in which to examine the adaptation patterns of Americans to Australia.[1]

SOME POLITICAL AND SOCIAL BEHAVIOR

American migrants in Australia do not have "natural" institutional structures in which they can maintain their identity: there is no single religious, social, sporting, cultural, musical, or other organizational structure that fulfills this function, as there is for most migrant groups like Italians, Greeks, Irish or Germans. These other ethnic communities have also become recipients of public funding as part of the multicultural settlement programs of the last two decades. Americans are too heterogeneous and do not have the ethnic cohesiveness of most migrant communities. The largest national organization is the Australian–American Association, founded in 1936, which has branches in all states and territories and was quite helpful to this study. It is primarily organized to promote friendship between the two nations, but it has a very high proportion of Australian members who have worked or traveled in the United States. The organization does provide an opportunity for Americans to celebrate the Fourth of July national day and Thanksgiving, but it is not an organization that provides for mass participation or ethnic cohesion.[2]

Other organizations in which American migrants can maintain ethnic ties include a variety of business groups, like the American Chamber of Commerce in Australia, and international groups such as the Lions, Kiwanis, and Rotarians, although these are not American organizations. Some migrants also belong to university alumni groups, such as the Harvard, Stanford, and Princeton clubs. In the 1993 sample, however, few Americans belonged to these organizations: only 13 percent reported membership in any American organization in Australia, and most of those were in the Australian–American Association. As discussed below, the correlation with membership and class was strong, with the highest rate of membership in the business professional groups, thus reflecting the business orientation of most Australian–American organizations.

One index of assimilation that has been examined in detail is the crossover of political behavior from the migrant culture to the host nation's political culture. B. and A. Finifter, in a study published in 1989 on American migrants in the 1970s, found that Americans transfer political and ideological preferences quite easily into Australian political conditions.[3] This propensity to shift quickly from one culture to another is an indication of the similarities between the cultures and therefore indicate a high level of adaptability.

Consistent with previous work on American migrants, the 1993 sample shows a very high cross-cultural pattern of political adaptation. Table 10.1 shows 78 percent of Republicans voting Liberal and 71 percent of Democrats voting

TABLE 10.1:   Political Preferences of 1993 Sample

American	%	Australian	%
Republican	23	Liberal	26
Democratic	68	Labour	52
Other	9	Democrat	13
		Other	9

Crossover of Political Preferences (%)

American	Liberal	Labour	Democrat	Other
Republican	78	10	6	6
Democratic	12	71	14	3
Other	16	11	20	53

Labour. Some of the Democratic vote has gone to the previously center and now left-wing Democrats. The majority of the sample is clearly on the social democratic end of the political spectrum, with 68 percent Democratic and 52 percent Labour in political preferences. This is also a reflection of the high proportion of academics in the sample (42 percent), who are 82 percent Democratic and 63 percent Labour, and thus the 1993 sample is probably somewhat to the left of the American community as a whole. The general social democratic orientation, however, is again consistent with previous studies.

The relatively easy transference of political preferences to Australian society does not, however, indicate that American migrants are politically active. As discussed above, there is a perceived hostility to American accents in political life, and only two politicians have been elected to the Federal Parliament from the American-born community. This may also indicate a reluctance for Americans to interject themselves into the political arena, where America is perceived, especially by the Left, as the "dominant" culture from which a sociopolitical distance should be maintained, if not actually extended. Although a number of respondents indicated participation in local government, few were involved at any level in state and federal politics.

The similarity in political ideology and cultural values across the two cultures is quite striking (as shown in Tables 6.3 and 9.1). The American social democratic migrant brings to Australian society a tradition going back to the New Deal of Franklin Delano Roosevelt in the 1930s. Two liberal American historians, Alonzo Hamby and William Chafe, have recently entitled their texts on American history *Liberalism and Its Challengers* (1992) and *The Unfinished Journey* (1991), reflecting this strong historicity and sense of continuity of the American Left. The social democratic migrant, therefore, sees the interventionist state in the United States and Australia as a consistent expansion of the promises of the New Deal, as continued in John F. Kennedy's New Frontier and Lyndon B. Johnson's Great Society.

The conservatives and hyperconservatives also appear to fit into the Australian political system on most issues. Although the American conservatives have a stronger republican tradition, on the issues of public sector spending, unions, sexism, race, defense, communism, and multiculturalism there is a general convergence of views. The conservatives of both cultures are split on the basis of differences between free-market, libertarian, economic rationalists and Christian fundamentalist state interventionists, but the nature of this split in the two traditions is roughly around identical issues. The most significant exception to this in the 1990s is the existence of a conservative Australian tradition favoring tariff protection and state economic regulation, as represented by Robert Manne, the editor (until 1997) of *Quadrant,* and stemming from the same liberal tradition as the one that drove the Deakinite Liberals to support an interventionist state in the first decade after federation.

There are other attitudinal correlates with political allegiances revealed in the 1993 empirical data. The social democrats are more likely to be willing to become citizens: 55 percent of social democrats indicated this intention, compared to 44 percent of conservatives and hyperconservatives. This is also illustrated in Tables 6.3 and 9.1, which show more positive views of Australia and less American chauvinism by the left than the right end of the political spectrum. The social democrats are less likely (6 percent) to join an American organization in Australia than are conservatives (26 percent), reflecting the business orientation of conservatives. In the executive occupation category, 36 percent voted Labour while 41 percent voted Liberal—the only category in which a majority were conservatives. The social democrats have a lower proportion of aged: among Labour voters, 5 percent were over 60 years of age, but among the Liberals 23 percent were over 60. The social democrats were strongest in the 1970s during the anti-Vietnam War period of social alienation—69 percent of those who came in this decade voting Labour—and weakest in the 1990s migrant group, of whom 23 percent were Labour voters. The social democrats are more likely to protest over alleged discrimination (43 percent) than are conservatives (29 percent) reflecting the higher expectations about the state in social democratic views, and the "rugged individualism" and antistatism professed by conservatives. The social democrats, on the other hand, are more likely to encourage Australianization in their children (49 percent) than are conservatives (35 percent), who more often perceived their children as maintaining an American identity.

These miscellaneous correlates point to a prototypical American migrant based upon ideology: the social democrats were more favorably disposed toward Australia and toward assimilation, while the conservative migrant tended to be more hostile to Australian culture and more prone to identify with traditional American chauvinistic values. As with social democrats, who are more likely to become citizens in Australia, anti-Communists are more likely to become citizens in the

United States—that is, migrants adapt faster to a host nation perceived to have an ideological structure that is more compatible with their own beliefs.[4] The long-serving Labour government of 1983–96 may have intensified these tendencies in the early- and mid-1990s.

TO BE OR NOT TO BE AN AUSTRALIAN

The most crucial test for an American migrant as a test for adaptation and assimilation is the question of whether to take out Australian citizenship. For an American to give up his/her nationality strikes at the very heart of that person's identity as part of the American tribe. Until the late 1980s, dual citizenship was not possible, but by the 1990s, through administrative changes in the United States, Americans could hold dual nationality. This has undoubtedly increased the number of Americans taking out Australian citizenship. As discussed in Chapter 1, American nationality has an almost fetishistic meaning for Americans as a kind of cement in a multicultural society that has always had enormous centrifugal racial/ethnic forces within it. American migrants (indeed, English-speaking migrants in general, including those from the United Kingdom, New Zealand, Ireland) show the lowest rate of taking up citizenship among the Australian migrant population: in 1991, U.S. migrants were at the bottom of the citizenship-rate table, with only 33 percent as citizens, slightly ahead of New Zealand (27 percent) and Japan (23 percent). In a Bureau of Immigration and Population Research survey in 1994, only 12 percent of American migrants professed an intention to become Australian citizens, and one-half of the U.S.-born surveyed did not intend to become Australian citizens.[5] Citizenship to an American, therefore, is an overarching symbol of national identity in a culture with few national ethnic institutions, and consequently it takes on an almost metaphysical meaning for most Americans. It is also difficult to retrieve, and as long as Australian citizenship conferred few benefits in addition to permanent residence status and involved the relinquishing of American citizenship, few Americans became Australians.

I don't think that I've ever lost my patriotism for the United States. In fact, I'm more patriotic than I think I have been in years. I think you have to get away from something to really evaluate it. And by getting away from the States, I'm much more, even though I know we've got problems over there, I think we'll work them out. I think that I'm proud to be an American. I resent the way the world has treated the United States much more now. I didn't really know the resentment that the world had, but I've felt it over here. I don't think we've ever done anything to warrant this. We've made plenty of mistakes, but at least we've done something. So I'm very proud to be an American.

—a migrant who arrived in the 1970s[6]

It is often argued that one can exaggerate the depth of American chauvinism: is not much of this political rhetoric and Hollywood schmaltz? In Australia the public is skeptical about the emotional outpouring of American jingoism and nationalism at events like the half-time entertainment of the annual gridiron Superbowl—and is also deeply suspicious of American policies of promoting human rights in other countries. Is this a true expression of American culture or a superficial delusion? The anecdotal and empirical evidence from the 1993 sample indicates that American chauvinism is "real" and alive and well in the 1990s—at least "real" to the extent that it is expressed, affects attitudes and behavior, and is the major factor in determining the relatively low rate of citizenship by American migrants here (and elsewhere). As is argued in the final chapter, it probably is also a major factor in Americans' returning to America at a rate that is high relative to other migrant groups.

As shown in Table 10.2, of American migrants in the 1993 sample, a large minority (45 percent) did not intend to become Australian citizens. Most believed that this would entail giving up U.S. citizenship, and even though this is no longer true, the knowledge of these American administrative changes had not been widely circulated. The proportion holding dual citizenship was 20 percent. Of those not intending to become Australian citizens, the majority expressed continuing ties to the United States, a need to be able to return to the United States quickly and easily, patriotic ideas about America, objections to Australian monarchism, and an unresolved ambivalence about giving up U.S. citizenship. Most migrants viewed the issue as serious, and, along with emotional anecdotal evidence concerning discrimination, this response produced the most emotive content of any category in the questionnaire. As shown, however, in Table 10.2, the length of residence was directly proportional to a decline in the proportion

TABLE 10.2:   Attitudes toward Citizenship

Australian Citizen or Intention to Become Citizen	%	The "No" Group	%
Yes	55	Practical[a]	42
No	45	Maybe[b]	23
		Patriotism[c]	22
		Anti-Australian[d]	8
		Indifferent[e]	5

Australian Citizen or Positive Intention by Length of Residence (%)

1960–64	76
1970–74	58
1980–84	56
1990–93	43

[a] *Practical*:   travel, financial, don't like forms, want quick exit, customs problems.

[b] *Maybe*:   may consider in future, unresolved ambivalence.

[c] *Patriotism*:   America best nation in world, can't give up identity, Australia not home.

[d] *Anti-Australian*:   against monarchy, Australia inferior nation, feel alien.

[e] *Indifferent*:   do not care either way, see no reason to do so.

who intend to remain U.S. citizens—familiarity breeds adaptability, and the longer in Australia, the greater the rate of citizenship intention. One may view this either as the adaptable migrant staying longer, or people becoming adaptable over time—the data will not decide this question, and previous work has shown a similar correlation with longevity.[7]

U.S. migrants to Australia do not seem to shake off strong emotional ties to their homeland. To many, America will "always be home," for their "roots are in the U.S. because we were a pioneer family," as one respondent wrote. One migrant "loves Australia and calls it home but deep down I am an American and paper doesn't change that." Chauvinism remains strong: "I just like the U.S.— U.S. the best place to live, don't you think?" Many cannot break from family associations: "Through early childhood training, I 'feel' American." Another places her feelings within an historical framework: "I'm blood related to J.F.K. I guess, with generations of Dad's family in the Massachusetts legislature and in that area, I feel tied to U.S." Norm Sanders, the former Democrat senator, professed anguish at becoming an Australian: "I felt a sense of loss when I ceased to be a U.S. citizen." After 40 years in Australia, one migrant with children ranging in age from 32 to 50 simply rejected Australian citizenship with the simple declaration "I just don't want to."[8]

To many Americans, the Australian attitude toward nationhood lacks emotional vitality and the sense of community. One basketball coach found that Australians were not interested in playing "Advance Australia Fair" before games the way Americans always play the "Star-Spangled Banner," and he was disappointed by the seeming lack of knowledge by Australians of the words of the national anthem. He also regretted the absence of the "lump-in-the-throat" nationalism of Americans. Many migrants believe nationality should be treasured and Australia should adopt American practices of teaching national history and saluting the flag every morning in schools. As in the job culture, Americans find the culture of nationalism in Australia lacking emotional vitality. This was summarized by one migrant: "Citizenship is not sufficiently understood and appreciated in Australia. It is too casual here. Too many foreigners are allowed to stay too long without taking out their citizenship papers. Kids are not being taught enough about it at school."[9]

Many respondents went to extraordinary lengths to hide their decision to take out Australian citizenship from their families, who would view this action as a kind of treason. One academic, resident for 25 years, just could not bring himself to take out citizenship because "my family would be disappointed." Another would be "unable to face my family at funerals, now becoming more frequent." Al Green, the basketball star, became a citizen but confessed that his disappointed mother "prays for him." The most elaborate story of evasion came from a migrant in her 60s:

I became an Australian citizen on 24 June this year! I had submitted an application to become naturalized in late 1978 and had my appointment for the interview scheduled for early January, 1979, but while visiting my mother in the US over Christmas, I discovered that my decision seemed to worry her more than I had expected. As she was then having at least one fairly major heart attack every year, I canceled my appointment as soon as I returned to Sydney after the holiday. After her death, I felt easier about making the break, but faced strong pressure from my only brother, who finds it impossible to think that an American could even consider relinquishing his/her citizenship! (I have not yet found the courage to tell him that I am now an Aussie!) It was not until I was interviewed this year for my naturalization that I learned that the United States was now granting some dual citizenships. I intend to visit the US Consulate next week to see if I might be able to maintain my US citizenship. If not, so be it!![10]

Many American migrants bring with them republican values that run across ideological lines from social democrat to hyperconservative. Of the 45 percent not intending to become citizens, about 5 percent expressed hostility to the constitutional monarchy. A migrant felt strongly that he "wouldn't raise my hand to Queen Elizabeth II"; another will "only become a citizen if Australia is a Republic." Other migrants objected to "an oath to the Queen," the "English monarchy," and "allegiance to the Queen." As most migrants appear to express republican views, it is especially ironic that the Liberal MHR Bob Charles —who, as discussed above, is a descendant of American Revolutionary patriots—supports the monarchy; in a phone interview, he agreed it was ironic but believed it was consistent with his conservative beliefs in the Liberal Party.[11]

Many migrants were reluctant to become Australian citizens for pragmatic reasons rather than motivations with an ideological content. These practical problems were highly varied and ran the spectrum from the consequential to the trivial. Some believed travel would be easier with a U.S. passport, while others had "problems managing properties here and in the U.S." Many had fears "about the tax structure," and a World War II veteran was concerned about "his U.S. Army pension and social security." Many academics worried whether they would lose eligibility for either Australian or American fellowships. Many of these fears would, of course, be alleviated by dual citizenship, but respondents were not always aware that this was now available to them.[12]

The majority of the 1993 sample, however, did intend to become, or already had become, Australian citizens (as shown in Table 10.2). Sometimes this was caused by political events. As one migrant stated: "Reagan was the final catalyst. I had been living in Australia ten years, and I felt that I should do it anyway." But the rate of citizenship for American migrants in Australia is relatively low compared to other groups, such as Italians and Germans. In studies of Americans in other countries, such as Canada and Israel, Americans again rank relatively low in the rate of taking out citizenship. This proclivity to avoid naturalization is judged to be caused by sentimental and ideological attachment to the United States and a persistent historical tradition of chauvinism and pride in U.S. nationality and nationhood.[13]

Other studies have suggested a variety of causes associated with rates of citizenship: place of origin, marriage to citizens of the host nation, and progeny born in the host nation. The 1993 sample shows an odd mixture of results when these variables are examined. Americans born in rural areas have the same citizenship intention rate as those from urban areas, and there does not appear to be any correlation with place of U.S. birth. Neither does having Australian-born progeny produce higher citizenship levels; the parents of Australian-born children profess the same rate of citizenship intention as do those without progeny. Marriage to an Australian spouse does affect citizenship intentions, but in the opposite direction as that suggested by other researchers: the 1993 sample shows a *lower* intention to become a citizen when married to an Australian. The probable reason for this is discussed below in the section on women, since the vast majority of Americans following spouses/partners are women.

The rate of citizenship, therefore, is determined by attachment to U.S. nationality, and the intention to become an Australian citizen is increased by length of time in Australia, a more social democratic ideological perspective, and a higher level of general satisfaction with Australian culture. Those who intend to become citizens show an 89 percent satisfaction with Australia compared to 67 percent for those who do not intend to become citizens—the total sample proportion is 76 percent. The pervasiveness of America in the political news as the dominant global power, of American domestic political news, and of American human-interest stories, as the major provider of world prepackaged news provision, and of American daily life as shown in film, TV, and music may also provide a disincentive for losing American citizenship, since, unlike other source countries for migrants, America can rarely be out of mind.

ARE ALL AMERICANS THE SAME?

People, of course, are not the same within any identifiable ethnic community. Sub-groups and individuals will have finite patterns of behavior, and within the ethnic group they will only share a constellation of general characteristics of language and some other values. When the 1993 American migrant sample is broken down into class, occupational, gender, and racial components, a variety of different social characteristics and adaptability patterns clearly emerge. Only once this is completed can one make a holistic judgment on whether Americans like Australia, how they adapt to the new culture, and why some reject the host nation.

SOCIAL CLASS AND OCCUPATION

One persistent methodological problem with all studies of American migrants is the difficulty of attaining a social spectrum of respondents that corresponds to the social composition of the group as a whole. In this study it was most difficult to obtain respondents in the lower socioeconomic occupational categories, and consequently suggestions made on correlations of class and adaptability can only be tentative.

Viewing the occupational structure shown in Table 5.8—from executive to student in 12 categories—a picture of relative adaptability that corresponds to occupational/class status does emerge. The highest three occupational categories—executive, professional, and academic—show a satisfaction rating of around 80 percent. As one moves down the occupational range, this falls to 55–60 percent in Category 5–8 (sales, clerical, service, and farm). A similar pattern occurs with respect to citizenship intention, with the higher occupational levels showing a 55–60 percent level of intention to become citizens, compared to 20–35 percent in the lower occupational groups. The higher educational/ occupational groups, therefore, appear to be more adaptable to Australian society, or the more adaptable migrants may be in the higher occupational groups because their intrinsic social abilities to adapt are greater.

The higher occupational groups also seem to have greater support systems as migrants. They have secure and highly paid jobs, which were obtained through an international labor market. The lower socioeconomic groups have less secure employment and, through anecdotal data, express strong attachments to the United States and have less experience in overseas travel and living. These findings, however, are only suggestive, and until methods can be found to obtain greater participation in migrant studies by blue-collar Americans, these conclusions must be considered with caution.[14]

ACADEMICS

One group that was not difficult to locate, nor shy, is that of academics. Of the 302 respondents, 128 were academics (42 percent) from 21 of the 36 universities in all eight states and territories. Recent literature on academics, such as *The Role of Immigration in the Australian Higher Education Labour Market* (1993), has made the American academic in Australia the subject of some controversy in these days of economic nationalism and anti-Americanism. Should Australia be recruiting North American academics? Are they "second-rate," bringing with them "second-rate" Ph.D.s? The data on American migrants in the 1993 sample, in addition to providing an insight into the American migrant community, sheds a good deal of light on these questions and others.[15]

The traditional Australian ties with the United Kingdom in tertiary education and training have shifted increasingly to North America. Australians and Americans travel across the Pacific for undergraduate, postgraduate, and postdoctoral work, and hundreds of academics from both nations now work and study in the libraries, archives, and universities of both America and Australia. As examined in the section on anti-Americanism, this has caused some ambivalent reactions to employing Americans and using American models in tertiary education. One letter writer to the *Adelaide Review* sees this as an invasion of second-rate

"American philosophies of education" and of American academics who have taken over "the trumped-up CAEs [Colleges of Advanced Education, which were made universities in the 1980s] and Institutes of Technology." Monash University, however, is excited by its new "elite United States-style think-tank for Australia's first Graduate School of Management." The rate of contact in the 1990s, in spite of cultural and social judgments, continues to increase, and the number of U.S. academics and students in Australia is projected to rise through- out the decade. As one author writing in the *Campus Review* on Professor Gene Likens, the American recipient of "Australia's richest and most prestigious prize for science in 1994," concludes: "although an American, Likens has a number of long-standing and continuing links with Australia," and this pattern is set to continue in the future.[16]

In spite of these ambivalent attitudes toward Americans, the academics from America working in Australia in the 1993 sample seem to be a particularly successful and contented lot. They are less prone to feel discrimination (63 percent say no) compared to the sample as a whole (60 percent), and this is reflected in their relatively high rate of promotion in the academic hierarchy, in which 32 percent are at levels above that of senior lecturer compared, to 17.5 percent for Australian academics as a whole (positions below that of pro- fessor at Australian—and British—universities are, in order of descending seniority: reader, senior lecturer, lecturer).[17] They are less likely to be at levels below that of senior lecturer (28 percent) than are academics as a group (58 percent). They are more likely to become Australian citizens, with 59 percent indicating a positive intention (55 percent as a whole), and their satisfaction rating is 82 percent—considerably higher than that of the total sample (76 percent). They are more likely to be social democratic in political ideology (83 percent Democratic Party and 63 percent Labour) compared to the group as a whole (68 percent Democratic, 52 percent Labour), and the higher levels of citizenship intention, satisfaction rating, and social democratic leanings all cor- relate with high adaptability to Australian society.

One is not surprised that this group of Americans, with high status, secure tenured positions, and living in some of the world's most appealing environ- ments (such as Canberra, the north coast of New South Wales, along the River Torrens in Adelaide) should be especially satisfied with life in Australia. They come to Australia with a clear desire for employment (92 percent) and adventure (60 percent), and they appear to have achieved their objectives, although in the mid-1990s the reform of the Australian education system, with the desire of making universities the same mass sector that had obtained in the United States for well over a generation, did provoke many complaints in anecdotal evidence about teaching loads, bureaucratization, and loss of international competitive- ness.

American academics, despite some rumors to the contrary, are recruited from very high-status institutions and had received their Ph.D.s from equally prestig- ious tertiary institutions. These include, in the 1993 sample, internationally elite

Ivy League universities such as Harvard, Yale, Princeton, Columbia, and other private universities of similar stature, such as M.I.T., Stanford, and Chicago. They are also products of America's best state universities, such as the University of California–Berkeley, UCLA, Michigan, Wisconsin, and most other major state university systems in America. In the 1993 sample, 85 percent received their highest degree from medium- to high-status universities (see note to Table 10.3), and 82 percent had previous employment in a medium- to high-status university in America or elsewhere (such as Oxford, Cambridge, and London). American academics, therefore, are numerous and successful in the Australian academic environment.[18]

Out of almost 30,000 academics in total in Australia in the 1990s, just over 1,100 are academics from North America .[19] As shown in Table 10.3, they have been successful in the promotional structure, but a social analysis of vice chancellors in 1994 reveals not one American-born vice chancellor, in spite of the large number of Americans in senior academic positions in all major Australian universities. Of the 36 vice chancellors, fewer than one in three were born overseas, and seven of these were British; the remaining four include one each from New Zealand, Canada, Ireland, and South Africa. The pattern for Americans revealed here is consistent with the level of Americans who are CEOs of large businesses, politicians, and communications specialists in the electronic media: if one has an American accent/nationality, the probability of achieving elite status in these areas is limited.[20] It should also be remarked that at a time when American ideas and culture are being criticized as right-wing and therefore inappropriate for Australian conditions, the single largest occupational group of American migrants to Australia, academics, is predominantly social democratic ideologically, with little sympathy with the dominant ideas being transmitted from America.

Table 10.3:   Status of Academics in 1993 Sample

Academic Rank	%	
Professor	14	} 32
Associate professor/reader[a]	18	
Senior lecturer	40	} 68
Lecturer	28	

Note: N = 128.

[a]Reader: highest position below that of professor in Australian (and British) universities.

High-status universities are elite private universities such as the Ivy League; regional elite universities such as North Western, Chicago, Duke, Rice, Stanford; small elite colleges like Williams, Kenyon, Amherst, Swarthmore; elite state universities like U.C.–Berkeley, Michigan, Wisconsin; and a few Catholic universities like Georgetown and Notre Dame. Medium-status universities are established state universities and colleges; many Catholic universities; private universities such as U.S.C. Low-status universities comprise the rest.

RURAL AMERICAN MIGRANTS

American migrants living in rural areas face the multiple problems of migrant adaptation, general economic pressures, and—especially for women—the social isolation of country living. The 1993 sample, however, does not provide a large enough number of respondents (as is the case with lower socioeconomic groups) to make anything but suggestive generalizations about a group that deserves more research attention in an area that focuses almost entirely on urban migrants. In studies in the 1970s it was found that rural migrants, in particular women, tended to be more dissatisfied than urban migrants, and the 1993 sample also revealed similar problems. A rural migrant "when living in a small country town and attempting to introduce 'new ideas' into a pre-school" encountered isolation and hostility. Another migrant likes country living, but "financial hardship for rural Australian families" makes life difficult. Others complained of jealousy from fellow farmers because the "Yanks worked too hard and succeeded"; several respondents reported cultural xenophobia directed at the more open personalities of Americans, especially negative reactions to "friendliness and effusiveness." But the most comprehensive description of rural life came from a female respondent who gives an extraordinarily complete analysis of rural life for women with the traditional cultural values of a rural American. It is produced in full:

I came to Australia in 1983 with my Australian husband. He came back to his family farm and we lived with his parents 18 months before being able to move to a house of our own. I knew nothing of Australia except what my mother in law had written and told me about when the in-laws came to our wedding in 1982. My husband rarely spoke of Australia only to say that Americans were very spoiled with all the "modern conveniences." I now know what he meant as I only just now after 10 years bought a second-hand clothes drier (to be used only on rainy days). And purchased my first "automatic" washing machine after 3 years of "twin tub." I would give anything for a dishwasher as it is my *worst chore* in life. I hate dish washing.

Living on the land in Australia was quite a shock. Even tho we were 40 miles from the coast our first 4 years and we only received a frost 5 or 6 times in winter: we weren't allowed a heater except to have a bath. And no cooling in summer except a fan. I find that still very hard now except we have a wood heater now. Much colder here. I missed not working in town and seeing people every day. When my 2 children came along it gave me something to do once again besides riding horses and doing housework. (We were training horses for the public at that time.)

I really hated moving to Australia for about the first 3 years. I swore if I had the chance I'd go back to America. I went back at [?] but returned. I found the *loneliness* was unbearable! I couldn't make close friends (ones you could tell "anything"). Everyone seemed to think if you let off steam or complained about something, you were making an official assault against *all* Australians and that included them. *I have since learned to be very careful what I say and to whom I say it.* I still do not have a *close* friend after 10 years here except my husband, of course.

Four years ago we had the opportunity to sell and move back to America. I had a very long look at what we were doing and what we wanted to do in the future and told my husband I wanted to stay here if he wanted to stay. I felt with our two children growing up on a property and going to a small country school it would give them a greater feel for people and life in general. I think country life is great for children and adults alike. It is hard; and we do without a lot of "modern conveniences," but we hope it will pay off in our own happiness in the long run. I also feared if we moved back before our children were in their teenage years and even 20s they would stand a greater chance of a drug problem in America. I have a real bad "thing" about fearing my children may try drugs. My husband and myself have never tried drugs. I drink very little and my husband not at all, so we want our children growing up in a drug-free life as well. I feel we have a better chance of doing that here than anywhere else by teaching them while they are young. I hope I am right about this!

So far we have had no problem with education here. Our eldest is in year 2 now. If we do find problems developing in that area I am prepared to move them to another school or teach them myself at home through correspondence. As it is available here.

I wish there was some sort of phone-line for Americans to ring up when they arrive to Australia to talk to other Americans about their problems. I found it so hard just to get people to understand what I wanted and how to find out things I needed to know. For example how the education system worked, not just for my children, but for myself to gain further education. I lost all self-confidence when I came here; some said I had *too* much to start with, but I really felt badly about myself until I spoke with a teacher from TAFE who helped me see where my life was going and what was *I* going to do to get there.

I felt like I had stepped back in time 20 years when I saw the way Australian women were treated by Australian men. Very down on women! very male chauvinistic attitudes. I used to get into great trouble for standing up for women.

I hope I have given you a good laugh if nothing else. Hope the information is useful.

P.S. One other thing that really sticks in my mind about first moving to Australia. I remember all thru school and on radio and TV in America how we were "proud" to be American or "proud" to be Texan. Perhaps it is ingrained into us from the day we were born that *there was no better place to be in the world*. It was not until I had moved to Australia and had to defend my country verbally for what it was doing that I realized just because it is done in America does not automatically make it right. We depend so much on others (politicians mainly) to say what is right for Americans instead of what I as an individual think.

What I actually started out to point out was that I was "proud" to be American, sort of like you are proud of your football team when they win a game. It's something from deep within that you really "feel" (like why we go to war to free others, because we feel it's right and we are "loyal" to our country). The majority of Australians my age or even under 40 that I have met, do not seem to feel that for Australia. Have things been so bad here for so long that no-one has faith in their government any longer? that they can only do all the wrong things? It's a puzzle to me, but I guess as an American I had put my total confidence in our American government to do *what was right* and I would follow whatever decision was made.

Perhaps now I would feel differently if we returned to America. Perhaps I should just say I am questioning government motives and being more adult (10 years down the track) than what I was when I left has more to do with how I feel. *Or are Americans really brainwashed from the time they are born to believe the U.S.A. is the best place on earth and we do everything that's right.*

I hear all the time: "how could you have lived in America with the crime rate the way it is." "Do people really kill one another like on the TV we saw yesterday." What can you say! It's the best place on earth to live???[21]

MEN AND WOMEN

As clearly illustrated in the above description of the life of a rural woman, the migrant experience for men and women is not identical. Female American migrants report a range of gender-specific problems—sexism, isolation, alienation, homesickness—which differentiate them from the men in degree and kind. They are more likely to be "involuntary" migrants in the sense that 90 percent of those respondents who came following an Australian spouse/partner were women; this will partly explain their higher levels of dissatisfaction compared to men, to be discussed below. Women, as 45 percent of the sample ($N = 136$), deserve and require a substantial level of analysis in order to arrive at a holistic understanding of the migrant American community.

Table 10.4 illustrates the variables associated with the relative adaptability and/or satisfaction among the 1993 American migrants when considered by gender: factors that have been observed by previous researchers in the field. In his analysis of 1970s migrants, Ray Aitchison found that American women complained about sexism, and they reported employment discrimination more often than did men. In the 1980s, M. D. R. Evans found that women missed family and friends more than did men living in Australia. And Arnold Dashefsky, writing in the 1990s, perceived a persistent pattern of greater dissatisfaction by American women than men with the migrant experience in Australia.[22]

Few areas in the 1993 study of American migrants produced more anecdotal data than did the issue of sexism. Table 10.4 reveals that while women, like men, are generally satisfied with life in Australia (69 percent), they are decidedly less satisfied than men. They are more likely to perceive discrimination, are less hostile to the United States, less likely to want to become Australian citizens, four times more likely to specify the importance of coming (reluctantly?) with a spouse/partner and to be somewhat lower in occupational and educational status than men. Politically they are slightly to the left of men, which generally would indicate a more favorable attitude to Australia, but this is negated by sexism. Women have similar motivations for coming to Australia as men, with the highest ratings for pursuit of employment and adventure. Female American migrants, therefore, like men, are well-educated, middle-class, and generally well adapted to Australian life; the level of perceived discrimination, however, differentiates them from their male counterparts.

TABLE 10.4:   Gender Variations (Percentages)

Category		Men	Women	Net Difference
Satisfaction		82	69	−13
Dissatisfaction		18	31	+13
Discrimination (medium to high)		33	47	+14
Hostile to U.S. (medium to high)		20	13	−7
Citizenship/intention	Yes	59	47	−12
	No	41	53	+12
Following spouse (medium to high)		12	56	+44
Political—U.S.	Republican	26	19	−7
	Democrat	64	74	+10
Political—Australia	Liberal	27	26	−1
	Labour	49	52	+3
Employment and Adventure	(medium to high)	60	61	+1
Academics	above senior lecturer	37	12	−25
	below senior lecturer	22	66	+44
Occupation	professionals	84	73	−11
BA and higher degree		94	85	−9

Note: Men: $N = 166$; women: $N = 136$.

"Australians are anti-American/anti-female/anti-divorcee/anti-successful/anti–working mother/anti-educated/totally paranoid."

                                                                —a dissatisfied female migrant

American migrant women respondents perceive sexism at every level of Australian society, ranging from a general cultural attitudinal hostility—"Yanks are pushy," "aggressive," "bitches"—to more concrete and finite discrimination in employment, promotion, and workplace social interactions. Their comments are so thorough and comprehensive, it would be an injustice to summarize them and thus reduce their impact. I, therefore, reproduce below a catalogue of sexism:

"American women are resented because of their style of presentation."

". . . subtle prejudice, both social and in employment, especially from elite British-educated/oriented males or left-wing male intellectuals in Universities."

"Australia is much more chauvinistic than I expected and racist and conforming except in painting, theater, and dance."

"Australian culture is more male-dominated than was apparent."

"Women in Australia are somewhat second-class citizens: it's hard for a woman to get credit even when she is employed. . . . This is slowly changing as more women go into the work force and get recognition as professionals."

"My accent causes males to call me 'pushy.'"

"Women in Australia are more role bound and there is subtle prejudice against professional women."

"Women are less happy here: now that I am home with our child, I find it frustrating as there are no incentives for women to opt out of the labor force in preference to raising a family."

"Australia is a paternalistic, hierarchical and chauvinistic society."

"Some Australians are resentful of American 'pushiness,' especially if you are a woman."

"There is lots of sexism at work."

"American women are referred to as 'too aggressive.'"[23]

One hardly needs to press the point: many American women feel Australian society to be not only anti-American but particularly anti-American female migrant.

It should be added, however, that were a similar survey to be undertaken of Australian women with a similar educational and professional background as that of the American women in this survey—that is, highly educated professional women pursuing a career in the Australia of the 1990s—similar results might well be obtained.

These stresses and strains exacerbate the adaptation problems of female migrants to Australia. Domestic tensions, marriage breakdown, and physical ailments were all reported as a consequence of these adaptation difficulties. One male respondent considered Australia to be the "best place to live in the civilized world," but his wife hates every minute. One married migrant wrote: "My husband wanted to stay. I didn't. I was homesick for 8 years but then I finally grew to like Australia." A divorcee tells a sad story: "As I came here to live with an Australian citizen who never gave up giving me a bad time about being American and who has subsequently left me—how could I not have mixed feelings about Australia?" The wife of a dentist who loves Australia admits "I am only here because of my husband!" And a final respondent experienced enormous cultural shock, which, she says, "eventually led to a divorce because of cultural differences" over living in Australia.[24]

These problems of adaptation are also manifested in other anecdotal and empirical results. Women married to Australians are even more reluctant to become citizens (61 percent say no) than those who are not (36 percent), indicating that those who came following an Australian spouse/partner are not always overwhelmingly happy about the decision (overall, 53 percent of women reject citizenship, compared to 41 percent for men). American female academics in Australia have a higher academic status on average than do female academics in general, with 12 percent above the level of senior lecturer compared to 5.5 percent of female academics as a whole. But they are still well behind the male American academics, with 37 percent above the level of senior lecturer compared with male academics as a whole at 22.8 percent. Women are concentrated in the lower academic ranks compared to men from America, with females below senior lecturer comprising 66 percent of the total compared to 22 percent for men (overall for academics the figures are also striking: 80.7 percent for women and 48.7 percent for men). American academics, as already discussed, do well in Australia, but they do less well if they are female.[25]

The differentiation of American migrants by gender reveals how cautious one must be in generalizations about the adaptability of Americans to Australia. The levels of dissatisfaction must be analyzed by ideology, class, and gender in order to produce a clear picture of *how and why* different groups and/or individuals are likely to react to the migrant experience. Women, generally, experience higher levels of discrimination and sexism and have fewer employment opportunities, and they have greater problems of adjustment than do men, the key factors being stronger ties to country of origin and family, alienation, and a greater propensity for homesickness. Migrant women as a whole adapt to these experiences in Australia in a pattern resembling the men's, but a significant minority of women can be differentiated by higher levels of dissatisfaction based upon gender-specific problems.

BLACK AMERICAN MIGRANTS

Black American migrants, like women and rural migrants, have problems of adaptability that are unique to their group and increase the difficulties of the adjustment that any migrant must make. The 1993 sample of black Americans was unfortunately not a large one, as only 12 respondents fell into this category. Although the anecdotal data from these respondents raises some crucial issues of race within both the American and the Australian cultural context, one can only draw suggestive conclusions from the relatively small sample.

Black Americans show up a whole series of paradoxes in Australian society, because they are simultaneously venerated and discriminated against—sometimes for being black Americans but also sometimes for being perceived as Australian Aborigines. They often appear in Australian advertisements, made both in the United States and in Australia (whereas, paradoxically, Aborigines rarely do). They are, as sportspeople and entertainers, given celebrity status, and a large part of imported American culture has black American origins, including jazz, blues and rap music, ritual overhead hand-clapping in sports, and "funky" language. Most of this language derives in turn from the black jazz and drug culture of the 1920s/30s, which was then popularized by the white beat culture and writers of the 1950s like Jack Kerouac and Allen Ginsberg. It is still alive and is now being transmitted to the next generation through American television characters like Bart Simpson—"hey man," "cool," "daddy-o"—and a whole generation of black film comedies featuring actors like Bill Cosby, Richard Pryor, and Eddie Murphy. Even though their image in advertisements is often stereotypical—like pizza-eating Italians, vegetable-selling Greeks, and Sumo-type Japanese—their general image in Australian society is associated with great athletic skill and socially "cool" sophistication. Although they are not subject to KKK-style American discrimination, there is, of course, more to the black American experience in Australia than these television-generated images.[26]

As discussed in Chapter 2, black Americans have been in Australia since the early colonial period, and their obvious visibility has always brought them special attention and elicited ambivalent reactions from Australians. This was true in the gold rushes, in nineteenth-century entertainment in the form of circuses and vaudeville from America, in touring black American minstrel shows in the 1870s, and during World War II. Rob Foster has drawn attention to a confusion in nineteenth-century Australia between stereotypical racist images of black Americans and Australian Aborigines. Aborigines were also subject to an American linguistic import, for they were increasingly referred to as "Darkies" and "Niggers"—a direct influence of racist Southern U.S. culture.[27] There was also an ambivalent response to American black performers in Australia in the 1920s, and after an interracial incident in 1928 involving black American vaudevillains and Australian women, the national Cabinet announced that no further entry permits could go to Negroes. The influence of black American culture in the World War II period, such as the introduction of jazz and hip culture in clubs like the Booker T. Washington Club in Sydney, also elicited a mixed response from Australians. These confused historical messages are clearly perceived by black American migrants.[28]

Herb McEachin, one of the first U.S. basketball players to come to Australia in the 1980s, points out that black Americans, especially if they are six feet nine inches tall, are difficult to hide, and he is keenly aware of the social and historical nuances of Australian racism. He views the differences between American and Australian racism as reflecting differences in style:

The difference between racial prejudice in Australia and at home is that it is less open in Australia. If a racist doesn't like you in America because you're black, most likely he'll let you know. In Australia they smile and conceal what they're thinking. I prefer the attitude of the Ku Klux Klan. Their hostility is more honest.

Some black Americans experience racism when confused with Aborigines: "In Queensland they treated me badly because I looked like an Aborigine; when I talked they knew I was an American and their behavior would change." Another said, "I came with my boyfriend and I would never have come because I think Australia is a racist country and worse than back home in South Carolina."

Many black Americans, however, have adapted well to Australian society, and some have even taken out citizenship. Among these are Marcia Hines and Chelsea Brown in television and entertainment; Steve Carfino of the Sydney

Kings and basketball television presenter (of an extraordinary multicultural background, with Italian, Puerto-Rican, black, and Native American ancestry); and scores of successful sportspeople of both sexes in baseball, basketball, and netball. A basketball player in South Australia, who has become an Australian citizen, maintains that racism is not a problem "on or off the court."[29] Another sportsman summarized his happiness in Australia thus: "I haven't found the racial bit here. Once you get a job and a circle of friends, you fit in." A black American computer specialist does not find any problems of race discrimination and is in "love with South Australian geography," and a Southern black American left America to escape "West Virginia crackers," and the only trouble he had in Australia with racism was "a punch up in a pub with some cracker American tourists."[30]

Black American culture has also had other influences on Australian society. Black American struggles in the 1960s civil rights era strongly affected Australian Aborigines. Radical activists like Gary Foley and Bobby Sykes—Dr. Roberta Sykes—were heavily influenced by the movement for equal rights in America, and both have brought back with them inspiration from travel and contacts with civil rights leaders in America. Charles Perkins, in an ABC TV documentary on his early activism, related his profound debt to the American civil rights movement and the ideas of Martin Luther King, which motivated the freedom rides in the mid-1960s to towns like Walgett in New South Wales, in which the song "We Shall Overcome," sung by Pete Seeger, provided inspiration.[31] Gary Foley has named a son Bruce Nemarluk Malcolm X after the civil rights and Muslim leader.

In the late 1990s the race and multicultural debates in Australia, sparked by Pauline Hanson's One Nation Party, attracted international attention, including a visit to Australia by a former minor Black Panther activist and convicted terrorist, Lorenzo Ervin, in July 1997. This heightened the attention paid to the growing racial divisions in Australia and prompted the conservative prime minister, yet again, to attack both international and domestic critics of Australia's racial and multicultural policies. Bennie Lewis, former basketball player, has begun a journal in Melbourne, *Shades of Black,* as a forum for black American and Australian issues. Lewis believes that in Australia there is a subtle but omnipresent level of racism toward all blacks, but he now intends, as an Australian citizen, to make his home here, which, compared to his former home in East St. Louis, is "a peaceful and pleasant lifestyle."[32]

For black American migrants, adaptation to Australia presents the same problems as those of American migrants in general, but with a racial twist. Skin color does not ever go unnoticed, and any generalizations about this migrant group must always deal with this indubitable fact. Black Americans must cope with multiple problems: being a migrant, a black migrant, and an American migrant. They may get reactions against one of these or sometimes all three: a sportswriter in *The Australian* warns Australians of the dangers of black American sportspeople as models when he condemns the "black bad asses who smoke

crack and beat their women"; other critics warn of the general corrupting influence of U.S. advertising in general, and black American models in particular.
The captain of the Geelong Supercats, Ray Borner, has claimed overt racial
harassment of his black American players by the Brisbane Bullets, even though
the Bullets have a black American captain in Leroy Loggins. In the 1990s the
issue of racism in Australian sport has received wide public attention, and action
has been taken against it in numerous sports (especially Australian Rules Football), although the problem has not been as acute in basketball. For black Americans living in Australia, therefore, representing both American culture and black
American culture simultaneously presents special challenges.[33]

ADAPTABILITY

To return to the original question posed at the beginning of this chapter, "Do
Americans like Australia," now seems an intellectually naive approach to the
topic. Which Americans does one mean? One must break this question into its
constituent elements both conceptually and in terms of social structure. In space
and time, therefore, the American migrant community will vary by differential
spatial characteristics of class, gender, race, and age; over time it must be broken
into differences in ideology, cultural values, and political propensities. Most
Americans in the 1993 sample do adapt well and are satisfied with Australia.
They like the climate, lifestyle, social services, and general employment opportunities and believe that Australia offers a relatively safe and secure future for
them and their families compared to the United States. The stereotypical minority migrant who is dissatisfied objects to the alleged "socialistic," union-domi-
nated, sexist, and low-work-ethic character of Australian society. The profile of
a satisfied migrant reveals a white male, slightly leaning toward the left wing, an
academic/professional who lives in an urban area; a dissatisfied migrant is more
likely to be a white female, slightly to the right, who is a middle-level white-
collar worker and lives in an urban area, but sometimes in smaller cities.

These, however, are generalizations about those who remain. What about
those who return to America? Does this act indicate *ipso facto* rejection of
Australia by dissatisfied migrants? If the majority of Americans return (as
shown by Table 5.3), does this indicate a failure of the migration program for
Americans? Are there alternative explanations for the high rates of return for
Americans: for example, did they never intend to stay, or do all migrants have
similar rates, or do they return for reasons other than rejection of Australia?

The conclusions about the adaptability of American migrants do not provide
an easy answer to the complex question of return rates for North American
migrants. There is no easy answer. J. and D. Bardo, sociologists from Wichita
State University, who carried out several detailed studies on the adaptability of
American migrants in Victoria in the early 1980s, concluded that "the data . . .
supports the position that adjustment of American migrants in Australia is a
complex social-psychological process involving several dimensions of adjust-

ment: alienation, degree of isolation, compatibility of work, orientations, perceptions of Australian amicability, and the degree of missing family and friends . . .
it is misleading to think in terms of a unitary 'adjustment' process."[34] In short,
people are complex, and some adjust and some don't. One can only describe the
general character of the process, but in terms of individuals, or even groups
of individuals, the individual cases will vary widely. With these caveats on
explanatory models for those who stay, one must, however, still attempt to
explain why those who leave the American migrant community do so in such
large—and consistently large—numbers.

Some migrants are extraordinarily unhappy with Australia, ranging from the
ambivalent to the desperately alienated. They are convinced that they have made
the wrong decision and want to get out of a declining, or even doomed, nation:

Individually (as neighbors, workmates, etc.) I find Australians delightful. The politics of the place—especially industrial relations—are wretched. People are overly
dependent on and respectful of government and politicians, when in fact the standards of performance are among the lowest of the Western world. The dole, paying
kids to go to school, the costly and inefficient medical system, the wage system,
over-regulation, and the over-representation of government at all levels and their
extensive bureaucracies (levels of public sector employment) will lead to a third
world economy in a shockingly short time. *Competition cannot be confined to sports*
if the country is to succeed.

Other migrants want to leave but cannot afford to do so: "The system of taxation
and socialist welfare mentality make life here frustrating—can't earn enough to
live as well as would in the United States. Can't afford to go back, don't qualify
for benefits. Too much of my earnings are to support too many pups on the
dole." And some migrants feel trapped in Australia:

Conclusion: To explain my feelings about staying in Australia: Although we have
lived outside the USA since 1961 . . . longer than we lived IN it, I am still fiercely
American and would love to return. However, the economics of the situation deem
that we will have to stay here. Neither my husband nor I worked enough quarters in
the USA to qualify for any more than the absolute minimum Social Security benefits . . . something like US$55 a month the last I checked 10 years ago! Because we
have lived in Australia for more than 10 years, we qualify for all the benefits of an
Australian citizen. We have not built up any appreciable superannuation, so here we
stay. Speaking for myself, if my husband predeceases me, his US$95,000 life
insurance policy will probably mean that I will hive myself back to the West Coast,
Seattle, where our daughter is living. Our son is living in Tasmania and is married to
a Tasmanian. I would miss him and his two children, but their much-different
lifestyle means that we don't see a lot of each other.

Primarily, I am tired of living in another country that is not my own. Despite all
its faults, I think America is the best country in the world, and I'm homesick for it.
I'm tired of either defending it or having to keep my mouth shut regarding any

criticisms of The Australian Way, be it politics, education or whatever. I went where my husband went, and this included 16 years in the Philippines and 3 years in the jungles of North Borneo (Sabah) before coming to Tasmania. I don't regret it, but I think it's time to go home. He does not share my feeling, but if he were sure of a job in the USA he would go, I'm sure. I think he feels that "it's better the devil you know . . . etc." I haven't really had the courage to ask him what he will do with the Aust$100,000 that he would receive from my insurance, should I predecease him.

Tasmania is a clean, unpolluted place to live. I have been accepted and made good friends here. There are many pluses, such as cheap meat and lack of serious crime. There is also a tendency to refuse to accept that the State needs to join the 20th century (refusal to extend shop hours . . . trying to reinvent the wheel when it comes to new procedures or processes) and the desire to stay just the way it always has been . . . frustrating to movers and shakers. As over-50s, the job market is dismal to say the least. I work for the State Public Service and wouldn't change for anything, because even though more jobs will be axed in the State Service, it's still safer than private enterprise, particularly during this time of economic strife. By the way, practically everything else BUT meat is more expensive in Tasmania than elsewhere in Australia.[35]

And, finally, many just want to go home; a sample:

"I miss my family."

"Constant perception of being outsider."

"Been here 10 years and it just isn't home."

"Although I will stay, homesickness will forever be a factor."

"Basically I am not expatriate material even after 22 years."

"After 20 years I am still socially isolated, especially now in my 50s."

"Miss the rural South."

"Fearful about aging parents in US."

"Miss my family and can only afford to visit once in 4 years."

"Anxious for my older and ill parents."

"I want to go home but can't afford it."

"Miss family and culture rituals in the US: sports, holidays, etc."[36]

Many migrants, therefore, believe that they have made a mistake. Some were misinformed, some were foolish, some miscalculated adaptation pressures, and some had come as half-hearted wives/husbands/partners; some came unwillingly, having been sent by employers, others because of family conflict. Now they lack the financial resources to return to America, even though they are dissatisfied in Australia. Many cling to tribal American identities that they cannot transcend. The policy of the Australian government toward American migrants has been that they do not need help. One report in the 1970s concluded:

American settlers were, on the whole, independent and require a modicum of assistance from official agencies. They showed considerable initiative in accommodation and employment matters and generally had little difficulty settling in, in the social sense. By virtue of their similar cultural background their migration had not required them to make any major adjustments in this regard. In possessing these characteristics, American settlers appear to present few problems from an integration point of view and it is not considered that any special recommendations dealing with post-arrival aspects are required.[37]

But the 1993 sample, especially from anecdotal data, clearly shows that this is not true for a large minority. Even more compelling is the large number of Americans who return home. In the case of these Americans, who were drawn back to "Yankeeland" by a variety of pressures, one must seek an explanation for a decision involving a large expenditure of emotion and capital being reversed.

NOTES

1. For a comprehensive discussion of the theoretical issues in analyzing American adaptation patterns for new migration, see Alejandro Portes and Ruben Rumbaut, *Immigrant America* (Berkeley, CA, 1990); for a recent Australian study, see Ann-Mari Jordens, *Redefining Australians: Immigration, Citizenship and National Identity* (Sydney, 1995).

2. *Australian–American Association, 1836–1956* (Sydney, 1986).

3. B. and A. Finifter, "Party Identification and Political Adaptation of American Migrants in Australia," *Journal of Politics*, 51 (1989), pp. 599–630.

4. See Portes and Rumbaut, *Immigrant America*, p. 124.

5. Department of Immigration and Ethnic Affairs, Submission to the Inquiry on the Enhancement of Citizenship, "Citizenship Rates for Those Likely to Be Residentially Eligible," 1994; *The Advertiser*, 13 July 1994, p. 7.

6. De: 235.

7. Baum, *Exchange of Migrants*, Table 7; Deamicis, "It Just Happens," p. 251.

8. Q: 113, 96, 138, 165, 234, 84; A: 143.

9. A: 16.

10. Q: 67, 98, 14, 18.

11. Q: 54, 61, 196, 231, 222; phone interview with Bob Charles, 10 June 1993.

12. Q: 195, 62, 277, 115, 121, 183.

13. A: 153; Borrie, *Italians and Germans*, pp. 141, 186; Dashefsky, *Americans Abroad*, pp. 38, 132–141; Deamicis, "It Just Happens," pp. 243–251. This is also true in comparison to migrants in the United States, where the citizenship rate for all migrants was in the 60–70 percent range and that for Italians, Poles, Hungarians, and Scandinavians in the 80-plus percent range: see S. Thernstrom, ed., *Harvard Encyclopedia of American Ethnic Groups* (Cambridge, MA, 1980), pp. 746–747.

14. This is consistent with U.S. studies that show a clear positive correlation between higher migrant educational levels and higher rates of citizenship: Portes and Rumbaut, *Immigrant America*, p. 132.

15. Sloan, *Higher Education*; *The Australian*, 1 June 1994, p. 21.

16. *The Adelaide Review* (November 1993), p. 10; *The Australian*, 18 December 93, p. 5; *Campus Review*, 11–17 November 1993, p. 4; 3–9 March 1994, p. 7. For the growing global

academic labor market, see W. G. Bowen and J. H. Schuster, *American Professors: A National Resource Imperiled* (New York, 1986); D. G. Brown, *The Mobile Professor* (Washington, DC, 1967); A. M. Cartler, *Ph.D.s and the Academic Labor Market* (New York, 1976); N. J. Smelser and R. Content, *The Changing Academic Market: General Trends and a Berkeley Case Study* (Berkeley, 1980).

17. Sloan, *Higher Education*, p. 9.

18. Also found to be true in the 1970s: Deamicis, "It Just Happens," pp. 214–215.

19. Based on Sloan, *Higher Education*, p. 14.

20. *Campus Review*, 28 October 1993, p. 11. A recent exception was Philip Lader, the vice chancellor of Bond University, who left in 1993 for a position in the Clinton administration: *Campus Review*, 11–17 February 1993, p. 5; Flinders University had an American vice chancellor in the turbulent 1970s—Professor Roger Russell, from the University of California. Professor Steven Schwartz, an American-born psychologist, was appointed vice chancellor of Murdoch University in June, 1995: *The Australian*, 28 June 1995, p. 23.

21. Cuddy, *Yanks*, p. 105; Q: 244, 18, 318, 285; phone interview 21 October 1994, with rural migrant in South Australia's Coonawarra district.

22. Aitchison, *Americans*, pp. 150–156; M. D. R. Evans, "Immigrant Women in Australia: Resources, Family and Work," *International Migration Review*, 18 (1984), pp. 1063–1090; Dashefsky, *Americans Abroad*, pp. 95–97.

23. Q: 255, 259, 262; R: 2; C: 141; Q: 216, 219, 120, 149, 206, 29, 147.

24. Q: 188, 216, 9, 119, 223.

25. Additional data from Sloan, *Higher Education*, p. 9; see also *Campus Review*, 20 October 1994, p. 7, for a general analysis of inequality for female academics in Australia. In 1995 these inequities were confirmed in *The Australian*, 28 June 1995, p. 23.

26. A recent thorough analysis of stereotyping in the media on racial, multicultural, and immigration issues found "non-Anglo, non-White images or verbal references are rare. The exclusion of (non-stereotyped) diversity is almost total in all the media studied": Philip Bell, *Multicultural Australia in the Media* (Canberra, 1994), p. 79.

27. Robert Foster, "An Imaginary Dominion: The Representation and Treatment of Aborigines in South Australia, 1834-1911," Unpublished Ph.D. dissertation (University of Adelaide, 1993), pp. 239–240; see also Richard Waterhouse, *From Minstrel Show to Vaudeville: The Australian Popular Stage, 1788–1914* (Sydney, 1990).

28. Stuart Macintyre, *Oxford History of Australia*, Vol. 4 (Melbourne, 1986–1990), p. 206; Bruce Johnson, *The Oxford Companion to Australian Jazz* (Melbourne, 1987), pp. 28, 79, 263–265; "Late Night Live," ABC Radio, 21 May 1997.

29. A: 13; Q: 89, 25; interview, 17 June 1994.

30. C: 108–109; Q: 311. When Marcia Hines took out Australian citizenship, this received front-page coverage in *The Australian*, 13 February 1995, p. 1. Interview by Mosler with computer specialist, 8 June 1995.

31. ABC TV, 4 November 1988. The thirtieth anniversary of these freedom rides was featured in *The Australian Magazine*, 4 March 1995, pp. 22–27.

32. *The Australian*, 9 August 1993, p. 3; phone interview by Mosler with Bennie Lewis, 12 January 1994; *The Australian*, 9 July 1997, p. 3.

33. Sportswriter quoted on "Media Watch," ABC TV, 25 April 1994; *Geelong Advertiser*, 11 May 1994; "World Today," ABC Radio, 9 November 1994. See the cartoon by Nicholson in *The Australian*, 29 April 1997, p. 14, on the subject, which implies that a racial attack on a giant American black would be too risky.

34. J. and D. Bardo, "American Migrants in Australia: An Exploratory Study of Adjustments," *Sociological Focus*, 14 (1981), pp. 147–156, quote 154; see also *idem*, "Adjustment of American Teachers in Victoria, Australia," *Psych. Reports*, 47 (1980), pp. 599–608;

"Dimensions of Adjustment for American Settlers in Melbourne," *Multi-variate Experimental Clinical Research*, 5 (1980), pp. 23–25; "From Settlers to Migrants," *Studies in Symbolic Interaction*, 3 (1980), pp. 194–232; "Note on Adjustment of Married American School Teachers in Victoria," *Psych. Reports,* 49 (1980), pp. 623–627; "Sociodemographic Correlates of Adjustment for American Migrants in Australia," *Journal of Social Psychology* 112 (1980), pp. 255–260; W. A. and R. Scott, *Adaptation of Immigrants* (Oxford, 1989).

    35. Q: 191, 233, 225.

    36. Q: 10, 25, 31, 42, 43, 61, 72, 77, 109, 131, 135, 197, 245.

    37. Quoted in Deamicis, "It Just Happens," p. 143.

11

Conclusion:
The Future

In the context of this study, three aspects of the future require final consideration: those Americans who remain in Australia; those Americans who have
returned home; and the future of the relationship between America and Australia.

FOR THOSE WHO STAY

Before examining those migrants who go home, a few suggestive results on
the future for those who remain can be explored. Certainly a critical element in
the decision to remain for American migrants is associated with a belief in the
future of their children. Australia is perceived as a safer and more hospitable
environment for their progeny, and most American parents do not envisage their
children as suffering the split cultural loyalties experienced by Europeans and
Asian migrants originating from more divergent cultures. But eventually Aus-
tralian-raised migrants from American backgrounds will know more about Sir
Donald Bradman than about Babe Ruth—some cultural clashes will occur, and
ultimately the American migrants will see their offspring mature as Australian
adults with different values and speech.

As indicated in Table 11.1, the overwhelming majority of respondents believed their children to be getting a "fair go": only 13 respondents, or 4 percent
of the total 1993 sample, believed that their children experienced major problems of discrimination. Almost one-half considered their children to have primary Australian identities, with only 16 percent retaining a primary identity as
Americans. Overall, 90 percent believed their progeny to have good life oppor-

TABLE 11.1: The Second Generation

Do Your Children Suffer Discrimination? (%)

Yes	17
No	83

Level of Discrimination Perceived by the "Yes" Group (%)

Trivial[a]	58	
Medium[b]	34	} 42
High[c]	8	

How Do Your Children Perceive Their Nationality? (%)

Australian	48
American	16
Both	36

Are You Satisfied with Their Life Opportunities? (%)

Yes	90
No	10

[a] Trivial: jokes, sneers, negative body language, odd remarks, not affecting life opportunities.
[b] Medium: persistent pattern of discrimination, belief that it affects life opportunities.
[c] High: overt job discrimination, refusal of a job or promotion, trauma, factor in leaving Australia.

tunities when questioned about their educational and employment future. The areas of difficulty, however, still must be examined, for they reveal a good deal about the problems faced in Australia by migrants in general and by American migrants in particular.

Migrants complain about their children being made to feel "different": accents, American parents, and different sporting interests are often cited. One respondent claimed that her child "had constant sense of being different," another was "teased at school as a Yank"; a very concerned mother claimed her "son was ridiculed at a C of E grammar school by his teacher because he didn't know the rules of cricket while not allowing the other guys to instruct him; he also 'smacked' him for not putting 'u's in 'labour' and 'neighbour' etc."; and several complained of "Americans loved or hated" and "discriminated against for working or achieving too hard." Parents felt that their children are pressurized to conform and assimilate: "pushed always to stop 'riding the hyphen' between the two cultures"; "pressured by state school teachers to ignore your American parents on accents, spelling, etc."; "one was cautioned about using 'Americanisms' by a teacher and caned for asking why; this same teacher at an all male school called an Italian immigrant student a 'wog'"; and another parent was distressed about assimilation and "would prefer more opportunities to expose my children to aspects of American life, culture and history."[1]

Problems result when children suffer more or less from homesickness than do their parents, and this often produces family splits. One parent was satisfied with life in Australia but "would return to the U.S. at the end of this year to be with my children who have chosen to be educated there." Another described how "my younger daughter (15) says she sometimes feels American there and Australian when in Australia; my eldest daughter (19) decided to retain American citizenship as an Australian resident. I think my Australian-born boy (17) considers himself Australian." One respondent saw a family breakdown looming: "My daughter has been to the United States 4 or 5 times and misses her relatives and friends there; she would like to attend university in the United States but changes day by day—she would live with U.S. relatives." Finally, another migrant has resigned herself to her daughter's wish to stay in the United States:

My daughter has had a particularly difficult time adjusting to life away from our family and her friends. She had developed a particularly close relationship with her grandparents and aunts and misses them a great deal. At 14, she plans to move back to California as soon as is possible, so I would anticipate her leaving after she finishes secondary school.[2]

Consequently, most migrants who stay in Australia—stayers—are satisfied with their lives and project satisfactory futures for their children. But one must not assume that stayers are necessarily satisfied or leavers dissatisfied, as the automatic corollary of the simple fact of staying or leaving. Many migrants who stay seem resigned to situations that are, on balance, acceptable, but without enthusiasm. One rural migrant, *before* the election of President Clinton, was staying but was "inclined to liken Australia to the State of Arkansas—very similar hillbilly living, especially in Queensland." Some are afraid of the "economy going downhill and creeping Americanism and could consider escaping to a less U.S.-influenced English-speaking country, less materialistic" [one wishes him luck!]. Another wonders about the future:

The quality of life outside of Sydney and Melbourne is quite high especially in terms of air and water quality. This is essentially due to low population levels, however. Standards will erode quickly with even moderate increases in population as infrastructure is poor and the country will not be able to afford it.

Australians' sense of fair play, multiculturalism and objective neutrality are admirable.

And an academic mixes intellectual rigor with humor:

Life in Oz has considerable negatives such as a basically limited view of the world and what can be attained in life. There is considerable discrimination against Americans, but also enough cultural cringe to mitigate this impact to a degree. In terms of my career, there are also limited opportunities to mix with fellow scientists and exciting individuals. Information access is difficult and becoming increasingly restricted due to cuts to library funding. On the other hand, fruit is fresher and better quality, cheese is dirt cheap, and the human population effect is behind the US. Criminals are less competent.

Some are even less sanguine:

Our material standard of living has slipped drastically and Aussie society is now racked by the drug problem one left behind in San Antonio in 1974. The shallowness of Australian life is a disappointment and I loathe *the lesbian mafia* and the grip homosexuals have on the AIDS money. The Aussie welfare state has gone too far but I *prefer* this system to the US system of ignoring the poor and processing huge amounts into the military.[3]

The children of American migrants offer an area for future research. As pointed out by Michael Tsounis in his work on Greeks, *all* Australian migrant communities (indeed, in every migrant-receiving nation) must face the problems of hybrid second-generation migrants.[4] Where does one live? How does one deal with aging parents in Australia and overseas? Where does one get educated? All of these questions press in on migrant families from all nations, and the American migrant community deserves follow-up research to examine the adaptation and/or assimilation of American–Australians in the process of adjusting to their parent's decision to stay in Australia.

FOR THOSE WHO LEAVE

The out-migration rate for Americans is unquestionably high, but considerable variations exist in the research literature on the rate and causes for re-migration. Dennis Cuddy found in the 1970s that 58 percent of his respondents desired to return to the United States, and he estimated the overall return rate to be 60 percent. Jan Deamicis, also in the 1970s, found that fewer than one-third of his respondents intended to stay in Australia, and even those in the group with migrant visas had weak intentions about permanency in Australia. Although Deamicis admits it is the "demonstration of the obvious," he found the stayers to be higher in indices of favorable attitudes and adaptation to Australia (family, jobs, children). J. and D. Bardo found the re-migration rate in the 1980s to be very high but suggested that more work was required to determine causes and levels. Arnold Dashefsky, surveying the literature in the 1990s, outlined a profile of stayers as having stronger family ties, being married to Australians, having friendship ties, high job satisfaction, and low assets in the United States, and feeling more at home in Australia than in America; the leavers felt more alien in Australia, had strong American identities, and clung more tenaciously to American values and institutions. He found the remigration rate to vary from 28 percent to 72 percent over the period of the 1970s to the 1980s, depending on the research methodology and statistical methods employed. He concludes that however one measures the American rate of return, it is high.[5]

As shown in Table 5.3, the conclusions drawn by Dashefsky are again demonstrated: despite the difficulties in determining the exact rate of permanency, it is low for Americans. O. Lukomskyj and P. Richards have estimated the overall staying rate for Australian migrant groups to be 80 percent, whereas most studies on Americans in Australia show the rate to be 25–30 percent. Studies of other migrant groups in Australia reveal fluctuations in staying rates, but those of Italians, Greeks, and other groups are much higher than those of Americans. The 1993 sample shows the reasons for the high rate of return to be consistent with previous work: American migrants have a relatively low level of knowledge when arriving, a high proportion did not intend to stay permanently, few are hostile to America, and their adaptation to Australia lacks conviction and urgency, given the capital and skills that make returning to America relatively painless. As the Green Paper (a detailed government document on a specific subject designed to generate public discussion and policy formulation) in 1977 noted, the return rate for Americans far exceeds the returnee rate for migrants generally in Australia, the United States, and Canada, and—no researcher could resist this conclusion—the whole area needs more research.[6]

In the most comprehensive study of emigration from Australia by Graeme Hugo in 1994, many previous research generalizations about Americans are confirmed, along with some characteristics about emigrants in general. Hugo argues that the act of emigration itself is a function of multiple causes and is not *ipso facto* an indication of the failure of a migration program or a maladaptive pattern by the migrant group (or individual). He cautions against the use of models for emigration (categorizing them by neo-classical, historical–structuralist, and a systems approaches) and identifies the methodological problems in emigration data. He also identifies Americans (and New Zealanders) as having especially high re-migration numbers, which, for Americans in the 1980s, were double that of their proportion of settlers (Americans represented 2.6 percent of settlers but 5.1 percent of emigrants). Hugo concludes that high levels of emigration in the 1990s may be intrinsic to the migration cycle, and one should not, with this multivariate phenomenon, necessarily alter existing immigration policies. The future pattern of global migration, he suggests, may include a high rate in the circulation of labor as well as higher rates of emigration in general, and in Australia in particular.[7]

The 1993 sample of returnees, however, reveals the enormous methodological problems in pursuing this topic. In 1993, over 70 questionnaires were sent to returnees in America and elsewhere around the world, as some had moved on to the United Kingdom, Hong Kong, and other places. It proved difficult to establish a list of potential respondents, as there is no record of returnees, respondents in the main 1993 study were reluctant to provide names or "dob in," returnees were un-cooperative respondents (only 22 responded), and they do not congregate in home villages or clubs in America where one could, as is the case with

Greeks or Italians, more easily locate them. The sample, therefore, is disappointingly small and provides only conclusions that must be suggestive; the anecdotal data provided was supplemented by direct follow-up interviews with one-half of the respondents living in the western states of America. One is, of course, immediately struck by the divergence of the results in Table 11.2 with previous generalizations concerning returnees: the 1993 sample shows high levels of satisfaction with Australia and a low level of hostility to their temporary host nation, the major reasons for returning to America being family crises and employment. One is tempted, therefore, simply to disregard these results as statistically irrelevant, and possibly the 22 respondents who bothered to respond were those who still had positive feelings about Australia and/or intended to return. However, before we discard these results, they deserve greater analysis and may indicate possible avenues for further research.

This small sample, however, does provide some intriguing and detailed stories of the vagaries of migration. With the small sample, we produce below some of the more detailed descriptions of the complex lives of individuals—complexities that should make historians and social scientists alike cautious about generalizing:

"Returned to earn more in America."

"I returned to reform US social policies."

"I may come back to Australia again because I am even more dissatisfied with the US."

"I went back solely because of sick parents."

"While in Australia my wife and I were divorced in 1984. Leaving Australia was one of the dumbest choices of my life, though the reasons seemed compelling at the

TABLE 11.2:   Returnees (Percentages)

Reasons for Returning to America (Medium to High Percentage)

Family crisis	64
Employment	46
Homesickness	27
Following spouse/partner	2
Boredom	14
Hostile to Australia	12

Satisfied with Life in Australia

Yes	82
No	18

Note: $N = 22$.

time: kids knowing their families and relations in America; learning about their American background; employment and career opportunities, especially for my daughter; and a general sense that if one were ever going to return, this was the time, when kids were starting high school. In retrospect, it was a *dumb* decision! See you in 1993!"

"Food shopping too difficult. Banking hard. Education system was too British. Role of women too regressive. I took a Teacher Refresher (summer) course and was assigned to a school miles and miles from our home. I felt unable to adapt to the more authoritarian system there and therefore gave up after a couple of months for my benefit and that of the 8 year old children. This was difficult for me to do, but it was entirely my choice."

"Leaving Australia was one of the hardest things I have done in my life because I was totally settled and satisfied with my lifestyle, friends, etc. The decision to leave came with the realization that I wanted the sense of "belonging" that only my family (father, brothers, nieces, etc.) could give me, and they lived in the US. Settlement back into the US (Southern California) has been extremely difficult, even harder than I'd anticipated. Life is more complex and very harsh."

"Many times I wished that I never left Australia, but my emotions bounce around too much. The College was wonderful to me, I met fantastic people, and the country is beautiful. It was very interesting learning about the USA from a foreign country. I wish you luck with your study."[8]

The empirical data in Table 11.2 shows family crises as the main reason for returning to America. The anecdotal data expand on these issues: problems of aging parents, fears and concerns about acculturation of their children as Australians, and desires for their children to be educated in and interact with families in the United States. Interviews with returnees confirmed these concerns but also revealed continuing *angst* about the United States and the way their children readapted to America.

To summarize the most illuminating points of the interviews:

An academic in Washington:
I basically wanted my children to be instructed in American culture and values. This has only had mixed results, because they seem unstable and split between the two nations. My divorce didn't help, but I can't help but feel I should have stayed in Australia. The United States right now is fairly depressing, and if I didn't live in this rural area I wouldn't be very satisfied.

A Seattle woman with home duties:
After my divorce I decided the kids should know their own country. The crucial turning point was when the oldest daughter began to speak like an Australian. But life here is harsh: crime and violence at school, no safety-net welfare, and we have trouble paying our bills. One of my son's friends (age 9) was shot by his mother! We may still go back to Queensland, but our kids definitely feel American. My second husband is Australian, and he really wants to go back to take care of his parents. These are all terribly hard problems to resolve.

A teacher in Oregon:

I only came home because of my parents. I wanted them to know their grandchildren, and I would love to go back to Australia. The United States has really gone backward: crime, drugs, breakdown of social consensus, and a lack of will to do *anything* about major problems. I think it is a real spiritual/family crisis, which won't get better. It is all downhill now.

An academic in the Bay Area (San Francisco):

I loved Australia and only came home because of a "broken heart." My romance with an Australian woman fell apart, and I couldn't stand living there. The Bay Area has much that is attractive, but population pressures and general social decay are much worse than when I left. I hope to spend time in Australia again and would be open to job offers.

A nurse in the Midwest:

After my Australian husband died I decided to go home. Some of my kids are staying here, and one is going back to America. I really am at loose ends, because the only job available was in America. When my mother dies (age 73), I may return to Australia. I really don't know at this stage.[9]

Both the anecdotal and the empirical data on these returnees suggest the complex patterns of human decision-making. American return rates are very high, but these data suggest that more work must be done before one can draw firm conclusions on the causality. Those returning clearly do so for reasons other than simple dissatisfaction with Australia, just as those remaining are not all uniform in their satisfaction and adaptation to Australian life. The myriad variations of human behavior in this area require more data and more subtle models for the explanatory causality in the decision to stay or to leave Australia. As Graeme Hugo concludes in his study on emigration, the act of emigrating results from many causes, some of which *may* be dissatisfaction with the host country and/or adaptation difficulties. In the globalization of labor markets in the 1990s, one will see greater ease and frequency of decisions to move about the globe in search of employment and life satisfaction opportunities, and the data in this study do not suggest any urgency to review migrant recruitment or settlement programs for U.S. migrants.

FOR AUSTRALIAN–AMERICAN RELATIONS

In March 1996 the Labour government of Paul Keating was defeated in a federal election; John Howard became prime minister and Alexander Downer foreign minister. Relations with America had received scant attention in the election debates between the two parties, who, insofar as they mentioned foreign relations at all, both assured the electorate they would be able to continue Australia's commercial thrust into the then booming economies of Asia Pacific. Both would be—and this was assumed by all concerned—decent allies of the United States and its handmaiden in the project of globalization. Shortly after the election, a top-level U.S. defense team visited Australia, and in a low-key way both sides reaffirmed their commitment to one another. Only the new defense minister, Ian McLachlan, broke the ice when later suggesting that China might be a regional security threat to watch, thereby revealing the real depth of the Australian–U.S. strategic congruence.

The Keating government was defeated because the electorate was resentful of his arrogant reform of the Australian economy and the resulting unemployment; most knew it to be unavoidable but resented it nonetheless. Voters took additional revenge on him for winning the 1993 election when they had refused to support his then Liberal opponent, John Hewson, who wanted to put up taxes. And in a sub-plot they voted against Keating for introducing what he called the "big picture," which they knew as the politically correct agenda—Aboriginal reconciliation, conjoining with Asia, promoting multiculturalism, and pursuing a republic. This was to produce the ugliest development in Australian politics for a generation, although it was of little consequence for the relationship with the Americans.

Pauline Hanson's large swing against Labour in the 1996 openly racist campaign soon lit a fire under the body of the old Australia. In April 1997 she launched the Pauline Hanson One Nation Party in sell-out rallies across the country, accompanied by some of the rowdiest left-wing-led demonstrations seen in years. Her supporters were mostly older Australian-born people, particularly from outside the major cities, bewildered by the changes forced on Australia during the last two decades. The strong vote received by the One Nation Party in the mid-1998 Queensland State elections, and the probability of the Party holding the balance of power in the Federal Parliament after the 12 October 1998 federal election, has jolted Australian politics. The national consensus among a civilized and increasingly multicultural society had survived rapid social, economic and cultural change in a way that only a civilized democracy can, but this will be tested in the future by the growing tensions in the body politic.

CONCLUSION

What does the total story of post–World War II American migration tell us about American and Australian culture and the relations between the two nations?

First, the historical data, both empirical and anecdotal, illuminate the texture of American society: its wandering people; its puritan millenarian culture with its sense of unique mission and destiny; its deep chauvinism and provincialism about America; and the capacity of Americans, even with this historical baggage, to pull up and go to a new "frontier."

Second, we see in operation the new globalization, with international labor markets, rapid transportation, and the spread of an American model of modernization.

Finally, we see revealed the character of Australia as a modern multicultural society that absorbs peoples from around the world into a progressive urban culture. American migrants, even with some tenacious attempts to retain their nationality, generally fit well into this modern Australia. Even though Australia is unquestionably flawed by racism, xenophobia, and conservatism, Americans, like most migrant groups, have been absorbed into the culture, and, relative to the rest of the world, Australia must be judged a reasonably successful multicultural society. Certainly the nation can improve on its migrant record, and there are danger signals for the future, but overall it is an enviable record.

What more needs to be done? The problems and pitfalls, methodological and theoretical, have been touched on throughout this study—small sample sizes for sub-groups, some biases in the 1993 sample, and so on. The areas that demand further research fall into two categories. In the first place, much more needs to be done on returnees. This is the greatest area of mystery: Why do so many people come halfway around the globe and then return? Second, the assimilation of the second generation should be followed up: do the American migrant progeny stay in Australia, and do they become assimilated Aussies? With more research in these areas in the future, one would be reasonably confident that most of the story of American migration was known. But for the details of each individual migrant, the history of American migration to Australia is the finite history of his or her experiences; to each of those who responded to our inquiries, thus permitting research into their private stories, we are most grateful. For these people, the story of migration is not that of some abstract "invisible migrants" but the concrete story of the trials and successes in life of finite people in a new land.

Perhaps paradoxically, the 50,000 American residents in Australia have had relatively little impact on relations between the two nation states. The modern Australian–American relationship has been determined chiefly by strategic considerations and then by economic and cultural factors. To the extent that Australians have resented that relationship—and many on the Left have—they have been supported by the majority of American migrants who have tended to be social democrat in disposition themselves. Indeed, many of the academics and intellectuals would have been educated in the cradle of the critique of U.S. laissez faire liberalism and state power—the U.S. university system.

In the end, the American migrant community in Australia has had a relatively minor impact on its host culture and seems unlikely to increase in numbers sufficiently to change this situation. This is in sharp contrast to the impact of America itself, which has arguably had a greater impact on modern Australia than has any other society.

NOTES

1. Q: 10, 45, 141, 237, 281, 312, 364, 169.
2. Q: 152, 192, 34.

3. C: 147; Q: 43, 191, 98, 78.

4. Tsounis, "Greeks," p. 530.

5. Cuddy, *Yanks,* pp. xix, 161, 165; Deamicis, "It Just Happens," pp. 42, 151; J. & D. Bardo, "American Migrants," p. 155; Dashefsky, *Americans Abroad,* pp. 111, 117, 120 140–141.

6. O. Lukomskyj and P. Richards, "Return Migration from Australia: A Case Study," *International Migration,* 24 (1986), pp. 603–632; Dashefsky, *Americans Abroad,* pp. 119, 140; Isaacs, *Greeks,* p. 108; C. A. Price, *Greeks in Australia* (Canberra, 1975), pp. 15–17; H. Ware, *A Profile of the Italian Community in Australia* (Canberra, 1981), p. 17; *Immigration Policies and Australia's Population: A Green Paper* (Canberra, 1977), p. 28. The most recent study, Baum, *Exchange of Migrants,* p. 7, shows a 60 percent American return rate; see also F. Bovenkerk, *The Sociology of Return Migration* (The Hague, 1974); R. T. Appleyard, "Determinants of Return Migration: A Social-Economic Study of United Kingdom Migrants Who Returned from Australia," *The Economic Record,* 38 (1962), pp. 352–681. This is reflected in a relatively low rate of home ownership for American migrants: Goldlust, *U.S.-Born, 1991,* p. 34.

7. Hugo, *Emigration,* pp. xvii, 7–12, 56-57, 65, 127–135; see also the discussion in Stephen Castles and Mark Miller, *The Age of Migration* (Basingstoke, 1993), pp. 18–26, 152–165, in which they analyze "migration in the new world disorder."

8. R: 1, 2, 3, 6, 7, 8, 13, 14.

9. R: 6, 22, 18, 14, 23, 24.

Appendix

QUESTIONNAIRE

1. Name: (optional)

2. Year born: Place:

3. Education:
   Public   Private   Diploma/degree   Institution
   High School
   University
   Postgraduate
   Other (specify)

4. Employment:
   Year   Position   Location

5. Married: Yes   No   Year
   Spouse living in Australia?   Yes   No
   Occupation of Spouse

6. Children:
   Number
   Sexes: Male
                 Female
   Ages:
   Place of Birth: Australia   Other

7. Year migrated to Australia:
   Assisted passage?   Yes   No

8. Why did you migrate?

> *Reason*   *Degree of Relevance*
>   (tick one in each category)
>   *Low*   *Medium*   *High*

> None
> Employment
> Family conflict
> General economy
> Hostility to United States
> Adventure
> Following spouse/partner
> Environment
> Crime
> Racial conflict
> Materialism in United States
> Family reunion
> Other (specify)

9. Why did you choose Australia?

> *Reason*   *Degree of Relevance*
>   (tick one in each category)
>   *Low*   *Medium*   *High*

> None
> Employment
> Family reunion
> General economic attraction
> Adventure
> Climate
> Environment
> Low crime
> Social harmony
> General life style
> Other (specify)

10. Are you a U.S. citizen?   Yes   No
    Will you become an Australian citizen?   Yes   No
    If not, why not? (specify)
    If you are now an Australian citizen, when (year) were you
           naturalized?

11. Political preference:
    U.S.:   Republican
             Democrat
             Other

     Australian: Labor
                  Liberal
                  Democrat
                  Other

12. Have you met discrimination as a migrant?   Yes No
     If so, what type of discrimination? (specify)

13. Do you belong to any American organization in Australia?   Yes No
     If yes, please specify

14. Do your children expect to live in Australia?   Yes No
    Have they suffered discrimination?   Yes No
     If yes, what type?
    Do they consider themselves Australian or American?
    Have they received the type of education and been offered the
     employment you expected them to get in Australia?   Yes No
    What is their highest educational qualification?
    What is their employment?

15. Would you be willing to do a follow-up interview?   Yes No

16. Names and addresses of other American migrants who you think may be
    interested in answering this questionnaire.

17. Names and addresses of returnees (those Americans who have returned to
    America) who may be interested in answering a questionnaire.

18. Conclusion: Are you satisfied with your life in Australia?

    Very satisfied
    Satisfied
    Mixed feelings
    Dissatisfied
    Very dissatisfied

    Please explain your response and feel free to add any further information
    on attached sheets.

Thank you very much for answering this questionnaire.

Bibliography

A Note Concerning Further Reading

The central concerns of this book—American–Australian relations, globalization, migration, multiculturalism, and ethnicity—have been topics of heated debates in both America and Australia in the 1990s. They have generated a vibrant and vast literature, which grows almost daily. The following bibliography, therefore, is only intended as an introductory guide and is by no means an exhaustive list of material on these subjects.

General Works on Australia

Bell, Philip, and Bell, Roger. *Implicated, the United States in Australia.* Melbourne, 1993.
Blainey, Geoffrey. *A Land Half Won.* Melbourne, 1980.
Crowley, Frank, ed. *A New History of Australia.* Melbourne, 1971.
Hughes, Robert. *The Fatal Shore.* New York, 1987.
Molony, John. *History of Australia.* Melbourne, 1988.
Russell, Ward. *A Nation for a Continent: The History of Australia, 1901–1975.* Richmond, 1985.
Younger, R. M. *Australia and the Australians: A New Concise History.* Melbourne, 1982.

American Identity and the Declinism Debate

Shafer, Byron. *Is America Different?* Oxford, 1991.
Walzer, Michael. "What Does it Mean to be an American?" *Social Research,* 57, 1990.

Migration of Americans to Australia and Americans in Australia

Aitchison, Ray. *The Americans in Australia.* Melbourne, 1986.

Bardo, J., and Bardo, D. "American Migrants in Australia: An Exploratory Study of Adjustment," *Sociological Focus,* 14, 1981.

Baum, Sam, and Young, Christabel. *The Exchange of Migrants Between Australia and the United States.* Canberra, 1989.

Catts, Dorothy. *King O'Malley: Man and Statesman.* Sydney, 1957.

Churchward, L. G. *Australia and America, 1788–1972, An Alternative History.* Sydney, 1979.

Cuddy, Dennis. *The Yanks Are Coming: American Migration to Australia.* San Francisco, 1977.

Dashefsky, Arnold. *Americans Abroad: A Comparative Study of Emigrants from the United States.* New York, 1992.

Deamicis, Jan. "It Just Happens: American Migration to Australia." Unpublished Ph.D. dissertation, University of Massachusetts, 1977.

Edwards, P. G. *Australia through American Eyes.* St. Lucia, 1979.

Finifter, Bernard, and Finifter, Ada. "Party Identification and Political Adaptation of American Migrants in Australia," *Journal of Politics,* 51, 1989.

Goldlust, John, et al. Bureau of Immigration and Population Research. *Community Profiles; 1991 Census; United States of America Born.* Canberra, 1995.

Grattan, C. Hartley. *The United States and the Southwest Pacific.* Melbourne, 1961.

Harper, Norman. *A Great and Powerful Friend: A Study of Australian–American Relations Between 1900 and 1975.* St. Lucia, 1987.

Jennings, Reece I. *William A. Webb.* Adelaide, 1973.

Moore, John. *Over-Sexed, Over-Paid and Over Here, Americans in Australia, 1941–45.* St. Lucia, 1981.

Phillips, D. *The Australian American Connection.* North Ryde, 1977.

Potts, E. D. and A. *Yanks Down Under.* Melbourne 1985.

Potts, E. D. and A. *Young America and Australian Gold, The Gold Rush of the 1850s.* St. Lucia, 1974.

General Books on Travel in Australia

Bevan, Ian. *The Sunburnt Country.* London, 1955.

Brewster, Barbara. *Down Under All Over.* Portland, 1991.

Grant, Don, and Seal, Graham, eds. *Australia in the World.* Perth, 1994.

Gunther, John. *Inside Australia and New Zealand.* London, 1972.

Linkletter, Art. *Linkletter Down Under.* Englewood Cliffs, NJ, 1968.

Wheeler, Tony. *Australia.* Sydney, 1977.

Ethnicity and Migrants in Australia

Appleyard, R. T. *British Emigration to Australia.* Canberra, 1964.

Bennett, Jim, and Fry, Ian. *Canadians in Australia.* Canberra, 1996.

Borrie, W. D. *Italians and Germans in Australia: A Study of Assimilation.* Melbourne, 1954.

Bottomley, G. *After the Odyssey: A Study of Greek Australians.* St. Lucia, 1979.

Cronin, C. *The Sting of Change: Sicilians in Sicily and America.* Chicago, 1970.

Huber, R. *From Pasta to Pavlova.* Sydney, 1977.

Huck, Arthur. *The Chinese in Australia.* Melbourne, 1968.

Inglis, Christine. *Asians in Australia.* Singapore, 1992.

Isaacs, Eva. *Greek Children in Sydney.* Canberra, 1976.

Lepervanche, M. De. *Indians in a White Australia.* Sydney, 1984.

Lyng, J. *Non-Britishers in Australia.* Melbourne, 1935.

Lyng, J. *The Scandinavians in Australia, New Zealand and the Western Pacific.* Melbourne, 1939.

MacDonagh, Oliver. *The Sharing of the Green: A Modern Irish History for Australians.* Sydney, 1996.

O'Brien, Ilma. *Australia's Italians, 1788–1988.* Carlton, 1989.

O'Farrell, P. *The Irish in Australia.* Sydney, 1986.

Prentice, M. P. *The Scots in Australia: A Study of New South Wales, Victoria and Queensland, 1788–1900.* Sydney, 1984.

Price, C. A. *The Ethnic Composition of the Australian People.* North Fitzroy, 1981.

Price, C. A. *Greeks in Australia.* Canberra, 1975.

Price, C. A. *Jewish Settlers in Australia.* Canberra, 1964.

Price, C. A. *Southern Europeans in Australia.* Melbourne, 1963.

Richardson, Alan. *British Immigrants and Australia.* Canberra, 1974.

Rubenstein, H. L. *The Jews in Australia.* Melbourne, 1991.

Rutland, Suzanne. *Edge of the Diaspora, Two Centuries of Jewish Settlement in Australia.* Sydney, 1988.

Thompson, S. L. *Australia through Italian Eyes: A Study of Settlers Returning from Australia to Italy.* Melbourne, 1980.

Tsounis, Michael. "Greek Communities in Australia." Unpublished Ph.D. dissertation, University of Adelaide, 1972.

Viviani, N. *The Long Journey: Vietnamese Migration and Settlement in Australia.* Melbourne, 1984.

Ware, Helen. *A Profile of the Italian Community in Australia.* Canberra, 1981.

Wegmann, Suzanne. *The Swiss in Australia.* Grusch, Switzerland, 1989.

Yarwood, A. T. *Asian Migration to Australia.* Melbourne, 1964.

Yarwood, A. T., and Knowling, M. J. *Race Relations in Australia.* North Ryde, 1983.

Aboriginal History

Blainey, Geoffrey. *The Triumph of the Nomads.* South Melbourne, 1975.

Broome, *Aboriginal Australians.* Sydney, 1982.

Reynolds, H., ed. *Aborigines and Settlers: The Australian Experience, 1788–1939.* Melbourne, 1972.

Reynolds, H. *The Other Side of the Frontier: Aboriginal Resistance to the European Invasion of Australia.* Ringwood, Victoria, 1982.

Rowley, C. D. *The Destruction of Aboriginal Society.* Canberra, 1970.

Yarwood, A. T., and Knowling, M. J. *Race Relations in Australia: A History.* Sydney, 1982.

Australian Identity and the Future of the Australian Nation

Blainey, Geoffrey. *The Tyranny of Distance.* Melbourne, 1966.

Boyd, Robin. *The Australian Ugliness.* Melbourne, 1956.

Carroll, John, ed. *Intruders in the Bush: The Australian Quest for Identity.* Melbourne, 1982.

Conway, Ronald. *The Great Australian Stupor.* Melbourne, 1971.

Grant, Bruce. *The Australian Dilemma: A New Kind of Western Society.* Sydney, 1983.

Grant, Bruce. *What Kind of Country.* Ringwood, Victoria, 1988.

Griffiths, Tony. *Beautiful Lies: Australia from Kokoda to Keating.* London, 1993.

Horne, Donald. *The Lucky Country.* Melbourne, 1964.

McGregor, Craig. *Profile of Australia.* London, 1966.

McQueen, Humphrey. *A New Britannia.* Melbourne, 1970.

Serle, Geoffrey. *From Deserts the Prophets Come, the Creative Spirit in Australia, 1788–1972.* Melbourne, 1974.

Walker, David. *Dream and Disillusion: A Search for the Australian Cultural Identity.* Canberra, 1976.

Ward, Russel. *The Australian Legend.* Melbourne, 1958.

White, Richard. *Inventing Australia: Images and Identity, 1688–1980.* Sydney, 1981.

Index

A Town Like Alice (1950), novel, 93
Aborigines, 13, 17, 28, 29, 44, 61, 88, 90, 94–95, 123, 144, 170–172, 187
academics, 67, 70, 73–74, 77, 79, 84, 95, 106, 108, 133, 141–144, 146–147, 150, 155, 159–160, 162–164, 169–170, 177, 181, 185–186, 188
ACT: *see* Australian Capital Territory
Adams & Company, 12–13
Adams, Philip, broadcaster, 135–136, 139
Adelaide, 20, 46, 60, 96, 103, 105, 113, 117, 132, 137, 141, 163
Adelaide University, 126
Aeroplane Jelly take-over, 116
Aitchison, Ray, 58, 167
Albinski, Henry, 43, 94, 96
Alexander, Fred, 42
Allen, H. C., 18, 35,
ALP: *see* Australian Labour Party
Altman, Dennis, writer, 95
America's Cup, 94
American Association of Australian Literary Studies, 94
American Chamber of Commerce in Australia, 154
American foreign policy, antagonism to, 112
American Immigration Acts, 14
anti-Americanism, 11, 26, 28, 36–37, 40, 41, 107–108, 110, 113, 135, 140, 162

anti-Australianism, 140–141
anti-Communism in America, 33, 143, 156
"anti-dago" riots, 59
anti-multiculturalism, 61; *see also* multiculturalism
ANZUS Treaty (1951), 34, 36
Archibald, W. O., 22
Arnotts take-over, 116
Asia Pacific Economic Cooperation (APEC), 50
assisted passage scheme, 45–46
Australasian Studies Center (Pennsylvania State), 94
Australian Arbitration Commission, 19
Australian Ballet, 94
Australian Capital Territory, 16, 21, 43, 103
Australian Consolidated Holdings, 21
Australian Constitution, 16–17
Australian Heritage Commission, 149
Australian Labour Party (ALP), 17, 18, 21, 34, 40, 46, 60, 61, 83, 113–114, 163, 155–156
Australian Mutual Provident Society (AMP), 116
Australian Rules Football, 173
Australian Shooters Party, 114
Australian War Memorial, 149
Australian–American Association, 81, 154
Australians Against Further Immigration, 60

Ballarat, 75
Baltic migrants, 62
Bardo, J. and D., sociologists, 173, 182
Barton, Prime Minister Edward, 20
"Battle of Brisbane," 28
Baum, S., 74
"big government," 145
Biggins, Barbara, 138
Bill of Rights, lack of Australian, 16, 17, 105, 116,
black Americans, 4, 13, 28, 57, 76, 123, 144, 170–173
"black-birding," 44
Blainey, Professor Geoffrey, 27, 35, 43, 48, 59
Bolkus, Nick, Minister for Immigration, 60–61
Booker T. Washington Club, Sydney, 171
Borner, Ray, 173
Borrie, W. D., 57–58
Boyd, Robin, artist, 41
Brewster, Barbara, writer, 99
Brisbane, 28, 46, 75, 77
British migrants, 82, 130, 146, 164
Brown, Bob, politician, 118
Brown, Chelsea, 123, 171
Bryce, James, Viscount, 4
Bulletin magazine, 20, 92, 128, 139
Burgess, Bob, 61
Burns, Tommy, pugilist, 17
Bush and Backwoods, 42
Bush, President George, 5, 23, 112, 114, 14

Cairns, Jim, politician, 37
California, 72, 79, 96, 106, 117, 142, 150, 181, 185
Calwell, Arthur, Labor Minister of Immigration, 45–46, 75
Campbell Soups, 116
Campbell, Graeme, politician, 61
Canberra, 21–22, 103, 118, 142–143, 163; *see also* Australian Capital Territory
Casey, Richard G., ambassador and politician, 26, 89
Cash, Pat, tennis-player, 94
Chafe, William, 155
Charles, Bob, politician, 150, 160
Chatwin, Bruce, writer, 95
Chinese migrants, 13–14, 58
Chomsky, Noam, 37
Chrysler Motor Company, 39
Central Intelligence Agency (CIA), 34, 52
Citizens Initiated Referenda (CIR), 61
Clark, Manning, historian, 35

Clinton, President Bill, 5
Cobb & Co., 13
Cold War, 3, 5, 17, 30, 38, 110, 113
Colleges of Advanced Education (CAEs), 163
Colombo Plan, 47
Commonwealth Bank of Australia, 19, 22, 49
Commonwealth Racial Discrimination Act (1975), 150
Communist Party of Australia (CPA), 35
conscription issue, 21
Coombs, H. C., 25
Coral Sea, battle of, 26, 34
Cordeaux, Jeremy, broadcaster, 113
Costello, Robert de, athlete, 94
Crocodile Dundee, film, 94
Cuddy, Dennis, 58, 74, 81, 98, 120, 182
cultural imperialism, 13, 122, 126, 138–139
Curthoys, Jean, 35
Curtin, Prime Minister John, 25, 28–29
Cutler, Samuel, 13

Darwin, 23, 25, 103
Dashefsky, Arnold, 58, 81, 167, 182
De Leon, Daniel, 15
De Tocqueville, Alexis, 2, 18,
Deakin, Prime Minister Alfred, 17, 20
Deamicis, Jan, 58, 74, 78, 81, 95, 182
Debs, Eugene V., 15
Democratic Party (U.S.), 15, 83, 154–155, 163
Democrat Party of Australia, 83
discrimination against American migrants, 145–151, 170
Down Under All Over (1991), 99
Downer, Alexander, politician, 83, 116, 186
draft resisters, 70
Dreiser, Theodore, 37
dual citizenship, 157, 158, 160
Dulles, Allen, 34
Dulles, John Foster, 34
Dunlap, Al, 21
Dyer, Bob, entertainer, 40

East India Company, 10
Eddy, Father John, 43, 95
education, 4, 88, 146, 166, 175; post-graduate, 92; pre-school, 165; secondary, 137, 143, 144, 166, 185; tertiary, 144, 162–163; U.S., 73, 133
Edwards, P. G., 25
Eisenhower, President Dwight D., 4, 33–34
Empire Settlement Act (UK), 45
Ervin, Lorenzo, 172

Export Enhancement Program (EEP), 113

Fares v. Box Hill College of TAFE and Orrs (1992), 150
Federal Capital Commission, 22
Festival of Light, 84
Fillmore, President Millard, 44
Finifter, Bernard and Ada, 58, 81
Fischer, Tim, National Party leader, 116, 121
Fisher, Prime Minister Andrew, 21
Foley, Gary, 172
Ford Motor Company, 39
Foster, Robert, 171
Fraser, Prime Minister Malcolm, 38, 49, 112
Fukuyama, Francis, 5

GATT, 24, 30, 40, 50, 115–117
General Motors Holden, 39
George, Henry, 15
Georgetown University, 43
German migrants, 57–58, 62, 68, 154, 160
Gibson, Mel, actor, 94
Glazer, Nathan, 64
globalization, 48
gold: discovered, N.S.W. (1851), 12; rushes, 11, 13, 14, 72
Goldman, Emma, 15
Gompers, Samuel, 15
Goolagong, Evonne, tennis-player, 93
Governor-General, office of, 16
Grassby, Al, politician, 47
Grattan, C. Hartley, historian, 24
Great Depression, 23, 24
Great Society program, 47, 156
Great White Fleet, 17
Greek migrants, 58–60, 63, 65, 68, 82, 154, 171, 182–184
Green, Al, 159
Green, Marshall, U.S. Ambassador to Australia, 6
Greer, Germaine, writer, 95
Griffin, Walter Burley, architect, 21–22
Gulf War, 7, 38, 112
gun laws, 136
Gunther, John, writer, 94

Hamby, Alonzo, historian, 155
Handlin, Oscar, historian, 56, 58
Hansen, Marcus, historian, 56
Hanson, Pauline, 59, 61, 64, 134, 172, 187; *see also* One Nation Party
Hargraves, Edward, gold-seeker, 12

Harper, Norman, historian, 34, 81
Harris, Max, 40
Hawke, Prime Minister Robert J., 38, 48, 49, 83, 112
Hayden, Bill, Labor Party Leader, 49
Haywood, Bill, union organizer, 15
Hewson, John, Liberal Party leader, 83, 113–114, 116, 150, 187
High Court of Australia, 16
Hill, Premier Lionel, 23
Hines, Marcia, singer, 171
Hispanic Americans, 57, 105
Hobart, 11, 77
Hogan, Paul, entertainer, 94
Hollywood, impact of, 24
Holt, Prime Minister Harold, 35, 47, 76, 91
Hoover, President Herbert Clark, 20
Hopkins, Frank, 89
Horne, Donald, writer, 27, 41
Housing Industry Association, 113
Howard, Prime Minister John, 44, 61, 83, 115, 136, 186
Hughes, Charles Evans, 23
Hughes, Helen, economist, 64
Hughes, Prime Minister Billy, 21, 22
Hughes, Robert, writer and critic, 95
Hugo, Graeme, demographer, 81, 183, 186
Hurford, Chris, 4

"I Am Australian" Foundation, 64
Immigration Bills (US), 44
immmigration: post-war, impact of, 43; quota, cuts to, 61
Immigration Restriction Act (1901), 44, 45
Industrial Workers of the World (IWW; Wobblies), 15, 16
International Refugee Organization, 46
Iran–Contra affair, 5
Irish migrants, 154
Isaacs, Eva, 59
Italian migrants, 57–58, 62, 68, 82, 154, 160, 176, 183

Japan, 23–24, 34
Japanese migrants, 14
Jenkins, Premier John Greely, South Australia, 19, 20
Jewish migrants, 58, 62–63, 70
Jim Crowism, 44
Johnson, David, 116
Johnson, Jack, pugilist, 17

Johnson, President Lyndon B., 4, 35, 47, 76,
    80–81, 92, 156
Jolley, Elizabeth, novelist, 93
Jones, Alan, broadcaster, 113
Jones, Barry, politician, 40
Jupp, James, 57

Kalgoorlie, 59, 61
Kangaroo Island, 11
Katter, Bob, politician, 61
Keating, Prime Minister Paul, 32, 38, 48–49,
    83, 112–116, 150, 186–187
Kennealy, Thomas, novelist, 93
Kennedy, President John F., 4, 149, 156
Kennedy, Senator Robert, assassinated, 75
King, Martin Luther, 75, 172
Kiwanis, 154
Know-Nothing (American) Party, 44
Korean War, 7, 30, 34, 35
Kruttschmitt, Julius, 20
Ku Klux Klan, 44, 64, 76, 171
Kynaston, Edward, writer, 93

Labour: *see* Australian Labour Party
language, Australian, 99, 147
Laver, Rod, tennis-player, 93
Laws, John, broadcaster, 113
League of Nations, 23
League of Rights, 61
Lenin, 18
Liberal Party, 34, 61, 76, 83–84, 113–114,
    116, 118, 123, 129, 136, 150, 154, 156,
    160, 187
Liberalism and Its Challengers (1992), 155
Lightfoot, Senator Ross, 44, 61
Likens, Gene, 163
Linkletter, Art, humorist, 91
Lions Clubs, 154
Loggins, Leroy, 173
London, Herb, 46
Lyffyt v. Capital Television (1993), 150–151

MacArthur, General Douglas, 25
Maloy, Maureen, 150
Manne, Robert, journalist and academic, 156
McCormack, Denis, 60
McCullough, Colleen, novelist, 94
McEachin, Herb, baseball player, 171
McGregor, Craig, 27, 41
McGuiness, Paddy, economic journalist, 116
McIntyre, Stuart, 35
McKell, Premier William J., 27

McLachlan, Ian, politician, 187
McMahon, Prime Minister William, 47
McQueen, Humphrey, historian, 27, 35
Meanjin quarterly, 105
Melbourne, 11, 13, 20, 21, 22, 26, 46, 75, 77,
    103
Melbourne University, 42
"melting pot," concept of, 3, 5, 75, 77, 103
Menzies, Prime Minister Sir Robert, 9, 10, 34–
    35, 39, 46, 47
Metin, Albert, 18
Michener, James, novelist, 90
Midway, Battle of, 26
Migration Act, 47
migration: historiography of, 55; internal
    (U.S.), 4; models for, 55
Moffat, J. Pierrepont, 25
monarchism, in Australia, 10, 143, 160
Monash University, 163
mono-culturalism, 64
Montesquieu, Charles de Secondat, Baron de, 18
Mount Isa Mines Ltd, 20
*Moving Frontier: An American Theme and Its
    Application to Australian History,* 42
multiculturalism, 27, 56, 58–60, 62, 64, 126,
    148, 156, 181, 187
multinational corporations, 117, 135, 137; *see
    also* Cambell Soups
Murphy, Paul, broadcaster, 115
Murray-Darling Basin, 11

National Bank (1911), 22
National Farmers Federation, 112
National Party of Australia, 59, 61, 84, 112,
    116
National Rifle Association (NRA), 114
native title issue, 61
neo-Fascism, 64
neo-Nazis: in Europe, 58; riot, 60
New Deal program, 4, 155–156
New Guinea, 34
Newcombe, John, tennis-player, 93
Newton-John, Olivia, 94
New Zealand migrants, 157, 164,
Nixon, President Richard, 92, 149
Norman, Greg, golfer, 94
Norris, Ron, historian, 45
North, Oliver, 136
North-West Cape, 36, 37
Northern Territory, 103
Novak, Michael, 59
Nurrungar, 36, 37

nurses as migrants, 106–107

O'Malley, King, Prime Minister, 19, 20–22, 31, 150
Oklahoma City bombing, 60
On the Beach, film, 89
One Nation Party, 59–61, 64, 84, 134, 172, 187
OPEC price rise, 49
Ottawa Agreement (1932), 24

Packer, Kerry, 21
Peace Party, 36
Perkins, Charles, 172
Perkins, Edward, U.S. ambassador, 116
Perth, 46, 103
Philippines, 17
Phillips, D., sociologist, 100
Pine Gap, 36, 37
Playford, Premier Thomas, 20
Polish migrants, 176
population, 1; of Australia, 2; of China, 3; of India, 3; of the U.S., 2, 3
Populist Party (U.S.), 15
Port Arthur massacre, 61, 136
Port Lincoln, 44
Price, C. A., 42, 57
privatization of prisons, 135
Privy Council (U.K.), 16
Progress and Poverty (1879), 15
push-polling criticized, 113

Qantas Airlines, 19, 49, 116
Quadrant magazine, 156
Queensland, 44, 45

Racial Discrimination Act (1975), 47, 151
Reagan, President Ronald, 4, 36, 112, 149
Reckless Kelly (1993), film, 113
republican debate, 114
Republican Party (U.S.), 15, 76, 83–84, 114, 116
return rates of migrants, 56, 173, 186
Road Warrior (1981), film, 94
Romper Stomper (1994), film, 65
Roosevelt, President Franklin Delano, 17, 24, 26, 28–29, 155
Roosevelt, President Theodore, 15, 17
Rotary Clubs, 154
Returned Services League (RSL), 59
Rutherford, James, 20

Sanders, Norm, politician, 150, 159
Sattler, Howard, 113
SBS Television station, 115
SEATO, 34
Serle, Geoffrey, historian, 27, 41
Shades of Black, 172
Sheldon, Joan, politician, 114
Sheridan, Greg, journalist, 116
Silver City, film, 62
Simpson, O. J., trial, 136
Sinclair, Upton, novelist, 37
Singapore, 24–25
Single Tax Leagues, 15
Siracusa, John, 89
Snowy Mountain Scheme, 46
Social Darwinism, 44
social democrats, American and Australian, defined, 83
Socialist Labor Party of America (1895), 15
Sombart, Werner, 3
South Australia, 11–12, 21, 22, 23
Southern Europeans in Australia (1963), 42
Soviet Union: *see* U.S.S.R.
Spencer, Herbert, 44
Stalin, Joseph, 33
standard of living, 55, 80, 103–104, 106, 142, 182
Steketee, Mike, 114
stock market, crash of, 1987, 41
Stone, Gerald, 91, 139
Summer, William Graham, Social Darwinist, 44
Summers, Anne, 95
Support Your Local Sheriff, film, 69
Sydney, 8, 11, 20, 21, 22, 26, 46, 75, 77
Sydney Dance Company, 94
Sykes, Dr. Roberta, 172

tall poppy syndrome, 142
tariff question, 18
Tasmania, 61, 103, 118, 136, 150, 174–175
television, 10
Terkel, Studs, writer, 26
The Legend of King O'Malley, 20
The Sundowners, film, 93
The Thorn Birds (1977), novel, 94
Thompson, Christina, editor, 105
Tiananmen Square massacre, 60
Townsville, Queensland, 25, 28
trade unions, 18, 94, 119, 142, 145, 156
Truman, President Harry S., 33
Tsounis, Michael, 59, 182

Tucson, Arizona, 141
Turkiewitz, Sophia, 62
Turner, Ian, historian, 15, 35
Twain, Mark (Samuel F. Clemens), 20

U.S.S.R., 5, 7, 33–35
un-American, concept of, 2
Unfinished Journey, The (1991), 155
unionism, 15
unions: *see* trade unions
United States Constitution, 16–17, 105, 110, 136
Uren, Tom, politician, 135

Vietnam War, 5, 7, 30, 34–38, 47, 69, 76, 81, 92–93, 104, 107, 149
Vietnamese, 58, 148; boat people, 62, 87
Viviani, Nancy, 59

Waco, Texas, siege, 60
war-brides, 29, 76
Ward, Russel, historian, 27, 35
Washington Naval Conference (1922), 23
Watergate crisis, 5, 69, 76

Webb, Sydney and Beatrice, 18
Webb, William A., 22–23
Wentworth, W. C., politician, 37
West Germany, 46
Western Australia, 12
Westminster "system," 16
whaling industry, 10, 11
Wheeler, Tony, journalist, 93
Wheelwright, Professor Ted, economist, 40
White Australia policy, 14, 19, 44, 45, 46, 47, 59, 91, 94–95
White, Patrick, novelist, 93
Whitlam, Prime Minister Gough, 6, 37, 38, 40, 47, 49, 50, 52, 112
Wicks, Harry, 35
Williams, Daryl, 114
Williams, James Hartwell, 11
Wilson, President Woodrow, 15, 23
Wolfe, Alan, sociologist, 64
World Trade Organization, 117
World War I, 3, 44
World War II, 3, 4, 25, 26, 28, 33, 38, 62, 89
Wright, Keith, politician, 150

Zoellick, Robert, Under Secretary of State, 6

About the Authors

DAVID MOSLER is Senior Lecturer in American History at the University of Adelaide. American-born, Dr. Mosler emigrated to Australia in 1971, where he began teaching history. His articles have appeared in numerous scholarly journals.

BOB CATLEY is Convenor of International Studies at the University of Adelaide. Born in England, he emigrated to Australia where he received his Ph.D. from the Australian National University. He has since held academic positions in a number of universities in Australia, Europe, Asia, and the United States. He has also served as a Member of the Australian House of Representatives and as a government official and Ministerial Adviser. He has authored nine earlier books.

ISBN 0-275-96252-0

9 0 0 0 0 >

EAN

9 780275 962524

HARDCOVER BAR CODE